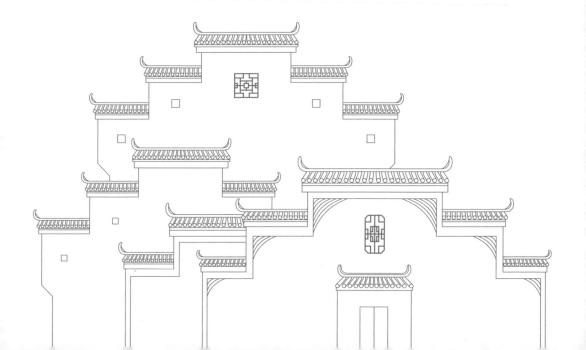

「中国式现代化的故事」丛书

张占斌 总主编

【汉英对照版】

方铭勇 主编

中共安徽省委党校（安徽行政学院） 组织编写

皖美跨越

GREAT LEAPS BETTER ANHUI
THE STORY OF CHINESE MODERNIZATION IN ANHUI

中国式现代化的安徽故事

国家行政学院出版社
NATIONAL ACADEMY OF GOVERNANCE PRESS

中央党校出版社集团
国家行政学院出版社

出版说明

党的二十大报告指出，从现在起，中国共产党的中心任务就是团结带领全国各族人民全面建成社会主义现代化强国、实现第二个百年奋斗目标，以中国式现代化全面推进中华民族伟大复兴。习近平总书记在中央党校建校90周年庆祝大会暨2023年春季学期开学典礼上的讲话中首次创造性提出"为党育才、为党献策"的党校初心。紧扣党的中心任务，践行党校初心，中央党校出版集团国家行政学院出版社和中央党校（国家行政学院）中国式现代化研究中心特别策划"中国式现代化的故事"系列丛书，邀请地方党校（行政学院）、宣传部门、新闻媒体、行业企业等方面共同参与策划和组织编写，从不同层次、不同维度、不同视角讲述中国式现代化的地方故事、企业故事、产业故事，生动展示各个地区、各个领域在大力拓展中国式现代化新征程上的理念创新、实践创新、制度创新、文化创新等，精彩呈现当代中国以中国式现代化全面推进中华民族伟大复兴的宏大历史叙事，以讲好中国式现代化的故事来讲好中国故事。

该丛书力求体现这样几个突出特点：

其一，文风活泼，以白描手法代入鲜活场景。本丛书区别于一般学术论著或理论读物严肃刻板的面孔，以生动鲜活的题材、清新温暖的笔触、富有现场感的表达和丰富精美的图片，将各地方、企业推进中国式现代化建设的理论思考、战略规划、重要举措、实践路径等向读者娓娓道来，使读者在沉浸式的阅读体验中获得共鸣、引发思考、受到启迪。

Publication Instructions

The 20th CPC National Congress Report points out that, from this day forward, the central task of the CPC will be to lead the Chinese people of all ethnic groups in a concerted effort to realize the Second Centenary Goal of building China into a great modern socialist country in all respects and to advance the rejuvenation of the Chinese nation on all fronts through a Chinese path to modernization. In the speech at the 90th anniversary celebration of the founding of the Party School of the Central Committee of C.P.C (CCPS) and the opening ceremony of its spring semester of 2023, President Xi Jinping first creatively underlined the original mission for Party schools to cultivate talent for and contribute wisdom to the CPC. In line with the central task of the CPC and the original mission for Party schools, National Academy of Governance Press and the Chinese Modernization Research Center of CCPS (National Academy of Governance) have specially planned the series of books "The Story of Chinese Modernization", inviting local Party schools (administration institutes), publicity departments, news media, industry enterprises, and other aspects to jointly participate in the planning and organizing of the writing. The books will tell the local stories, enterprise stories, and industry stories of Chinese modernization from different levels, perspectives, and dimensions, vividly showcasing the innovative ideas, practices, systems, and culture in various regions and fields in the new journey of expanding Chinese modernization. It will present a magnificent historical narrative of the promotion of the rejuvenation of the Chinese nation on all fronts through a Chinese path to modernization, and better tell China's story to the world by better telling the story of Chinese modernization.

其二，视野开阔，以小切口反映大主题。丛书中既有历史人文风貌、经济地理特质的纵深概述，也有改革创新举措、转型升级案例的细节剖解，既讲天下事，又讲身边事，以点带面、以小见大，用故事提炼经验，以案例支撑理论，从而兼顾理论厚度、思想深度、实践力度和情感温度。

其三，层次丰富，以一域之光映衬全域风采。丛书有开风气之先的上海气度，也有立开放潮头的南粤之声；有沉稳构筑首都经济圈的京津冀足音，也有聚力谱写东北全面振兴的黑吉辽篇章；有在长江三角洲区域一体化发展中厚积薄发的安徽样板，也有在成渝地区双城经济圈中走深走实的川渝实践；有生态高颜值、发展高质量齐头并进的云南画卷，也有以"数"为笔、逐浪蓝海的贵州答卷；有"强富美高"的南京路径，也有"七个新天堂"的杭州示范……。丛书还将陆续推出各企业、各行业的现代化故事，带读者领略中国式现代化的深厚底蕴、辽阔风光和壮美前景。

"中国式现代化的故事"系列丛书既是各地方、企业推进中国式现代化建设充满生机活力的形象展示，也是以地方、企业发展缩影印证中国式现代化理论科学性的多维解码。希望本丛书的出版，能够为各地方、企业搭建学习交流平台，将一地一域的现代化建设融入全面建设社会主义现代化国家的大局，步伐一致奋力谱写中国式现代化的历史新篇章。

国家行政学院出版社

"中国式现代化的故事"丛书策划编辑组

This series of books strives to embody the following prominent features:

First, the writing style is lively, using vivid descriptions to depict vivid scenes. This series of books differs from the serious and rigid face of general academic works or theoretical readings. With lively and vivid subjects, fresh and warm brushstrokes, expression of a sense of presence, and rich and exquisite images, it narrates the theoretical thinking, strategic planning, important measures, and practical paths of promoting construction of Chinese modernization by various regions and enterprises, allowing readers to resonate, think, and be inspired through immersive reading experiences.

Second, it has a broad vision and reflects major themes through small perspectives. The series of books includes both a deep overview of the historical and cultural characteristics and economic geography traits, as well as detailed analysis of reform and innovation measures and transformation and upgrading cases. It talks about both national affairs and local affairs, uses specific stories to extract experiences, supports theories with cases, and thus takes into account the thickness of theory, the depth of thought, the intensity of practice, and the warmth of emotions.

Third, it has rich levels, reflecting the regional brilliance against the backdrop of the overall picture. The series of books include the elegance of Shanghai, which leads the trend, and the voice of innovation and openness in Guangdong; the sound of Beijing, Tianjin, and Hebei, which steadily builds the capital economic zone, and the chapters of Heilongjiang, Jilin, and Liaoning that gather strength for the comprehensive revitalization of Northeast China; the Anhui model that accumulates strength and breakthroughs in the development of the Yangtze River Delta regional integration, and the practical exploration of Chengdu-Chongqing economic zone; the Yunnan picture with high ecological value and simultaneous high-quality development, and the Guizhou paper that uses "numbers" as brushes to explore blue oceans; the development goal towards "strong economy, rich people, beautiful environment and a high degree of social civilization" in

Nanjing, and the demonstration of construction of seven types of new paradise in Hangzhou... The series of books will also gradually launch the modernization stories of various enterprises and industries, allowing readers to appreciate the profound heritage, vast scenery, and magnificent prospects of Chinese modernization.

The series of books "The Story of Chinese Modernization" is not only a vibrant display of promoting construction of Chinese modernization by various regions and enterprises, but also a multi-dimensional decoding of the scientificity of Chinese modernization theory through the epitome of local and enterprise development. It is hoped that the publication of this series of books can provide a platform for learning and exchange for various regions and enterprises, integrate the modernization construction of single place and single region into the overall construction of a modern socialist country, and strive to write a new chapter in the history of Chinese modernization with consistent steps.

Planned and Editorial Team of

the series of books "The Story of Chinese Modernization",

National Academy of Governance Press

总 序

　　党的二十大擘画了全面建成社会主义现代化强国、以中国式现代化全面推进中华民族伟大复兴的宏伟蓝图。中国式现代化是前无古人的开创性事业，是强国建设、民族复兴的康庄大道。回顾过去，中国共产党带领人民艰辛探索、铸就辉煌，用几十年时间走完西方发达国家几百年走过的工业化历程，创造了经济快速发展和社会长期稳定的两大奇迹，实践有力证明了中国式现代化走得通、行得稳；面向未来，在以习近平同志为核心的党中央坚强领导下，各地方各企业立足各自的资源禀赋、区位优势和产业基础、发展规划，精心谋划、奋勇争先，在推进中国式现代化过程中将展现出一系列生动场景，一步一个脚印地把美好蓝图变为现实形态。

　　中国式现代化，是中国共产党领导的社会主义现代化，既有各国现代化的共同特征，又有基于自己国情的中国特色。中国式现代化，是人口规模巨大的现代化，是全体人民共同富裕的现代化，是物质文明和精神文明相协调的现代化，是人与自然和谐共生的现代化，是走和平发展道路的现代化。这五个方面的中国特色，不仅深刻揭示了中国式现代化的科学内涵，也体现在不同地方、企业推进现代化建设可感可知可行的实际成果中。中国式现代化理论为地方、企业现代化的实践探索提供了不竭动力，地方、企业推进中国式现代化建设的成就也印证了中国式现代化道路行稳致远的时代必然。

　　为讲好中国式现代化的故事，更加全面、立体、直观地呈现中国式

The General Prologue

The 20th CPC National Congress had planed the grand blueprint to build China into a great modern socialist country in all respects, and to advance rejuvenation of the Chinese nation on all fronts through a Chinese path to modernization. Chinese modernization is an unprecedented pioneering endeavor, which represents the grand path towards building a strong nation and achieving national rejuvenation. Looking back, we have led the people through arduous exploration and achieved brilliance, completing the industrialization process that took Western developed countries hundreds of years in just a few decades. We have created two miracles of rapid economic development and long-term social stability, proving that Chinese modernization is feasible and sustainable. Looking towards the future, under the strong leadership of the CPC Central Committee with Xi Jinping at the core, each region and enterprise will rely on their respective resources, geographical advantages, industrial foundations, and development plans to carefully plan and strive to be at the forefront. In the process of advancing Chinese modernization, a series of vivid scenes will be presented, step by step, transforming the beautiful blueprint into a tangible reality.

Chinese modernization is a socialist modernization under the leadership of the CPC that combines common features of modernization in various countries with Chinese characteristics based on its own national conditions. Chinese modernization is characterized by a large population, shared prosperity for all its people, the harmonious coordination of material and spiritual civilization, the harmonious coexistence of humans and nature, and the pursuit of peaceful development. These five aspects of Chinese characteristics not only reveal the scientific connotation of Chinese modernization, but also reflect tangible

现代化的丰富内涵和万千气象，中央党校（国家行政学院）中国式现代化研究中心和中央党校出版集团国家行政学院出版社联合策划推出"中国式现代化的故事"系列丛书，展现各地方、企业等在着眼全国大局、立足地方实际、发挥自身优势，推进中国式现代化建设上的新突破新作为新担当，总结贯穿其中的完整准确全面贯彻新发展理念、构建新发展格局、推动高质量发展的新理念新方法新经验。我们希望该系列丛书一本一本的出下去，能够为各地更好推进中国式现代化建设以启迪和思考，为以中国式现代化全面推进中华民族伟大复兴凝聚更加巩固的思想基础，为进一步推进中国式现代化的新实践、书写中国式现代化的新篇章汇聚磅礴力量。

中央党校（国家行政学院）中国式现代化研究中心主任

2023 年 10 月

achievements in the modernization efforts of different regions and enterprises. The theory of Chinese modernization provides endless motivation for the practical exploration of modernization in different regions and enterprises, and the achievements of localities and enterprises in advancing construction of Chinese modernization confirm the inevitability of the steady and far-reaching path of Chinese modernization in this era.

To tell the story of Chinese modernization, and to showcase the rich connotations and diverse aspects of Chinese modernization more comprehensively, vividly, and intuitively, the Chinese Modernization Research Center of CCPS and National Academy of Governance Press have jointly planned and launched the series of books "The Story of Chinese Modernization". These books aim to demonstrate the new breakthroughs, achievements, and responsibilities of various regions, enterprises, etc., in promoting Chinese modernization, by focusing on the overall national situation, local realities, and leveraging their own advantages. They also summarize and implement the new development concepts, new development patterns, and new ideas, methods, and experiences for promoting high-quality development. We hope that this series of books will be published one by one, to inspire and stimulate thinking, and to better promote construction of Chinese modernization in various regions. They will serve as a solid ideological foundation for the advancement of the rejuvenation of the Chinese nation on all fronts through a Chinese path to modernization. This will gather tremendous strength for further advancing new practices and writing new chapters of Chinese modernization.

Zhang Zhanbin
The chief director of
Chinese Modernization Research Center of CCPS
October, 2023

目 录 CONTENTS

Chapter 1

Anhui, a Wonderful Province Shining in History and Present

Chapter 2

Innovation Promoting High-quality Economic Development

Chapter 3

Beautiful Scenery with Good Mountains and Waters

Chapter 4

Anhui Culture Blooming in the New Era

第五章　幸福安居

贵治理

第六章　活力开放

添新翼

Chapter 5
Governance for a Better Life

Chapter 6
Building a Vibrant and Open Anhui

第七章　党建引领

写新章

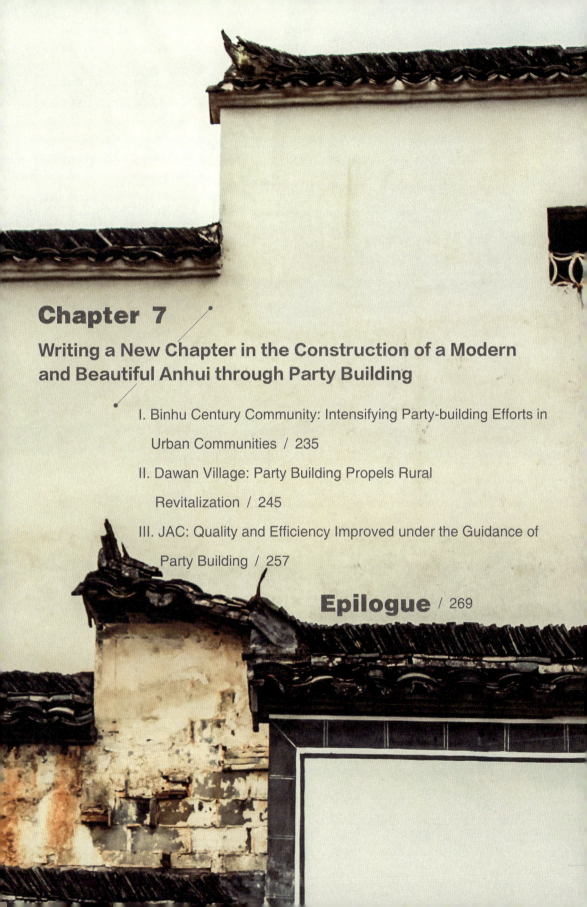

Chapter 7

Writing a New Chapter in the Construction of a Modern and Beautiful Anhui through Party Building

第一章
江淮胜地映古今

安徽，简称"皖"，地处中国东中部，东连江苏，西接河南、湖北，东南接浙江，南邻江西，北靠山东，面积14万平方公里，人口约7200万人，辖16个市，省会合肥，省名取古时安庆、徽州两府首字合成。安徽是中华文明的重要发祥地，人文底蕴深厚。安徽是中国革命的红色热土，见证了中国共产党百年筚路蓝缕。安徽是敢为人先的改革先锋，开放融通、重信重义，正加快建设科技强省、制造强省、农业强省、生态强省、人才强省、教育强省、文化强省，在中国式现代化进程中奋力走出新时代安徽高质量发展新路。

Chapter 1

Anhui, a Wonderful Province Shining in History and Present

Anhui Province, referred to as "Wan", located in the east-central China, is neighbored by six provinces which are Jiangsu, Henan, Hubei, Zhejiang, Jiangxi, and Shandong. It covers 140,000 square kilometers, and the population is about 72 million. Anhui administers 16 cities, with Hefei City as its provincial capital. The name Anhui originated from the initial word of two ancient municipalities which were Anqing and Huizhou. Anhui is an important birthplace of Chinese civilization and has a profound fundamental of humanity. Furthermore, Anhui is a red-hot land of the Chinese revolution, witnessing the Communist Party of China (CPC)'s great hardships in blazing a trail over 100 years. Anhui is a pioneer of reform, showing its openness and integration, honesty and righteousness. It is accelerating the construction of a strong province on science and technology, manufacturing, agriculture, ecology, talents, education, and culture. Anhui is striving for high-quality development on the new journey in a new era of the process of Chinese modernization.

一、古韵安徽

安徽的考古发现和研究成果实证了我国百万年的人类史、一万年的文化史、五千多年的文明史。在芜湖市繁昌区人字洞发现的距今约 250 万年的人类活动遗址，及在和县龙潭洞发掘的三四十万年前旧石器时代的"和县猿人"遗址，表明远古时期我们的祖先就在安徽这块土地上生息繁衍。在潜山市发掘的薛家岗遗址，距今有五六千年历史，是一处以新石器时代遗存为主的古文化遗址，

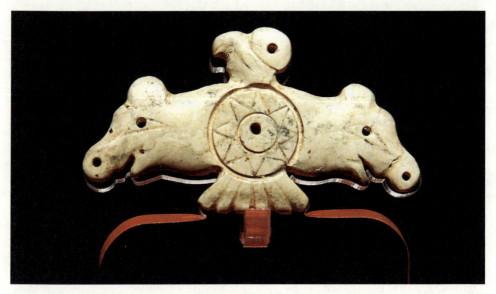

凌家滩遗址墓葬祭祀区的发现——玉鹰（徐旻昊 摄）

Jade Hawk, discovered in the Lingjiatan Site (Photo by Xu Minhao)

I. Ancient Anhui

The archaeological discoveries and research results in Anhui confirmed millions of years of human history, 10,000 years of cultural history, and more than 5,000 years of civilization in China. Human activities about 2.5 million years ago having been discovered in Renzidong Site, Fanchang District, Wuhu City, and the excavation of the 300,000 to 400,000 years old Paleolithic "Ape Man in He Xian County" in Longtandong Site both indicate that our ancestors lived and prospered in Anhui in ancient times. The Xuejiagang Site excavated in Qianshan City with a history of 5,000 to 6,000 years is an ancient cultural site with Neolithic remains, which has an important academic value for the study of primitive culture to the middle and lower reaches of the Yangtze River. The Lingjiatan Site discovered in Hanshan County, is a central settlement site in the late Neolithic period 5,800~5,300 years ago, which occupies a symbolic position in the origin and formation of Chinese civilization and provides physical evidence for the study of 5,000 years of Chinese civilization. The historical records testified that "Yu the Great (Xia Dynasty) met the chiefs in Tushan, and ten thousand chiefs paid tributes of jade and silk to him". Tushan is the ancient Dangtu in Matou City, southeast of Huaiyuan City, Anhui. The meeting in Tushan is regarded as a gradual unification of various clans and tribes of the Chinese nation and the establishment of ancient China, as well as the landmark of the founding of the Xia Dynasty.

There were many celebrities in the long history of Anhui, shining in the splendid Chinese traditional culture. It was the birthplace of Laozi, the ancient

对研究长江中下游地区原始文化有着重要的学术价值。在含山县发现的凌家滩遗址，是一处距今 5800～5300 年的新石器时代晚期中心聚落遗址，在中华文明起源和形成过程中具有标志性地位，为研究五千多年中华文明提供了实物例证。史书记载"（夏）禹会诸侯于涂山，执玉帛者万国"，涂山即今安徽怀远东南马头城的古当涂。涂山之会被认为是华夏民族各氏族部落逐步走向一体、华夏民族统一、夏王朝建立的标志。

安徽历史上名人辈出，在灿烂的中华优秀传统文化中熠熠生辉。安徽是中国古代思想家、哲学家、道家学派创始人老子的出生地。唯一发源于中国、由中国人创立的本土宗教道教尊老子为道祖。老子的著作《道德经》是全球文字出版发行量最大的著作之一。老子提出"道法自然""以百姓之心为心"，老子思想对中国的政治、经济和文化都发生过深刻的影响，是全人类共同的精神财富。

春秋时期齐国著名的政治家、军事家、经济学家管仲是安徽颍上人。管仲史称管子，他提出"仓廪实则知礼节，衣食足则知荣辱""政之所兴，在顺民心；政之所废，在逆民心"。他辅佐齐桓公从政治、经济、军事、民风等各方面进行改革，抵御外族侵扰，成就了一代霸业，为中华文明的存续作出了巨大贡献，其管理智慧为后世治理经济提供了可贵的借鉴，被誉为"华夏第一相""华夏文明的保护者"。

中国家喻户晓的历史人物曹操是安徽亳州人。他身处乱世、雄才大略，主张法治、唯才是举，抑制豪强、发展生产，改革了东汉末年的许多恶政，将破碎的河山重新整合，统一了北方，为中华民族大一统奠定了基础。曹操不仅是杰出的政治家、军事家，还是文学家。"往事越千年，魏武挥鞭，东临碣石有遗篇。"毛泽东曾在诗词中这样感叹。以曹操、曹丕、曹植父子为代表的建安文学，直抒胸臆、俊爽刚健，形成了中国文学史上"建安风骨"的独特风格，被后人尊为典范，是后代文人对文学追求的理想境界。

Chinese thinker, philosopher, and founder of the Taoist school of thought. Daoism, the only native religion that originated in China and was founded by Chinese people, honors Laozi as the primogenitor. Laozi's masterpiece – *Tao Te Ching*, is one of the world's most widely published and distributed works. Laozi suggests that "Human beings should follow the rules of nature," and "To follow the heart of the people". His thought has had a profound impact on China's politics, economy, and culture, and is the common spiritual wealth of all mankind.

During the Spring and Autumn Period, Guan Zhong, a famous politician, military strategist, and economist of Qi State, was a native of Yingshang County, Anhui. Guan Zhong, known as Guanzi in history, put forward the idea that "When the granaries are full, the people follow appropriate rules of conduct," and "The success and failure of politics depend on whether satisfying the aspiration of the people." He aided Duke Huan of Qi to carry out reforms in the aspects of politics, economy, military, and people's morals, as well as to ward off the foreign clans' invasion, and to achieve a generation of hegemony. He made great contributions to the survival of Chinese civilization, and his management wisdom provided a valuable reference for administration of future generations. He was known as the top Chinese prime minister and the protector of Chinese civilization.

Cao Cao, a well-known historical figure in China, was a native of Bozhou City, Anhui. He was a man of great talent and bold vision in chaos, advocated the rule of law and meritocracy, curbed overpowered clans and tribes, developed production, and reformed much misgovernment implemented in the last years of the Eastern Han Dynasty. He reintegrated the shattered homeland, and unified the northern area, thus, laying the groundwork for the great unification of the Chinese nation. Cao was not only an outstanding politician and military strategist, but also a litterateur. "More than a thousand years ago, Cao wielded his whip on a horse heading east, and left a poem on Jieshi Mountain for us," Mao Zedong once exclaimed in his poem. Cao and his two sons, Cao Pi and Cao Zhi, together referred to as the representatives of Jian'an Literature, with a style of

北宋时期的包拯廉洁公正、不附权贵、铁面无私，以"包青天"及"包公"名垂青史。包拯是安徽合肥人，并长期在安徽任职。近代洋务派代表人物、台湾省首任巡抚刘铭传是安徽肥西人，他率领中国军民击败外国侵略者对台湾地区的进犯，维护了国家统一、领土完整，是推动台湾现代化建设的先驱者，有台湾洋务运动之父和台湾近代化之父之誉，是深受两岸民众敬仰的民族英雄。晚清安徽歙县人王茂荫的货币理论及其施行结果受到了当时正在从事资本研究的马克思的关注，成为《资本论》中提到的唯一的中国人。

　　经过长期的积淀与传承，安徽形成了极具地方特色的区域文化，包括徽州文化、淮河文化、皖江文化。以方苞、姚鼐、刘大櫆为代表的重要文化流派——桐城派起源于安徽。研究徽州文化的徽学，与藏学、敦煌学并称中国三大地域文化显学。中华美食豆腐产自安徽，如今已成为全世界人民的舌尖最爱。

农作物与徽派建筑融为一体（沈道银 摄）
Crops and Huizhou architecture (Photo by Shen Daoyin)

straightforward, beautiful, and robust, formed a unique style in Chinese literary history – Jian'an Style, which was honored as a mode by descendants and the ideal realm of the pursuit of literature for future generations of literati.

In the Northern Song Dynasty, Bao Zheng, who was incorruptible and just, and not attached to dignitaries, was famous in history as Bao Qingtian and Lord Bao. He was a native of Hefei, Anhui, where he served for a long period. Liu Mingchuan, the representative figure of modern foreign affairs and the first governor of Taiwan Province, was born in Feixi County, Anhui. He led the Chinese army and people to defeat the foreign invaders in Taiwan, defended national unity and territorial integrity, as well as the pioneer in promoting the modernization of Taiwan's construction. He was commemorated as both the father of Taiwan's Westernization Movement and Taiwan's modernization. People across the Taiwan Strait deeply admire him as a national hero. In the late Qing Dynasty, Wang Maoyin, a native of She County, Anhui, had his monetary theories and the results of its implementation arouse Karl Marx's concern, who was engaged in the study of capital at that time. Wang became the only Chinese person mentioned in *Capital*.

After a long period of accumulation and inheritance, Anhui has cultivated a regional culture with great local characteristics, including various cultures of Huizhou, Huaihe, and Wanjiang. The Tongcheng School of thought, an important cultural theory school represented by Fang Bao, Yao Nai, and Liu Dakui, originated in Anhui. The studies of Huizhou culture, along with Xizang Studies and Dunhuang Studies, were jointly named as the three important practical schools of regional cultures in China. The Chinese delicacy Tofu, produced in Anhui, has become a favorite food of people all over the world. Huizhou cuisine, which originated in the mountainous countryside of ancient Huizhou and concentrated the flavors and characteristics of different parts of Anhui, is unique among Chinese dishes. Huizhou cuisine, together with the cuisines of Sichuan, Shandong, Guangdong, Jiangsu, Zhejiang, Fujian, and Hunan, were called the Eight Traditional Chinese Cuisines. Huizhou architecture is located in lucid

黄山宏村徽州古建筑群落（温沁 摄）

Huizhou ancient architecture clusters in Hongcun Village, Huangshan Mountain (Photo by Wen Qin)

起源于古徽州的山乡风味、集中了安徽各地风味特色的徽菜，在中国菜系中独树一帜，与川菜、鲁菜、粤菜、苏菜、浙菜、闽菜、湘菜并列被称为中国八大菜系。徽州建筑坐落于绿水青山之间，集山川风景之灵气，融风俗文化之精华，村镇规划构思精巧，平面空间处理得当，砖木石雕刻精美，依山就势、自然得体，成为中国建筑艺术的一大派系。粉墙、青瓦、马头墙也成为中国南方建筑的一个典型符号。

另外，安徽文房四宝（宣笔、徽墨、宣纸、歙砚）驰名中外，"中国的乡村音乐"黄梅戏唱响全球华人圈。安徽"三山三江两湖"山水秀美，尤其是黄山更以"五岳归来不看山，黄山归来不看岳"闻名天下。安徽的人物、故事、风光、物产数不胜数。

waters and lush mountains, gathering the spirit of the mountains and rivers of the scenery, integrating the essence of customs and culture, presenting delicate village planning, properly handling the space both horizontally and vertically, exquisitely engraving brick, wood, and stone. In accordance with mountains on the terrain, Huizhou architecture is designed naturally and appropriately, becoming a major school of Chinese architectural art. The white walls, black tiles, and horse-head gabbles have also become typical symbols of Southern Chinese architecture.

In addition, the Four Treasures of Study (Chinese Brush, Black Ink, Xuan Paper and Ink Stone) are famous worldwide. Huangmei Opera, China's "country music", has been sung by Chinese people all over the world. Anhui boasts beautiful landscapes of "three mountains, three rivers, and two lakes". Especially, the Huangshan Mountain enjoys the reputation of "One doesn't want to visit other mountains after returning from Huangshan Mountain," which is known globally. Celebrities, stories, scenery, and resources are countless in Anhui.

二、红色安徽

安徽是红色革命文化资源大省。百年以来，江淮大地在一个个重要历史节点上发生了一系列重大事件，镌刻下了深深的安徽印记。

新文化运动的倡导者、发起者和主要旗手，"五四运动的总司令"，中国共产党的主要创始人之一和党早期主要领导人陈独秀是安徽安庆人。他的长子陈延年、次子陈乔年也是中共早期重要领导人和优秀党员，先后为中国革命献出

金寨县红军广场（王尚云 摄）
Red Army Square of Jinzhai County (Photo by Wang Shangyun)

II. Red Anhui

Anhui is rich in red cultural resources. Over the past one hundred years, a series of major events have taken place here at different critical historical junctures, which were deeply engraved with imprints of Anhui.

Chen Duxiu, the advocator, initiator, and main flag-bearer of the New Culture Movement, respected as the Commander-in-Chief of the May Fourth Movement, was one of the main founders and an early major leader of the CPC, who was a native of Anqing, Anhui. His eldest son Chen Yannian, and his second son Chen Qiaonian, were also important leaders and outstanding members of the CPC in its early days. They sacrificed their lives for the Chinese revolution successively. Both of them died under the age of 30 at the time.

Jinzhai County, Anhui, is known as the Cradle of the Red Army, and the Hometown of Chinese Generals. It is an old revolutionary area, an important source of the Chinese Revolution, and the prominent birthplace of the People's Army. In the 1950s and 1960s, among all the Generals awarded the title in the People's Liberation Army (PLA), there were 59 from Jinzhai, thus, it nationally renowned as the Generals' County. Among them, Hong Xuezhi was the only one who had been awarded the highest rank of General twice since the establishment of the PLA.

During the War of Resistance Against Japan, the New Fourth Army – the armed force led by the CPC directly, fought against Japan in Anhui long-termly.

了生命，牺牲时皆不满 30 岁。

安徽金寨县被誉为"红军的摇篮、将军的故乡"，是革命老区，是中国革命的重要策源地、人民军队的重要发源地。在 20 世纪五六十年代授衔的中国人民解放军将军中，金寨籍就有 59 名，是全国著名的"将军县"，其中洪学智将军是解放军建成以来唯一一位两次授上将军衔的将军。

抗日战争时期，中国共产党直接领导的抗日武装力量新四军长期战斗在安徽。新四军转战大江南北、淮河两岸，出征后的首战在巢县蒋家河口，震惊中外的皖南事变发生在泾县茂林。新四军在华中地区共创建 8 块抗日根据地，其中安徽就有淮北、淮南、皖江 3 块抗日根据地，为抗日战争的胜利作出了重大贡献。

渡江战役纪念馆（温沁 摄）
The Yangtze Crossing Campaign Memorial in Hefei, Anhui (Photo by Wen Qin)

安徽，是当年渡江战役的练兵场、出发地、主战场。1949 年 4 月 21 日，毛泽东主席、朱德总司令发布了《向全国进军的命令》，号令解放全中国，将革命进行到底。人民解放军百万雄师千帆竞渡，迅速突破国民党军苦心经营的长江防线，彻底粉碎了国民党反动派凭借长江天险，实现"划江而治"的图谋。仅

The New Fourth Army battled from the north to the south of the Yangtze River and on both sides of the Huaihe River. Its first battle after the expedition took place in Jiangjiahekou of Chaoxian County. The Southern Anhui Incident, which shocked the whole world, took place in Maolin of Jingxian County. The New Fourth Army created 8 bases of resistance against Japan in central China, among which, 3 bases were in Anhui, including Huaibei, Huainan, and Wanjiang, and made great contributions to the victory of the War of Resistance Against Japan.

Once, Anhui was the training ground, starting point, and main battlefield of the Campaign of Crossing the Yangtze River. On April 21, 1949, Chairman Mao Zedong and Commander-in-Chief of the PLA, Zhu De, jointly issued *An Order to March Towards the Whole Nation*, commanding to liberate China on the whole and carrying the revolution through to the end. The PLA, with its millions of troops, quickly broke through the defense line of the Yangtze River, which had been painstakingly operated by the Kuomintang (KMT) army, and completely crushed the KMT reactionaries' plan of Separately Rule by the River by virtue of the heavenly danger of the Yangtze River. In only 3 days, the PLA liberated Nanjing– the ruling center of the KMT, marking a comprehensive victory in the War of Liberation. The PLA crossed the Yangtze River over 500 kilometers, of which more than 400 kilometers accounted for Anhui. During the Campaign of Crossing the Yangtze River, the people of Anhui supported the front-line actively and positively, demonstrating the inestimable power of the People's War. On August 19, 2020, during a visit to the Yangtze Crossing Campaign Memorial in Hefei, Anhui, President Xi Jinping said that the victory of the Campaign of Crossing the Yangtze River was won by the common people who rowed with a small boat. At no time could we forget the people as our roots, and we must always be loyal servants to the people.

China's reform began in the countryside, and the reform of the countryside began in Anhui. On a cold winter night in 1978, in Xiaogang Village, Fengyang County, Anhui, 18 hungry peasants, taking the risk of their lives, with the courage

用三天，解放军就解放了国民党统治中心南京，标志着解放战争走向全面胜利。人民解放军横渡千里长江，皖江占了八百余里。在渡江战役中，安徽人民积极展开如火如荼的支前运动，展现出人民战争不可估量的强大威力。2020 年 8 月 19 日，习近平总书记在安徽合肥考察渡江战役纪念馆时说，渡江战役的胜利是靠老百姓用小船划出来的。任何时候我们都不能忘了人民这个根，要永远做忠诚的人民服务员。

中国的改革是从农村开始的，而农村的改革又是从安徽开始的。1978 年的一个寒冬之夜，安徽省凤阳县小岗村 18 个饥肠辘辘的农民，不惜拿性命作赌注，以敢为人先的胆识，按下了"红手印"，打破极端化平均主义组织形式，搞起了"大包干"。次年，小岗村即获得大丰收。邓小平肯定了这一源自安徽农民的改革创举。由此，"当年贴着身家性命干的事，变成中国改革的一声春雷，成为中国改革的一个标志"，揭开了中国改革开放的序幕。

从开天辟地的建党伟业，到改天换地的建国大业，再到翻天覆地的改革宏业，安徽在共和国的历史上留下浓墨重彩的光彩篇章。

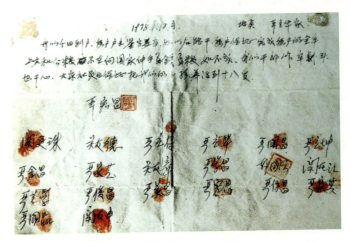

小岗村红手印（吴文兵 摄）

Red handprint pressed by 18 peasants in Xiaogang Village (Photo by Wu Wenbing)

to surpass all, pressed the "red hand-prints" on Land Contract Responsibility Letter, breaking the extremist egalitarian form of organization, and launched the All-round Responsibility System. In the following year, Xiaogang reaped a bumper harvest. Deng Xiaoping recognized this reform initiative from Anhui peasants. As a result, "What was done at that time risking the lives of the family, turned into a spring thunder and became a symbol of China's reform," unveiling the prelude to China's reform and opening-up.

From the great establishment of the CPC to the magnificent founding of the People's Republic of China, and then to the grand cause of China's reform, Anhui has written a splendid chapter in the history of China.

三、奋进安徽

　　党的十八大以来，习近平总书记两次亲临安徽考察，为安徽发展全方位把脉定向、把舵领航。安徽坚持以习近平新时代中国特色社会主义思想为指导，全面贯彻落实习近平总书记关于安徽工作的重要讲话、重要指示精神，立足新发展阶段，贯彻新发展理念，构建新发展格局，全力打造具有重要影响力的"科技创新策源地、新兴产业聚集地、改革开放新高地、经济社会发展全面绿色转型区"，取得了新的重大成就。

　　实现了"总量居中、人均靠后"向"总量靠前、人均居中"的历史性跨越，在区域发展格局中的地位和形象均显著提升，在国家发展全局中的战略地位进一步凸显。全省生产总值连跨 2 个万亿元台阶达到 4.5 万亿元左右，跻身全国十强，人均地区生产总值突破 1 万美元。粮食产量稳定在 800 亿斤以上，跃升至全国第 4 位。社会消费品零售总额突破 2 万亿元，进出口总额突破 1000 亿美元。

　　实现了"科教大省"向"科技创新策源地"的跨越发展。合肥是全国 4 个综合性国家科学中心之一，首个国家实验室落地安徽，已建、在建、拟建大科学装置 12 个，数量位居全国前列。量子通信、动态存储芯片等领域科技创新和产业发展并跑领跑。加快科技成果转化应用，推进建设"科大硅谷"、安徽科技大市场，运行全国首家以创新为主题的安徽创新馆。2022 年，安徽区域创新能力跃居全国第 7 位，已连续 11 年稳居全国第一方阵。

III. Advancing Anhui

Since the 18th National Congress of the CPC, President Xi Jinping has inspected Anhui twice, directing the development of Anhui in an all-round way. Under the guidance of Xi Jinping Thoughts on Socialism with Chinese Characteristics for a New Era, Anhui comprehensively implements Xi Jinping's important speeches and instructions on the work of Anhui, grounds its effort in the new development stage, applies the new development philosophy and builds a new pattern of development, and makes full efforts to construct "an influential cradle of sci-tech innovation, a hub of emerging industries, a highland of reform and opening-up, and a demonstration area for eco-friendly development" with great influence, which has made new significant achievements.

Anhui has realized a historic leap from "GDP at the middle level and per capita GDP backward" to "GDP at the front level and per capita GDP at the middle level". Its position and image in the regional development pattern have been significantly enhanced, and its strategic position in the overall situation of China's development has been further highlighted. Anhui's GDP has crossed RMB 2 trillion in a row, and increased remarkably to about RMB 4.5 trillion, ranking among the Top 10 in China, and the per capita GDP has exceeded USD 10,000. Grain output has stabilized at more than 40 million metric tons, jumping to the 4th place of China. The total retail sales of consumer goods exceeded RMB 2 trillion, and the total volume of imports and exports exceeded USD 100 billion.

Anhui has fulfilled a forward span from a large province of science and

大科学装置（温沁 摄）
Large-scale scientific facility (Photo by Wen Qin)

实现了"传统农业大省"向"新兴产业聚集地"的跨越发展。新能源汽车、先进光伏和新型储能、新一代信息和通信技术、人工智能、生命健康、绿色食品、新材料、高端装备制造、智能家电（居）、数字创意等战略性新兴产业聚链成群、集群成势，高技术制造业增加值年均增长 19.6%，数字经济增加值突破 1 万亿元，战略性新兴产业产值达 2 万亿元，对全省工业经济增长的贡献率达 60%。

实现了"内陆腹地"向"改革开放新高地"的跨越发展。安徽沿江近海、居中靠东，是连接长三角和中部地区的枢纽，拥有内畅外联、四通八达的综合交通运输体系，拥有自贸试验区、综合保税区、合肥国际陆港、芜湖专业航空货运枢纽港等对外开放平台，成功举办世界制造业大会等重要国际性展会。经贸朋友圈覆盖全球 97% 的国家和地区。合肥中欧班列覆盖 18 个国家、122 个国际站点城市。

education to an influential cradle of sci-tech innovation. Hefei is one of the 4 comprehensive national science centers around the nation. The first state laboratory has been located in Anhui, and 12 large-scale scientific facilities have been built or are under construction, or are proposed to be built, the number of which is among the highest in China. Quantum communication, dynamic storage chips, and other areas of sci-tech innovation and industrial development are co-leading or leading in China. Anhui accelerates the transformation and application of sci-tech achievements, promotes the construction of the Silicon Valley of the University of Science and Technology of China as well as Anhui Sci-Tech Market, and runs Anhui Innovation Pavilion – China's first innovation-themed pavilion. In 2022, Anhui's regional innovation capacity ranked 7th in the country and has been at the national forefront for 11 years consecutively.

Anhui has realized the stride from a traditional agricultural province to a hub of emerging industries. The province gathered industry chains into groups, clustered groups into a trend on new energy vehicles, advanced photovoltaic and new energy storage, new generation of information and communication technology, artificial intelligence, life and health, green food, new materials, high-end equipment manufacturing, intelligent home appliances and furniture, digital creativity, etc. The added value of the high-tech manufacturing industry grew at 19.6% on annual average. The added value of the digital economy exceeded RMB 1 trillion. The output value of strategic emerging industries amounted to RMB 2 trillion. All of the above contributed to the growth of the provincial industrial economy at 60%.

Anhui has actualized the leapfrogging development from hinterlands to a highland of reform and opening-up. Along the Yangtze River and near the Yellow Sea, as well as located in central China to the east, Anhui is a pivot connecting the Yangtze River Delta with the central region of China, and has a comprehensive transportation system known as straightway connections from internal to external and accessible in all directions. Anhui owns open platforms such as the Pilot Free

合肥新桥机场（温沁 摄）

Hefei Xinqiao International Airport (Photo by Wen Qin)

安徽的发展充分体现了中国式现代化人口规模巨大、全体人民共同富裕、物质文明与精神文明相协调、人与自然和谐共生、走和平发展道路的特征。从安徽的生动实践中，我们深切感受到，安徽发展之所以取得这样的进步，最根本的是习近平总书记的掌舵领航，是习近平新时代中国特色社会主义思想的科学指引。江淮大地日新月异的变化充分彰显了中国特色社会主义的无比优越性和强大生机活力，深刻揭示了中国共产党的领导是中国特色社会主义的最本质特征和最大优势。

唯有奋进，才有机遇。当前，安徽发展面临难得的历史机遇。一是多重国家战略叠加催生的新机遇。长三角一体化发展、中部地区高质量发展、长江经济带发展、"一带一路"建设等国家战略覆盖安徽，借上了长三角的"东风"、搭上了一体化的"快车"，这是安徽发展的最大机遇、最大势能、最大红利。二是科技革命和产业变革深入推进孕育的新机遇。当前，新一代信息和通信技术加速突破应用，新能源产业等异军突起，安徽在这些领域已深耕多年，完全有条件在开辟发展新领域新赛道上迈出更大步伐，抢占发展制高点，实现弯道超

Trade Zone, Comprehensive Bonded Zone, Hefei International Land Port, and Wuhu Professional Air Cargo Hub Port, and has successfully hosted important international exhibitions such as the World Manufacturing Convention. Partners of economic and trade circles cover 97% of the countries and regions in the world. The China–Europe Railway Express (Hefei) covers 18 countries and 122 international station cities.

The development of Anhui fully embodies the characteristics of Chinese modernization with a huge population, common prosperity for all, material and cultural-ethical advancement, harmony between humanity and nature, as well as peaceful development. We deeply feel that under the overall leadership of President Xi Jinping and the scientific guidance of Xi Jinping Thought on Socialism with Chinese Characteristics for a New Era, Anhui has made such vivid progress. Changing rapidly with each passing day, Anhui has fully demonstrated the unparalleled superiority and strong vitality of socialism with Chinese characteristics and profoundly revealed that the most essential feature and the greatest advantage of socialism with Chinese characteristics is under the leadership of the CPC.

Only by striving forward can there be opportunities. At present, the development of Anhui is facing rare historical opportunities. Firstly, new opportunities arise from the superposition of multiple national strategies. The integrated development of the Yangtze River Delta, high-quality development of the central region, the development of the Yangtze Economic Belt, the Belt and Road Initiative, and other national strategies wreathed Anhui. Under the great strategy of the Yangtze River Delta and its integrated development, this is Anhui's greatest opportunity, potential, and dividend for development. Secondly, new opportunities are bred out by the sci-tech revolution and industrial transformation. Currently, a new generation of information and communication technology accelerates the breakthrough in the application, and other industries like new energy rise drastically. Anhui has been deeply plowed in these areas for many

车和跨越式发展。三是加快构建新发展格局带来的新机遇。安徽连接沪苏浙、辐射中西部，位于"两个扇面"的交汇点上，开放通道持续加密扩容，市市通高铁、县县通高速全面实现，引江济淮世纪工程通水通航，综合性智慧化物流交通体系加快建设，有利于深度融入大循环。安徽，中国中东部这个创新活跃强劲、制造特色鲜明、生态资源良好、内陆腹地广阔、历史文化底蕴深厚的省份，正处于厚积薄发、动能强劲、大有可为的上升期、关键期，推动高质量发展其时已至、其势已成。

"水上立交"展雄风——引江济淮世纪工程（蒋常虹 摄）
Magnificent "Above-water Flyover" – the Yangtze-to-Huaihe Water Diversion Project (Photo by Jiang Changhong)

党的二十大擘画了全面建成社会主义现代化强国、以中国式现代化全面推进中华民族伟大复兴的宏伟蓝图，描绘了促进世界和平与发展、推动构建人类命运共同体的美好画卷。站在新的历史起点上，安徽将立足自身优势，奋发有为、勇毅前行，推动党的二十大战略部署在安徽落地生根，奋力走出新时代质量更高、效益更好、结构更优、活力更强、优势充分释放的发展新路，全力谱写中国式现代化建设安徽篇章。

years and is fully equipped to open up new areas and new arenas in development, control commanding points of development, overtake on a bend and leapfrog in development. Thirdly, new opportunities emerge from accelerating the creation of a new development pattern. Anhui links Shanghai, Jiangsu, and Zhejiang, radiating to the central and western region, located in the intersection of "two sectors". The open channels continue to expand intensively, with all cities connecting the high-speed rail network and all counties connecting to highways, as well as successfully achieving the Yangtze-to-Huaihe Water Diversion Project and speeding up comprehensive intelligent logistics and transportation system. All of these benefit the integration into the domestic economy deeply. Anhui, a province in east-central China, with strong innovation, distinctive characteristics in manufacturing, rich ecological resources, vast hinterlands, profound historical and cultural heritage, is in an ascending and critical period of spurring with long accumulations, strong energy, and promising potential. The time to promote high-quality development has come, and the trend has formed.

The 20th National Congress of the CPC draws a grand blueprint for building a great modern socialist country in all respects and advancing the rejuvenation of the Chinese nation on all fronts through Chinese modernization, depicts a splendid prospect of promoting world peace and development as well as building a human community with a shared future. Standing on a new historical starting point and acting on its own advantages, Anhui will make great efforts and forge ahead with enterprise and fortitude. It will facilitate the strategic plan of the 20th National Congress of the CPC to take root, strive for a development path in the new era with higher quality, better efficiency, more optimized structure, more vitality, and full release of advantages, and make every effort to write the Anhui chapter of Chinese modernization.

朱晓婷 摄
Photo by Zhu Xiaoting

第二章
创新驱动助腾飞

　　创新是中国经济高质量发展的重要底色。安徽下好创新"先手棋"，以重点突破带动整体推进，区域创新能力显著提升，战略性新兴产业加快集聚，经济结构持续优化。全球 10% 的笔记本电脑、20% 的液晶显示屏在安徽生产，全国 20% 的光伏组件、15% 的家电、10% 的新能源汽车是安徽制造。《2023 年安徽省政府工作报告》提到，过去 5 年，安徽的服务业增加值占地区生产总值比重超 50%；数字经济增加值突破 1 万亿元；粮食产量稳定在 800 亿斤以上，跃升至全国第 4 位。安徽是如何通过创新实现这些突破的？

　　下面介绍三个故事："科创之城"合肥市在产业发展上勇于开辟新赛道，与新兴产业双向奔赴；以羚羊工业互联网为代表的数字经济为企业转型升级提供新动能，是现代服务业与制造业深度融合的范例；"百亿江淮粮仓"阜阳市将科技广泛应用于农业，给农业现代化插上科技的翅膀。读者可借此一窥安徽以创新引领经济高质量发展的具体做法。

Chapter 2

Innovation Promoting High-quality Economic Development

Innovation is an important influencing factor of China's high-quality economic development. Anhui Province gains its competitive edge by innovation, drives the overall progress by key breakthroughs, and significantly improves the regional innovation capacity. Strategic emerging industries gather with faster speed, and the economic structure of the province is continuously optimized. 10% of the world's laptop computers, and 20% of the world's LCD screens are produced in Anhui. Also in China, 20% of photovoltaic modules, 15% of the home appliances, 10% of the new energy vehicles are made here. *Anhui Provincial Government Work Report 2023* mentions that over the past five years, the added value of the service industry in Anhui has accounted for more than 50% of the regional GDP, and the added value of the digital economy has exceeded RMB 1 trillion. Grain output has stabilized above 40 billion kg, jumping to No. 4 in the country. How did Anhui achieve these breakthroughs with innovation?

Here are three stories: Hefei, "the city of sci-tech innovation", is brave enough to open up new tracks in industrial development, engaging in a two-way rush with emerging industries. Ling Yang Industrial Internet, a representative of digital economy, provides new drive for the transformation and upgrading of enterprises, and is an example of deep integration of modern service and manufacturing industry. Fuyang City, known as "the granary of Anhui", widely applies sci-tech in agriculture, attaching sci-tech wings to agricultural modernization. From these stories, readers can get a glimpse of Anhui's specific approach to leading high-quality economic development through innovation.

一、产业兴市：新兴产业与
"科创之城"的双向奔赴

　　合肥，安徽省省会，全国重要的科教基地之一，中国第二个综合性国家科学中心城市①，被人们誉为"科创之城"。21世纪初的合肥，虽身为省会城市，但重点产业并不突出，GDP（国内生产总值）全国城市排名还在80名开外。如今，这座内陆城市像新兴产业的"强磁场"一样吸引着众多相关企业纷至沓来，已形成新型显示、集成电路、人工智能、新能源汽车等新兴产业集群。

　　众所周知，新兴产业对经济具有明显的拉动作用。飞速发展的新兴产业，助推合肥在追求更高质量增长的道路上阔步迈进。2012年到2022年，合肥GDP年均增速超过8%，2023年上半年GDP总额位列全国20强。随着"合肥速度"不断上演，许多城市前来学习考察，国外知名媒体《经济学人》专门刊文分析，称"合肥模式"赋能城市经济高质量发展，并为中国其他城市发展提供了实践范例。从平平无奇的低调小城到国内外瞩目的"新一线城市"，合肥逆袭式的发展究竟隐藏着怎样的奥秘？新兴产业又为何选择与之结缘？

---

　　① 综合性国家科学中心是国家创新体系建设的基础平台。目前国内在建的有上海张江、安徽合肥、北京怀柔、粤港澳大湾区、陕西西安5个综合性国家科学中心。

I. City Thriving with Industry: The Two-way Rush Between Emerging Industries and "the City of Sci-Tech Innovation"

Hefei, the capital of Anhui Province, one of the country's important science and education bases, China's second comprehensive national science center[1] city, is renowned as "the city of sci-tech innovation". However, at the beginning of the 21st century, as the capital city, its key industries were not prominent enough, with its GDP national ranking still behind Top 80. Today, this inland city is like a strong magnet for emerging industries, attracting many related enterprises, and has formed emerging industry clusters in the fields such as new display, integrated circuits, artificial intelligence, and new energy vehicles.

As we all know, emerging industries have an obvious pulling effect on the economy. The rapid development of emerging industries pushes Hefei in big strides in the pursuit of high-quality growth. From 2012 to 2022, Hefei's GDP average annual growth rate is more than 8%. In the first half of 2023, its total GDP ranked among the Top 20 in China. As the "Hefei speed" continues to happen, many cities come to study and investigate. The well-known foreign media *The Economist*

---

[1] The comprehensive national science center is the fundamental platform of the national innovation system. Currently, there are five such centers under construction in China, located in Shanghai, Hefei, Beijing, the Greater Bay Area, and Xi'an.

（一）无中生有的"神操作"

让我们先从一块屏说起。曾经，家电生产是合肥的代表性产业。2004 年初，时任合肥经济开发区副主任王厚亮走访家电企业海尔，询问他们有什么困难。海尔负责人把心病说了出来："我们迫切需要大尺寸的液晶显示屏。"当时国内有自主产权的产线，只有京东方的 5 代线，而大尺寸电视液晶屏幕至少需要 6 代线来生产，只能依赖进口。在合肥市政府看来，引入京东方 6 代线可以把家电版图中缺少的屏给补上，更可以借此推动产业升级。通过牵线搭桥，合肥主动与京东方建立联系，洽谈新产线布局事宜，可惜当时有比合肥更有优势的城市在与京东方接触。

机会在 2008 年来了。京东方寻找新产线所在地的过程并非一帆风顺，而是几经波折、屡屡碰壁，此时又逢全球金融危机，京东方由盈转亏，资金压力巨大。合肥决定抓住机会，一旦看好产业未来，就算砸锅卖铁也要把事情办成。当时全市的财政收入归属地方的部分仅 100 多亿元，合肥宁可停建地铁，也承诺为京东方提供投资 90 亿元。最终，这条国内首条液晶面板 6 代线项目成功落户合肥。因发挥国有资本引导作用，撬动 8 家社会投资机构出资 90 亿元，合肥市政府实际出资 30 亿元，这种招商引资模式是合肥市探索出的一条独特的发展之路。此外，合肥市政府还向京东方提供了土地、能源、税收等方面的政策支持。

这次大胆的尝试不仅解决了家电企业的显示屏供应问题，还带动 100 多家配套企业落地，新型显示全产业链就这样无中生有地在合肥的土地上扎下了根，合肥成为世界上最大的显示屏基地之一。

analyzes in its article that the Hefei mode empowers high-quality development of the urban economy, and provides a practical example for the development of other cities in China. From a mediocre low-profile city to a new first-tier city drawing both attention from domestic and abroad, what are the mysteries of Hefei's development? And why do emerging industries choose to settle in this city?

i. The Story of "Starting from Scratch"

The story begins with a piece of screen. Once, the production of home appliances was Hefei's representative industry. In early 2004, Wang Houliang, the Deputy Director of Hefei Economic Development Zone at that time, visited home appliance company Haier, and asked what difficulties they had. The person in charge of Haier said, "We urgently need large-size LCD (liquid crystal display) screens." Among domestic enterprises at that time, only BOE (Beijing Oriental Electronics) had 5th generation line with independent property rights, but large-size TV LCD screen, which needed at least 6th generation line to produce, had to rely on imports. In the view of the Hefei municipal government, the introduction of BOE's 6th generation line could make up for the missing screens in the home appliances industry puzzle, but also be beneficial to promote industrial upgrading. Hefei took the initiative to establish contact with BOE to discuss the new production line, but unfortunately, there were cities with more competitiveness in contact with BOE.

However, the opportunity came in 2008. The process of BOE finding the location of the new production line was not smooth. Also, with the global financial crisis occurring, BOE turned from profit to loss and suffered huge financial pressure. Being optimistic about the future of the industry, Hefei decided to seize the opportunity and get things done at all costs. At that time, the local portion of the city's fiscal revenue was only over RMB 10 billion, but it would rather suspend the construction of subways and promise to invest RMB 9 billion in

合肥京东方（李博 摄）
BOE factory in Hefei (Photo by Li Bo)

　　合肥产业转型升级的序幕就此拉开，这座城市再续传奇。2016 年"投注"长鑫存储芯片，2020 年"接盘"跌入低谷的蔚来汽车……每一次投资，引一个龙头，带一串链条，兴一片产业。这些"神操作"让合肥一度被认为是"最牛风投城市"。

　　对此，合肥有自己的方法论：合肥不是"风投"是"产投"，不是"赌博"是"拼搏"——赌博靠的是手气，拼搏靠的是手艺。

（二）产业创新：产业发展的合肥模式

　　合肥的产业发展可以总结为政府领投，带动社会资本参与的"以投带引"模式，瞄准产业发展方向和国家政策导向进行投资，被人们称为"合肥模式"。

　　"与普通风投不同，政府通过设立引导基金'以投带引'具有较强的政策意图，其目的不是高额投资回报，而是引导促进地方产业发展，通过引导基金招引优质产业项目，进而推动调整产业结构、促进产业集聚、引导区域经济转型。"市国资委相关负责人说。目前，合肥已构建"政府引导母基金 + 天使 / 科

BOE. Finally, the first domestic 6th generation line of LCD panel was successfully settled in Hefei. Due to the guidance of state-owned capital, 8 social investment institutions were mobilized to invest RMB 9 billion, while the Hefei municipal government actually invested RMB 3 billion. This investment attraction mode is a unique development path explored by Hefei. In addition, the government also had provided policy support for BOE in terms of land, energy, tax and other aspects.

This bold attempt not only solved the supply problem of display screens for home appliance enterprises, but also led to the landing of more than 100 supporting enterprises. The new display industry chain has taken root in the land of Hefei starting from scratch, and the city becomes one of the largest display screen bases in the world.

The transformation and upgrading of Hefei's industry has therefore begun. The legend continues. In 2016, it "bet" on Changxin storage chips, and in 2020, it took over NIO Motors which was at a low point... Every investment has brought a leading enterprise, and then an industry chain, and a thriving industry. These successful operations has made Hefei be considered as the most impressive venture capital city.

Hefei has its own methodology for this – it is not venture capital investment but industrial investment, not gambling but striving. Gambling relies merely on luck, while striving relies more on abilities.

ii. Industrial Innovation: the Hefei Mode of Industrial Development

The industrial development of Hefei can be summarized as the "investment led" mode that the government takes the lead in the investment and motivates social capital to participate, targeting towards the industry developing and policy-oriented direction. Such industrial development way is known as the Hefei mode.

"Unlike ordinary venture capitalists, the government has a strong policy

创／种子基金＋市场化基金"的国有"基金丛林"。

"成立之初,团队根本找不到一家愿意投资我们的企业。"本源量子总经理张辉说道。正当团队举步维艰的时候,一笔政府产业投资资金注入,让企业活了下来。短短几年,本源量子已经成为国内第一家量子计算独角兽企业。

这一模式还构建了国有资本退出机制,待项目成熟后,国有资本以市场化方式安全退出,循环支持新的产业项目投资。合肥在京东方 6 代线、8.5 代线项目完成投资退出时收益近 200 亿元。

在具体的产业招商过程中,人是关键因素。针对重点产业,合肥认真梳理产业链的链主企业和核心配套企业招引清单,实施靶向招商,并由政府相关负责人任产业链"链长",各县区也比照建立。"链长"的职责不少,包括完善产业发展规划、政策和服务,帮助协调解决企业招商、运营中的各种问题等。

为了不说"外行话",不做"外行事",合肥从市领导到普通招商人员,都深入学习研究产业投融资政策、行业发展报告、上市企业招股等各种与产业相关的信息。合肥的《重点产业招商指南》厚达 250 页,详细分析了合肥市重点产业链的产业趋势、市场布局、产业政策,并列出产业链全景图、重点目标企业和招商对接平台等。这本资料的编写者并不是专业机构,而是合肥市投促局的工作人员。

（三）服务创新:为企服务的"合肥温度"

近年来,合肥树立"营商环境只有更好、没有最好"的理念,连续 5 年实施 676 项改革措施,致力于打造一流营商环境,让各行各业的众多投资者、企业家们都感受到了"合肥温度"。

合肥比亚迪汽车有限公司是安徽省重点招商引资项目。2021 年 7 月,比亚迪与合肥一拍即合,比亚迪合肥基地项目从洽谈到签约用时仅 23 天,从签约到

intention of setting up guiding funds for the 'investment led' mode. Its purpose is not to achieve high investment returns, but to guide and promote the development of local industries. By guiding the funds to attract high-quality industrial projects, it can promote the adjustment of industrial structure, industrial agglomeration, and regional economic transformation," said the relevant person in charge of the municipal state-owned assets management office. At present, Hefei has established a state-owned "funds forest" composed of "government guiding funds+angel/innovation/seed funds+market-oriented funds".

"At the beginning, our team couldn't find an investor," said Zhang Hui, general manager of Origin Quantum. However, when the team was struggling, an injection of industrial investment funds from the government saved the company. In just a few years, Origin Quantum has become the first quantum computing unicorn in China.

This mode also establishes a state-owned capital exit mechanism. When the project is mature, state-owned capital can exit safely in a market-based approach, and support new industrial project investment in a circular way. Hefei earned nearly RMB 20 billion when the investment of BOE 6th and 8.5th generation line were completed.

In the process of attracting industrial investment, people play an important role. For key industries, Hefei carefully sorts out the list of leading enterprises and core supporting enterprises of the industrial chain, implementing targeted investment promotion. The relevant responsible person of the government acts as the "chain leader". Such mechanisms are also established in the counties and districts by reference. The "chain leader" has many responsibilities, such as improving the development of industrial development planning, policies and services, helping to coordinate for various problems occurring in business attraction and enterprise operation.

In order to present more professionalism, from city leaders to ordinary investment attraction personnel, Hefei has done in-depth study on industrial

开工用时 42 天，从签约到整车下线用时 10 个月，再次刷新了"合肥速度"。该项目总投资达 150 亿元，预计可带动上下游产业链总产值 1000 亿元。比亚迪的决心和底气正是来自当地政府的有力支持和高效服务，省、市、县顶格调度，及时协调解决项目土地、资金、用工等要素需求。

2021 年 8 月 19 日，距离比亚迪合肥基地项目开工仅有十几个小时，项目方提出项目区地势低洼，急需巨量土方填平。面对突如其来的难题，项目所在地合肥市长丰县下塘镇连夜协调运输公司来镇"作战"，1200 多辆渣土车彻夜忙碌。第二天，一块平整的土地交付给项目方，项目得以如期开工。项目建成后，为了方便员工生活，在比亚迪合肥基地项目对面专门建起一条商业街；当地政府每周还召开一次"周六解题会"，企业提问题，部门来解答……通过一件件小事，可以看出地方干部为了发展"撸起袖子加油干"的拼搏和时时处处为企业

比亚迪合肥基地第一辆整车下线（范柏文 摄）
The first car off the line in BYD Hefei Base (Photo by Fan Baiwen)

investment and financing policies, industry development reports, listed companies offering and other industry-related information. *The Key Industry Investment Guide* of Hefei, as thick as 250 pages, is a detailed analysis of the Hefei key industry chains on industry trend, market layout, and industrial policy, listing the industry chain panoramic maps, key target enterprises and investment docking platform. The compilers of this information are the staff of Hefei Investment Promotion Bureau, instead of an investment institution.

iii. Service Innovation: The "Hefei Temperature" Warming Enterprises

In recent years, Hefei has upheld the idea that the business environment can only be better, implemented 676 reform measures for 5 consecutive years, and are committed to creating a first-class business environment, so that investors and entrepreneurs from all walks of life have felt the "Hefei temperature".

Hefei BYD Auto Co., Ltd. is a key investment project in Anhui Province. In July 2021, BYD and Hefei reached cooperation. The BYD Hefei Base project took only 23 days from negotiation to agreement signing, 42 days from signing to construction, and then 10 months from signing to the cars off the line, which once again refreshed the "Hefei speed". The total investment of the project reached RMB 15 billion, and it was expected to drive the total output value of the upstream and downstream industrial chain to RMB 100 billion. BYD's determination and confidence come right from the strong support and efficient services of the local government. The provincial, municipal and county level government leaders always timely coordinate the needs of the project on land, capital, labor and other factors.

On August 19, 2021, only a dozen hours before the BYD Hefei Base project kicking off, the project side mentioned an urgent situation that the project area was low-lying and in need of a huge amount of earth filling. In the face of sudden

考虑的真情实意。

有了龙头企业带动，再加上政府的大力支持，相关产业链企业主动向合肥靠拢。目前，合肥已集聚新能源汽车产业链企业 500 余家，从业人员约 10 万人，具有国际影响力的"新能源汽车之都"正逐渐形成。

（四）科技创新："科里科气"的"合肥气质"

科技创新是合肥的"金字招牌"。从世界首颗量子通信卫星"墨子号"，到拥有突破性计算速度的量子计算机"九章"，再到给人类带来清洁能源的"人造小太阳"，合肥在许多重大科研领域实现全球领跑，"科里科气"的科创氛围成为合肥吸引企业的重要因素。

安徽创新馆（程兆 摄）
The Anhui Innovation Pavilion (Photo by Cheng Zhao)

difficulties, the government of Xiatang Town, Changfeng County, Hefei City, where the project is located in, coordinated transportation companies to the site overnight, and more than 1,200 muck trucks were busy all night. The next day, a flat piece of land was delivered to the project side, and the project was able to start on schedule. After the completion of the plant, in order to facilitate the life of employees, a shopping street was specially built opposite to the BYD Hefei Base; the local government also held "problem solving meeting on Saturday" every week, where enterprises raised questions and government gave the solution... Through one thing and another, we can see that local officials roll up their sleeves and get down to work to promote development and always consider for the enterprise.

Driven by leading enterprises and with strong support from the government, related industrial chain enterprises actively move to Hefei. At present, more than 500 new energy automobiles industrial chain enterprises, with about 100,000 employees have gathered in Hefei. The capital of new energy automobile with international influence is gradually taking shape.

iv. Sci-Tech Innovation: The Innovative "Hefei Quality"

Sci-tech innovation is the representative edge of Hefei. From the world's first quantum communication satellite "Micius", to the quantum computer "Jiuzhang" with breakthrough computing speed, to the "artificial sun" that brings clean energy to human beings, Hefei has achieved global leadership in many major scientific research fields. The innovative atmosphere of sci-tech has become an important factor to attract enterprises in Hefei.

Hefei not only has the innovative talent resources provided by the University of Science and Technology of China and other institutions of higher learning, but also invests about 17% of its financial resources in scientific and technological

合肥不仅拥有中国科学技术大学等高等院校提供的创新人才资源，而且将17%左右的财政投入科技创新，布局建设12个大科学装置，创新实力跃居全球"科研城市"第16位。同时，合肥不断推动科技成果的转化应用，让企业和高端技术的距离更近。

位于巢湖之畔的安徽创新馆，不仅是高端科技的展示窗口，还肩负着科技大市场的职能。2023年7月2日，这里举行了一场关键核心技术需求发布活动，覆盖11个重点产业领域。企业发布自身的技术需求，高校院所的技术成果在这里找到应用场景。类似这样帮助解决企业技术需求、促进科技成果转化的对接活动，在合肥一直常态化举行。

合肥的专业"手艺"到底是什么？创新或许就是其"独门秘籍"。合肥用产业创新、服务创新和科技创新共同塑造了与新兴产业之间的良性互动。今天的合肥，坚持创新驱动发展战略，围绕产业发展目标不断开辟新领域、抢占新赛道。这座敢于创新、饱含真诚的城市，不断书写着与新兴产业双向奔赴的美好故事！

innovation, and builds 12 large-scale scientific facilities. Its innovation capacity rises to the 16th place among the world's "research cities". At the same time, it constantly promotes the transformation and application of scientific and technological achievements, so that enterprises are closer to high-end technology.

The Anhui Innovation Pavilion, located by the Chaohu Lake, is not only a showcase for high-end technology, but also a major market for sci-tech. On July 2, 2023, a core technology demand release event was held here, covering 11 key industrial fields. Enterprises released their own technical needs, and technological achievements of universities and institutes found application scenarios here. Similar docking activities to help solve enterprise technical needs and promote the transformation of scientific and technological achievements have been held regularly in Hefei.

What are the special abilities of Hefei? Innovation may be its "secret weapon". Hefei uses industrial innovation, service innovation, and scientific and technological innovation to create a positive interaction with emerging industries. It adheres to the innovation-driven development strategy, and constantly opens up new areas and new arenas around the goal of industrial development. The city, innovative and sincere, keeps writing a splendid story of two-way rush with emerging industries.

二、数字赋能：羚羊工业互联网平台推动企业跨越"数字鸿沟"

在自然界生活着一种视觉和听觉发达、灵活机敏的动物，善于在不同的栖居环境中生存，它们叫作羚羊。有一家来自安徽的工业互联网平台，正是以"羚羊"命名，凭借其发达的工业感知、灵活广泛的服务内容满足了广大企业数字化转型的需求，让越来越多企业成为数字经济的"领头羊"。羚羊工业互联网综合服务平台（以下简称"羚羊平台"）是安徽扶持培育的众多工业互联网平台的一个突出代表。2023 年 6 月，《互联网周刊》发布"2023 工业互联网 500 强"榜单，安徽共有 9 家企业上榜，其中羚羊平台闯入前五。这只从安徽跑出的"羚羊"是如何诞生的？又为何能够脱颖而出呢？

（一）生而不凡的"羚羊"

这只"羚羊"是政企合作的结晶，诞生于 2021 年 9 月。在此之前，安徽的工业互联网平台不仅数量少，规模也很小。为了不错过数字化转型的风口，提升企业运营效能，增强竞争力，有的大企业投入大量资源打造了专属本企业、本行业的工业互联网平台。然而，中小企业是数量最大、最具活力的企业群体，它们是实体经济转型升级的主力军，也是我国制造业数字化转型的主战场。对

II. Digital Empowerment: Ling Yang Industrial Internet Platform Promotes Enterprises to Cross the "Digital Divide"

There is an creature in nature with developed vision and hearing, flexible and agile, good at surviving in different habitats, called Ling Yang (Chinese expression of "antelope"). An industrial internet platform from Anhui took the name after this animal. With its developed industrial perception, flexible and extensive service, it meets the needs of digital transformation of enterprises, and makes more and more enterprises take the lead in digital economy. Ling Yang Industrial Internet platform (hereinafter referred to as "Ling Yang platform") is an outstanding representative of many similar platforms supported and cultivated in Anhui. In June 2023, the magazine *China Internet Weekly* released the list of "2023 Top 500 Industrial Internet", and a total of 9 enterprises in Anhui were listed, among which Ling Yang platform broke into the top 5. How was this "Ling Yang" born in Anhui, and why can it stand out?

i. "Ling Yang", Born to Be Extraordinary

The Ling Yang platform is a result of government-enterprise cooperation, born in September 2021. Before it, the industrial internet platforms in Anhui were lack in quantity and small in scale. In order to catch the opportunity of digital transformation, and improve operation efficiency and competitiveness, some large

于数字化转型，大多数中小企业要么是没有认识到其能给企业带来哪些变化，同时对价格较敏感，不敢转；要么是找不着门路，缺资源、少技术，不会转。安徽的中小企业总量超 200 万户，难道它们就注定要被数字化浪潮所抛弃？

为了解决这个问题，安徽省经信厅携手国内人工智能领军企业科大讯飞，联合打造了羚羊平台，实行市场化运作。平台不仅可以服务中小企业，也可以服务大企业，同时还能帮助企业、科技成果、资本之间建立联系，提升科技成果转化和产业化水平。有了政府背书和推动，企业、服务商、人才、资本以更大的体量在羚羊平台汇聚一堂，碰撞出资源对接的最大效能。

（二）为中小企业提供数字化工具包

针对中小企业，羚羊平台甄选了一系列轻便好用、可快速上手的数字化工具，覆盖生产制造、仓储物流、综合管理等环节。政府和羚羊平台共同与软件服务商进行洽谈，集中采购，有效降低了采购成本。同时政府在平台为企业发放 1 万元的消费券，企业第一年的使用往往都是免费的。

安徽海森汽车零部件有限公司成立于 2022 年 3 月，是一家专注于汽车零部件的年轻公司，具有 500 万套刹车片的年生产能力。在遇到羚羊平台之前，车间生产一直使用纸质人工报单。"使用纸质人工报单易出错、耗时多、数据延后，严重影响工作效率。"公司生产部负责人李刚说。

通过参加羚羊平台的选品会，安徽海森发现了一款适合工厂生产管理的应用——黑湖小工单[①]。选用这款应用后，安徽海森告别了效率低下且容易出错的纸质手工报单，实现电子下发生产任务、实时跟进生产数据、提前预警订单延

---

① 黑湖小工单是上海黑湖网络科技有限公司的一款应用程序，为制造业提供计划排产、生产执行、质量管理等协同管理功能。

enterprises invested huge resources to create industrial Internet platforms designed for their own enterprises or industries. However, SMEs (small and medium-size enterprises) are the largest and most dynamic group of enterprises. They are the main force of the transformation and upgrading of the real economy, and should be the main fields where most of the digital transformation of China's manufacturing industry happens. However, for digital transformation, most SMEs are not willing or not prepared enough. They either do not realize what changes can be brought and are price-sensitive, or are in lack of resources and technology. The total number of SMEs in Anhui exceeds 2 million, are they doomed to be left behind by the digital wave?

In order to solve this problem, Anhui Provincial Department of Economy and Information Technology, together with the domestic artificial intelligence leading enterprise iFlytek, jointly built the Ling Yang platform, and implemented market-oriented operation. The platform cannot only serve SMEs, but also large enterprises. At the same time, it can help establish a connection among enterprises, sci-tech achievements and capital, improving the transformation and industrialization of sci-tech achievements. With government's endorsement and promotion, enterprises, service providers, talents and capital gather together in the platform with a larger volume, reaching the maximum efficiency of resource docking.

ii. Providing Digital Toolkit for SMEs

For SMEs, the Ling Yang platform has selected a series of digital tools that are easy and quick to use, covering sectors such as manufacturing, warehousing and logistics, and comprehensive management. The government and the platform jointly negotiate with software service providers and centralize procurement, effectively reducing procuring costs. Meanwhile, the government distributes a consumption coupon of RMB 10,000 for enterprises on the platform, which allows enterprises to use many digital tools for free in the first year.

Anhui Haisen Auto Parts Ltd., founded in March 2022, is a young company

期等智能化操作，效率提升 5 倍。如今企业设备高效运转，产品流转井然有序，登录手机云端，产品数量、生产进度、合格率等数据信息一目了然。

良好的使用体验坚定了企业负责人继续选择羚羊平台的信心，该负责人表

改善前：手工报单烦琐易出错、数据延后

Before: Manual reporting is complicated and error-prone with data delay

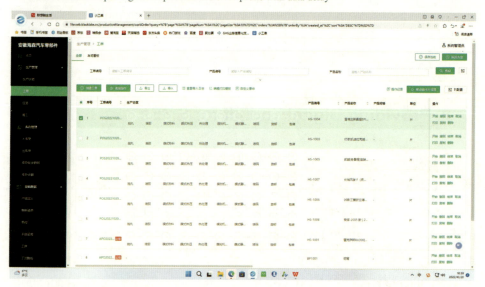

改善后：电子报单清晰明了，数据实时更新（来源："羚羊工业互联网"公众号）

After: Electronic reporting is clear and concise with data updated in real time (Source: WeChat official auount of Ling Yang Industrial Internet)

with annual production capacity of 5 million sets of brake pads. Before encountering the Ling Yang platform, its production has been using paper manual reporting. "Using paper manual reporting is error-prone, time-consuming, data delayed, and seriously affects work efficiency," said Li Gang, head of the company's production department.

By participating in a product selection fair of the Ling Yang platform, Anhui Haisen found an application suitable for factory production management – Blacklake Work Order[①]. After using this application, Anhui Haisen bid farewell to the inefficient and error-prone paper manual reports, realizing intelligent operations, such as electronic issuance of production task, real-time follow-up of production data, and early warning of order delay, and production efficiency improved by 5 times. Now, enterprise equipment operates efficiently, and product flow becomes orderly. Data information such as product quantity, production progress, and pass rate is clear at a glance by logging into the mobile phone.

The fine experience of usage has strengthened the confidence of the enterprise to continue choosing the Ling Yang platform. The person in charge said that the follow-up plan was to introduce the inventory and financial system from the Ling Yang platform, connecting the inventory and financial data, so as to further upgrade the digital level.

iii. Building "Industrial Brain" with Leading Enterprises

As a global leader in photoelectric intelligent identification equipment, Meyer's products such as color sorter for foods and oral CT machines have

---

① Blacklake Work Order: An application of Shanghai Black Lake Network Technology Co., Ltd., providing collaborative management functions, such as production planning and scheduling, production execution, quality management and so on.

示，后续计划在羚羊平台引入进销存和财务系统，将库存财务数据打通，进一步升级数字化水平。

（三）与龙头企业共同打造"工业大脑"

美亚光电是全球领先的光电智能识别装备提供商，生产的食品色选机、口腔 CT 机等产品在国内市场占有率均处于领先地位。然而，如何借助数字化转型，长久保持市场竞争优势并寻找新的营收增长点呢？

羚羊平台为美亚光电专门组建了项目团队，团队由项目负责人陈珍珍和 7 名成员组成。经过分析业务情况，他们帮助美亚光电打造了"1+2"数字化运营体系，"1"即美亚数据中台，"2"则是以数据中台为基础衍生的美亚智联与美亚智云两个平台。

美亚光电数据中台（来源："羚羊工业互联网"公众号）

Meyer data center (Source:We Chat official auount of Ling Yang Industrial Internet)

a leading market share in domestic market. However, how to maintain market competitiveness and find new revenue growth with the help of digital transformation?

The Ling Yang platform specially set up a project team for Meyer, which was composed of project leader Chen Zhenzhen and seven team members. After analyzing the business situation, they helped Meyer to create a "1+2" digital operation system, in which "1" representing the Meyer data center, and "2" referring to two platforms based on the data center called Meyer Link and Meyer Cloud.

The data center extended more than 30,000 data, covering all operation sections such as R&D, production, quality, service and finance, and becoming the "industrial brain" that supported the digitalization of all internal factors and the whole industrial chain externally. The company's original 800 business statements have been reduced to 8 statement systems, and the accuracy of sales forecast has increased by 30%, the comprehensive rate of equipment by 15%, and the efficiency of production scheduling by 50%. Before, the data of each department in the enterprise was like an isolated island, which could not be interconnected.

The Meyer Link platform effectively links the upstream and downstream of the food processing industry. Meyer started from food color sorter. By installing sensors and automatic control systems on each color sorter, the machine can be real-time docked with the Meyer Link platform, making production more scientific and efficient. The platform has connected more than 60,000 manufacturers and more than 100,000 in-use equipment, solving many problems for food processing enterprises, such as mass customized production. The product category can be expanded from original 6 to hundreds, and the delivery time cycle of the product can be shortened from original 15 days to a few hours.

The Meyer Cloud platform is connected with more than 10,000 imaging devices in dental clinics produced and sold by Meyer. The devices can provide AI-assisted diagnosis and treatment, and the industry ecology is linked through the platform, greatly improving the efficiency of diagnosis and operation.

数据中台延伸出超 3 万项数据，汇聚研发、生产、质量、服务、财务等运营全环节，成为支撑企业内部全要素数字化和企业外部的全产业链数字化的"工业大脑"。公司原先 800 张业务报表被精减成 8 张报表体系，且销售预测准确率提升 30%、设备综合率提升 15%、排产作业效率提升 50%。在此之前，企业各部门的信息数据犹如一个个孤岛，无法互联互通。

美亚智联平台实现了食品加工产业上下游的有效链接。美亚光电是做食品色选机起家的，通过给每一台色选机加装传感器和自动化控制系统，机器可以和美亚智联平台实时对接，生产变得更加科学、高效。平台已连接 6 万多个厂商、10 万多台在用设备，解决了食品加工企业的很多难题，比如大规模定制化生产的问题，产品的品类从原来的 6 种可以扩充至上百种，产品的交付周期从原来的 15 天缩短到几个小时。

美亚智云平台连接了美亚光电生产销售的 1 万多台口腔诊所的影像设备，设备可提供 AI 辅助诊疗，行业生态通过平台建立联系，诊疗和运营效率大大提高。

与羚羊平台的合作，让美亚光电成功实现从单一的设备制造商向产业综合服务商转型。结合不同行业特点，羚羊平台已携手 30 多家龙头企业打造定制化的"工业大脑"。

（四）助"科技之花"结出"产业之果"

安徽省科技资源丰富，对于如何依托工业互联网平台，推进科技成果和产业的高效对接，羚羊平台专门设立了"羚羊科产"板块。

高校院所和企业之间往往存在供需信息不对称的情况。一方面，企业不了解高校院所，有技术需求却找不到解决办法；另一方面，高校院所不了解企业需求，不少科研成果被束之高阁。羚羊平台为科研与产业之间搭建了连接渠道，

The cooperation with the Ling Yang platform has enabled Meyer to successfully transform from an equipment manufacturer to an integrated industrial service provider. Adapting to the characteristics of different industries, the Ling Yang platform has joined hands with more than 30 leading enterprises to create customized "industrial brains".

iv. Helping the "Sci-Tech Flowers" Bear "Industrial Fruits"

Anhui Province is rich in sci-tech resources. The Ling Yang platform has specially set up the Sci-Tech to Industry section, in order to promote the efficient docking between sci-tech achievements with the support of industrial internet platform.

There is often a supply-demand information asymmetry among universities, institutes and enterprises. Universities and institutions do not understand enterprise needs, and many research achievements are put on the shelf. On the other hand, enterprises feel difficult to find technical solutions. The Ling Yang platform has built a connection channel between research and industry. The technical problems of enterprises and the innovation achievements of universities and institutions can be conveniently released and precisely docked on the platform.

AIMS is a provider of overall solutions for smart manufacturing. In August 2022, the company encountered a technical bottleneck, the precision of steel pipe surface defect monitoring being difficult to meet the standard, and the customer were not satisfied. Wang Xiaopu, vice president of R&D of the company, was so anxious that he tried to post the project requirements on the newly established Ling Yang platform. There were more than 17,000 university teachers and 80,000 university student makers from Anhui, who had logged their research directions or achievements when they registered.

Zeng Weihui, a teacher from Anhui University, has done in-depth research in the fields of intelligent information processing and computer vision. When she

企业的技术难题和高校院所的创新成果都可以在平台便捷发布、精准对接。

科大智能物联是一家智能制造整体解决方案提供商。2022 年 8 月，公司遇到技术瓶颈，钢管表面瑕疵监测精度难以达标，客户对此不满意。公司研发副总裁王筱圃心急如焚，试着把项目需求发布在了新成立的羚羊平台。平台上有来自安徽全省 1.7 万多名高校教师和 8 万多名高校学生创客，他们注册时都登记了自己的研究方向或科研成果。

安徽大学的曾伟辉老师在智能信息处理和计算机视觉领域有深入研究，她在浏览羚羊平台"羚羊科产"板块时看到科大智联的企业需求，发现自己的专长与该企业发布的待解问题的技术需求匹配度很高。经羚羊平台撮合，曾老师与科大智联进一步对接交流，双方签订技术服务合同，总金额为 100 万元。寒假期间，曾老师工作地点变成了科创产业园，她和大学同事与企业的科研人员组成一个攻关小组，通过优化计算机算法，提升钢铁材料表面的检测技术，预计可将成品出厂的次品率降低 80%。"感觉又有了一片新的天地，我们要把论文的成果应用到我们的实际的生产和实际的经济发展中。"曾伟辉老师说。

羚羊平台依托人工智能、大数据和技术经理人，实现海量供需精准匹配，助力越来越多企业降本增效，驶上数字经济的"快车道"。作为国家级跨行业跨领域工业互联网平台，截至 2023 年 8 月，羚羊平台已拥有超 35.2 万用户，累计服务企业 113.2 万次，成为企业跨越"数字鸿沟"的重要桥梁。

数字赋能推进新型工业化，类似羚羊平台这样的数字经济正在给中国生产制造带来翻天覆地的改变。数字经济是继农业经济、工业经济之后人类经济形态的又一次飞跃。安徽省锚定数字经济新赛道，使其成为推动高质量发展的重要引擎。未来，安徽省将继续大力发展工业互联网，推动数字经济和实体经济深度融合，让制造业朝高端化、智能化、绿色化的方向加速发展，全面建设数字安徽。

browsed the Sci-Tech to Industry section of the Ling Yang platform, she saw the enterprise demand of AIMS, and found that her expertise was highly matched with the technical demand released by the enterprise. After the matchmaking of the Ling Yang platform, Zeng and AIMS further communicated with each other, and the two sides signed a technical service contract with a total amount of RMB 1 million. During the winter vacation, Zeng worked in the science and innovation industrial park. She, her colleagues from the university and the scientific researchers from the enterprise formed a research team. By optimizing the computer algorithm, they improved the detection technology of the surface of steel materials, which was expected to reduce the defective rate of the finished products by 80%. "It feels like opening a new world. We need to apply the paper findings to practical production and economic development," said Zeng Weihui.

Relying on AI, big data and technical managers, the Ling Yang platform realizes the accurate matching of massive supply and demand, helping more and more enterprises reduce costs, enhance efficiency, and drive into the "fast lane" of the digital economy. Based on data as of August 2023, as a national cross-industry and cross-field industrial internet platform, the total number of users of the Ling Yang platform has exceeded 352,000, and the cumulative service times for enterprises has reached 1.132 million times, becoming an important bridge for enterprises to cross the "digital divide".

Digital empowerment promotes new industrialization, and digital economy like the Ling Yang platform is bringing substantial changes to China's manufacturing industry. Digital economy makes a new leap in human economic form after agricultural economy and industrial economy. Anhui Province has anchored this new track, making digital economy an important engine to promote high-quality development. In the future, the province will continue to vigorously develop the industrial internet, promote deep integration of digital economy and real economy, accelerate manufacturing towards high-end, intelligent and green direction, and comprehensively build a digitized Anhui.

三、科技强农："百亿江淮粮仓" 插上"科技翅膀"

阜阳市位于安徽省西北部，因地势平坦气候适宜，粮食总产量多年保持在100亿斤以上，被誉为"百亿江淮粮仓"。2022年阜阳粮食播种面积1459.41万亩，粮食种植面积、产量均稳居全省第一位。每年春末夏初，随着麦收时节临近，皖北阜阳大地金黄一片，麦浪滚滚，一派丰收景象。

中国式现代化离不开农业的现代化。近年来，阜阳大力推进科技强农、机械强农，突出良种、良法、良机，全力提升以现代农业科技为支撑的粮食综合生产能力，科技种粮路子越走越稳，"百亿江淮粮仓"越筑越牢。

（一）良种：种子是农业的"芯片"

在阜阳市太和县，种粮大户徐淙祥一有空就来到田头。在种粮这块，年近七旬的他已耕耘50余年。他建立的农作物绿色高效试验示范田，屡屡创下小麦、玉米、大豆的安徽省单产纪录。多年的亲身实践，让徐淙祥坚信，良种是丰收的关键。2011年，他与安徽省农科院合作，承接国家粮食丰产科技工程。从那时起，徐淙祥每年都会试种10个至20个小麦新品种。

2022年，新品种之一"皖垦麦22号"夏收亩产超过800公斤，比常规品种

III. Strengthening Agriculture: Fuyang Attaching "Sci-Tech Wings" to Agricultural Modernization

Fuyang City is located in northwest Anhui Province. Due to flat terrain and favorable climate, its total grain output has maintained above 5 billion kg for many years, and therefore it is known as the "the granary of Anhui". In 2022, Fuyang's grain sown area is 14.5941 million mu[①], ranking first in the province in terms of grain planting area and output. Every year in late spring and early summer, as the wheat harvest season approaches, the earth in Fuyang turns golden yellow, and the wheat waves are rolling, picturing a beautiful harvest scene.

Chinese modernization is inseparable from the modernization of agriculture. In recent years, Fuyang has vigorously promoted the strengthening of agriculture by sci-tech and machinery, highlighted "good seeds, good methods and good machinery", and made every effort to enhance the comprehensive grain production capacity supported by modern agricultural sci-tech. Therefore, its road of scientific planting becomes more stable, and the "granary" getting more secured.

i. Good Seeds: the "Chips" of Agriculture

In Taihe County of Fuyang, Xu Congxiang, a large-scale grain grower,

① 1 mu nearly equals to 666.667 square kilometers.

提高将近 100 公斤。"现在小麦 800 公斤不倒伏，以前 800 斤就倒了，更别说刚干农业那会儿了。"年近七旬的徐淙祥回忆说。20 世纪 70 年代，小麦亩产大都不足 300 公斤，一遇灾年，收成更不理想。

因夏粮喜获丰收，徐淙祥提笔给习近平总书记写了一封信，汇报了 10 多年来从事粮食生产、帮助群众脱贫的情况和体会。2022 年 6 月 27 日，习近平总书记在给他的回信中说，希望种粮大户发挥规模经营优势，积极应用现代农业科技，带动广大小农户多种粮、种好粮，一起为国家粮食安全贡献力量。收到习近平总书记的回信，徐淙祥备受鼓舞，带领其他农户应用现代农业科技的劲头更足了。

"脚下这块田里的小麦品种，叫'安科 1804'，是安徽省农科院研发的新品种，今年秋种首次进行大规模示范试验。""那个是'阜航麦 1 号'，阜阳市农科

种粮大户徐淙祥（李博 摄）
Xu Congxiang (Photo by Li Bo)

comes to the fields whenever available. The man, nearly 70 years old, has been working hard for more than 50 years in growing grains. His green and efficient demonstration fields have repeatedly set records for the yield per unit area of wheat, corn and soybeans in Anhui Province. With years of experience, Xu firmly believes that good seeds are the key to a bumper harvest. In 2011, he cooperated with the Anhui Academy of Agricultural Sciences to undertake the national grain yield sci-tech project. Since then, Xu has tried to grow 10 to 20 new varieties of wheat every year.

In 2022, one of the new varieties, "Wankenmai No. 22", had a yield of more than 800 kg per mu in summer harvest, nearly 100 kg higher than the conventional variety. "Now, wheat with 800 kg yield per mu does not fall, but before, it would fall with only half the yield, not to mention the time when I just started to involve in agriculture." Xu, recalled that in 1970s, the wheat yield was mostly less than 300 kg per mu, and the harvest was even worse in disaster years.

Because of a bumper harvest in summer, Xu wrote a letter to President Xi Jinping, reporting his experience for more than 10 years of growing grain and helping fellow villagers shake off poverty. On June 27, 2023, Xi Jinping replied that large-scale grain growers should leverage the advantages in scale operations, actively apply modern agricultural technologies and encourage small household farmers to jointly contribute to national food security by expanding grain production and improving grain quality. Receiving the letter, Xu felt quite inspired, getting more strength to lead other farmers to apply modern agricultural technology.

"The wheat here in this field, called 'Anke 1804', is a new variety from Anhui Academy of Agricultural Sciences, carried out this autumn for the first time in large-scale demonstration experiments." "That is 'Fuhangmai No. 1', a new seed from Fuyang Academy of Agricultural Sciences. This year I plant 32 varieties of wheat here, and many are sowed in large area for the first time..." In the morning, Xu came to the planting cooperative base, demonstrating and explaining for more

院选育的新品种。今年我这儿有32个小麦品种，不少是第一次大面积播种……"一早，徐淙祥来到自家牵头的种植专业合作社基地，为太和县30多位种粮大户代表示范讲解。

2023年夏粮收割时节，有些地区的小麦收割因连续降雨，需要紧急抢收，否则就会减产损产。但这对徐淙祥的小麦影响不大，因为他种的是晚熟优良品种，成熟期错开了降雨，抵御自然灾害的能力也较强。

种子是农业的"芯片"，要想高产就要研发、选用好的"芯片"。阜阳市大力实施种业振兴行动，通过加强与省内外高校院所对接合作等方式，加快良种研发、繁育、推广。一批高产、优质的良种正破土而出，让这个农业大市、粮食大市的丰收底气更足。

（二）良法：科技特派员下田忙

徐淙祥种了几十年的地，深知"良种不良法，种了也白搭"，所以他非常感谢来自安徽省农科院的科技特派员给予他长期的技术指导。在阜阳市基层农村，常年活跃着一支科技特派员队伍。他们带着新技术、新理念，走村入户，传经送宝，帮助群众解决生产中的难题，助力增收致富，受到群众欢迎。

在阜阳市颍泉区的一片玉米地里，两个身影格外醒目——科技特派员牛峰正俯下身子，对着年轻的钱鑫磊嘱咐注意事项："离成熟还有25天左右，收获宜晚不宜早……"

钱鑫磊是阜阳红旗农业综合服务合作社的副理事长，虽未满30岁，但已和农业打交道有9个年头了。他回忆说，"过去玉米种植品种多且杂，每年种了收、收了种，也没有统一标准，有时候甚至是盲目选种。而且玉米收得早，含水量高，容易出现霉变。自从牛叔来了之后，很多玉米种植难题都解决了，亩均产量也明显提高了"。

than 30 large-scale grain growers in Taihe County.

In the summer harvest season of 2023, the wheat harvest in some areas needs to be urgently harvested due to continuous rain, otherwise the yield will be reduced or lost. However, there has been little impact on Xu's crops, which belong to a late-maturing superior variety. The maturation comes later than rain period, and the ability to withstand natural disasters is also strong.

Seeds are the "chips" of agriculture. In order to achieve high yield, it is necessary to develop and select good "chips". Fuyang vigorously implements the seed industry revitalization action, and speeds up R&D, breeding and promotion of fine varieties by strengthening cooperation with universities and institutes inside and outside the province. As a result, a number of high-yield and high-quality varieties of wheat are breaking upward through the soil, ensuring the abundant harvest for this large agricultural and grain city.

ii. Good Methods: Technical Professionals Active in the Fields

Xu has been planting for decades, knowing that good seeds but bad methods will get nowhere. He is grateful to the technical professional from Anhui Academy of Agricultural Sciences for his long-term technical guidance. In villages of Fuyang, there is a team of technical professionals active all year round. With new technologies and ideas, they go to the villages, pass on farming knowledge, and help villagers solve problems in production and increase income. They are much welcomed by the villagers.

In a corn field in Yingquan District of Fuyang, two figures are noticeable – technical professional Niu Feng is bending down and telling young man Qian Xinlei about precautions, "There are still about 25 days left before the corn is ripe, and the harvest would rather be late than early..."

Qian Xinlei is the vice chairman of Fuyang Hongqi Agricultural

　　2018 年，在阜阳市农科院玉米中心工作的牛峰作为阜阳市第一批科技特派员被下派基层，开始他的科技帮扶，为农民解决产业难题。此后数年，牛峰一月两次雷打不动送技术下乡，帮着农民指导耕种、改良品种，调整结构、发展种植。

　　"株高控制在 2.5 米以下，不宜过高，果穗低于 1.2 米，株型要紧凑。""带状复合种植，要充分发挥玉米、大豆间作的互补效益，提高复种指数和土地生产率……"

　　在牛峰的精心指导下，当地的玉米品质得到明显提高，价格迎来上涨，产量还得到大幅增长。几年下来，农民实现了稳产增收，牛峰也成了村民口中的牛叔、牛老师、牛专家。

　　像牛峰这样的科技特派员，阜阳已经发展了 1300 多名。这些科技特派员多

科技特派员指导农户（沈云鹏 摄）

The technical professional is instructing farmers (Photo by Shen Yunpeng)

Comprehensive Service Cooperative. Although not yet 30 years old, he has been dealing with agriculture for nine years. Qian recalls, "In the past, there were many and miscellaneous varieties of corns. Every year, we planted and harvested, and then planted again, but there was no unified standard, and sometimes we just chose seeds randomly. Moreover, the corn was often harvested early, so it's easy to have mildew because of high water content. Since uncle Niu came, a lot of corn planting problems have been solved, and average yield per mu has increased obviously."

In 2018, Niu Feng, who worked in the corn center of Fuyang Academy of Agricultural Sciences, was assigned to villages in the first batch of technical professionals in Fuyang, and began his technical assistance to solve agricultural problems for farmers. In the following years, Niu Feng unremittingly sent technology to the countryside twice a month, helping farmers do planting, improve varieties, adjust the structure and develop planting.

"The height of corn should be controlled below 2.5 meters, not too high. The ear of corn should be below 1.2 meters, and the plants should be compact." "The strip composite planting of corn and soybean should give full play to their complementary benefits, improving the multiple cropping index and land productivity..."

Under Niu Feng's careful guidance, the quality of local corn has been improved significantly, the price increases, and the output has been enhanced substantially. Over the past few years, farmers have achieved stable production and income increase, and Niu Feng has been called by villagers as uncle Niu, teacher Niu and expert Niu.

In Fuyang, there are more than 1,300 technical professionals like Niu Feng. These technical professionals have deeply rooted in the rural land for many years, giving on-site guidance in the fields. They have cultivated a group of local farming experts and technicians, and promoted scientific and technological achievements to application, constantly improving the planting performance of local farmers.

年深深扎根农村一线，到田间地头进行现场指导，为当地培养了一批种田能手和技术骨干，推动科技成果落地生根，不断提高农户种植水平。

（三）良机：效率升了成本降了

在阜阳颍上县，随着夏收工作的结束，全县 67.86 万亩水稻开始栽插。新技术、新机械的推广应用让 2023 年当地的夏种充满了"科技范"，全县机插率达到 50% 左右，大幅提升作业效率和耕作质量，还降低了生产成本。

在颍上县现代农业产业园，种粮大户宋廷周正组织工人驾驶智慧插秧机在他的 800 多亩水田里作业。传统的插秧机需要两个人操作，一个负责驾驶、一个负责摆放秧盘。为了降本增效，老宋给他的 10 台插秧机加装了北斗导航系统，每台插秧机可减少一个人工，一天就能节省 2000 元钱。对老宋这样的种粮大户来说这减少了不少生产性投入，让他很开心。无人驾驶的插秧机自动规划作业路径，在稻田中智能避让障碍物，希望的田野焕发出勃勃生机。

更让老宋开心的是，原来不看好农业生产的儿子宋小强，放弃了在外发展的机会，选择回来当上了"90 后新农人"。新农人对智慧型科技机械设备接受快，使用起来也十分得心应手。宋小强说："这种新机具上手非常快，一教就会，基本上小半天就可以上手熟练地操作了，可以实现无人驾驶，一个人操作，不起早，不摸黑，一天就能插秧 50 亩。2023 年实行的是宽窄行技术，这种技术能提高秧苗的通风透光性，产量比老一代的插秧机提高 10% 左右。"

在应用新机具上，太和县的徐淙祥自然也不会落后。除了使用无人机等现代农机具，在他的示范园区，他还将孢子捕捉仪、农业自动监测与控制系统、虫情自动监测系统等应用在田间管理一线，通过手机应用就能实时掌握田间土壤墒情、虫情、降雨量等。他的孙子徐旭东也是新农人，用起这些智能化工具比他要熟练得多。

iii. Good Machinery: Efficiency Up and Costs Down

In Yingshang County, Fuyang, after the summer harvest, the county's 678,600 mu of rice began to be planted. The promotion and application of new technologies and new machinery have made this year's summer planting full of technique. The county's machine planting rate has reached about 50%, greatly improving operation efficiency and farming quality, and reducing production costs.

In the modern agricultural industrial park in Yingshang County, Song Tingzhou, a large-scale grain grower, is organizing workers to drive the intelligent rice transplanter in his 800 mu paddy fields. The traditional rice transplanter needs two persons to operate, one responsible for driving, the other for placing the rice tray. In order to reduce costs and increase efficiency, Song Tingzhou installed the Beidou navigation system on his 10 transplanters. Each machine can reduce one manpower, saving RMB 2000 a day. For Song Tingzhou, this reduces a lot of productive investment, which makes him very happy. The unmanned rice transplanter automatically plans the operation path and intelligently avoids obstacles in the rice field, making the field full of vitality.

What makes Song Tingzhou happier is that his son Song Xiaoqiang, who had not been optimistic about agricultural production before, gave up the opportunity to develop in the city and chose to come back as a post-90s new farmer. The new farmers like him accept the intelligent technology and machinery quickly and use them very easily. Song Xiaoqiang said, "This new machine is very easy to learn. It can be used skillfully in half a day and can realize unmanned driving. One person can transplant 50 mu of rice seedlings a day without working from dawn to dusk. This year, the wide and narrow line technology is implemented, which improves the ventilation and light condition of seedlings, and the output will be about 10% higher than the previous generation of rice transplanters."

In the application of new machinery and tools, Xu Congxiang in Taihe

阜阳应用植保无人机（沈云鹏 摄）

The drones are applied to plant protection in Fuyang (Photo by Shen Yunpeng)

　　"以后的农业，应该是规模化、机械化、智能化的，坐在屋里就能把地种好。"徐淙祥曾经这样描述他心中未来的种粮场景。如今，他心中的场景正在逐渐转变为现实。

　　新机具的推广应用大大提升了农业生产效率，为阜阳的粮食稳产增产提供了关键助力。阜阳以机械强农为抓手，稳步提升粮食生产全程机械化和信息化水平，加强农机社会化服务，有力有效推动了农业生产节本增效和农业生产智能化发展。

County certainly hasn't lagged behind. In addition to using modern agricultural machinery such as drones, he has also applied spores capture device, agricultural automatic monitoring and control system, and insect automatic monitoring system, etc. to the field management in his demonstration fields. Through mobile Apps, he can grasp real-time soil moisture, insect condition, and rainfall amount in the field. His grandson Xu Xudong is also a "new farmer", much more skilled in using these intelligent tools than he.

"Agriculture in the future must be large-scale, mechanized and intelligent. You can grow crops while sitting at homes." Xu described the future grain-growing scene he once dreamed for, which is now gradually turning into reality.

The promotion and application of new machines and tools greatly improve the efficiency of agricultural production, providing key support for stable and increased grain production in Fuyang. Fuyang steadily improves the mechanization and informatization level in whole process of grain production, strengthens socialized services of agricultural machinery, and therefore effectively promotes cost saving, efficiency increase, and intelligent production in agriculture development.

Food security is among a country's most fundamental interests. Fuyang, "the granary of Anhui", is an epitome of strengthening agriculture with sci-tech in Anhui. In 2022, the total grain output of Anhui Province reached 41.001 billion kg, a new record high; the contribution rate for agricultural sci-tech progress reached 66%, 3.6% higher than national level; the comprehensive mechanization rate of crop cultivation and harvest reached 83%, 10% higher than the national level. Anhui will adhere to the instructions of President Xi Jinping – actively applying modern agricultural technologies, implement seed industry revitalization, strengthen scientific and technological and equipment support, promote modern advanced technology in agriculture, inserting wings of technology to agricultural modernization. By accelerating the construction of a high-quality and efficient province with strong agriculture, national food security will be effectively

粮食安全，是国之大者。"百亿江淮粮仓"阜阳市是安徽科技强农的缩影。2022年，安徽全省粮食总产量达820.02亿斤，再创历史新高；农业科技进步贡献率达66%，比全国高3.6个百分点；农作物耕种收综合机械化率达83%，比全国高10个百分点。安徽将持续落实习近平总书记"积极应用现代农业科技"的嘱托，深入实施种业振兴行动，强化科技和装备支撑，推广现代农业先进技术，给农业现代化插上科技的翅膀。通过加快建设高质高效的农业强省，切实维护国家粮食安全。

当前，"高质量发展"已成为读懂中国的关键词。中国坚持创新、协调、绿色、开放、共享的新发展理念，努力推动更高质量的发展。创新发展注重解决发展动力问题，协调发展注重解决发展不平衡问题，绿色发展注重解决人与自然和谐问题，开放发展注重解决发展内外联动问题，共享发展注重解决社会公平正义问题。

安徽牢记高质量发展这一首要任务，在新发展理念的引领下，积极服务和融入新发展格局。以上三个故事仅从创新视角，展示安徽对高质量发展进行的积极探索。未来，安徽将坚持创新在现代化建设全局中的核心地位，推进高水平创新型省份建设，加快建设以实体经济为支撑的现代化产业体系，在中国式现代化进程中奋力走出新时代安徽高质量发展新路。

safeguarded.

High-quality development has become a key word to understand China. China is committed to the new development philosophy of innovative, coordinated, green, open and shared development, and strives to promote development of higher quality. Innovative development is focused on addressing the issue of growth drivers, coordinated development on redressing imbalances, green development on creating harmony between humanity and nature, open development on coordinating internal and external development, and shared development on ensuring social equity and justice.

Keeping in mind the primary task of high-quality development, Anhui actively serves and integrates into the new development pattern under the guidance of the new development philosophy. The three stories above reflect Anhui's active exploration of high-quality development only from the perspective of innovation. In the new era, Anhui will uphold that innovation remains at the heart of modernization drive, promote the construction of a high-level innovative province, accelerate the modernization of industrial system supported by real economy, and strive to explore Anhui's path of high-quality development in the process of Chinese modernization.

第三章
好山好水好风光

　　安徽山水资源丰富，自然风光美好。全省上下牢牢把握习近平总书记"要把好山好水保护好"的要求，实现绿水青山和金山银山的有机统一，建设绿色江淮美好家园，打造山水秀美生态强省，在加强生态文明建设上树立安徽样板。

　　下面是关于安徽生态文明建设的三个有代表性的故事：安庆林长制改革全国首创，是我国生态文明建设的重大制度创新；马鞍山把长江大保护与推动产业转型升级结合起来，走出了统筹生态环境高水平保护和产业高质量发展的新路径；合肥坚持不懈治理巢湖蓝藻，建起了环湖十大湿地，创造了大湖名城的奇迹。

　　让我们来到怀宁，共赏蓝莓花开；来到薛家洼，和微笑天使江豚打声招呼；来到巢湖，看东方白鹳展翅飞翔……让我们共赏美景，聆听这块大地上的辛勤劳动者为了守护好山好水奋斗拼搏的故事吧。

Chapter 3

Beautiful Scenery with Good Mountains and Waters

Anhui boasts abundant landscape resources with breathtaking natural scenery. The whole province implements the instruction "to protect our beautiful mountains and waters" made by President Xi Jinping, realizing that "Lucid waters and lush mountains are invaluable assets." Anhui has built a green Jianghuai (referring to Anhui) and better home, created an ecological province with a beautiful landscape, and set up the Anhui mode in eco-civilization.

Here are three representative stories about eco-civilization in Anhui: Forest Chief Scheme of Anqing City is the national initiative and the major institutional innovation in eco-civilization in our country. Ma'anshan City combines the protection of the Yangtze River with industrial restructuring and upgrading and has explored a new path to coordinating high-level protection of the eco-environment with high-quality development of industries. Hefei City has made unremitting efforts to control the blue-green algae in Chaohu Lake and built ten wetlands, creating the miracle of a famous lake city.

Let's come to Huaining County to enjoy the blueberry blossoms, to Xuejiawa in Ma'anshan City to say hello to the smiling angel porpoise, and to Chaohu Lake to watch the white stork spreading their wings and flying... Let's enjoy the beautiful scenery as listening to the stories of the diligent workers on this land to protect our beautiful mountains and waters.

一、安庆以"林长制"促"林长治"

林长制改革是生态文明建设安徽样板的一个很好的例证。所谓"林长制"，是指把保护发展森林资源落实为党政主要领导的主体责任，建立省、市、县、乡、村五级林长，实现山有人管、林有人造、树有人护、责有人担，确保一山一坡、一园一林、一区一域都有专人专管。

安徽省把"五绿"确定为林长的五大任务：围绕"护绿"加强林业生态保护修复，围绕"增绿"推进城乡造林绿化，围绕"管绿"预防治理森林灾害，围绕"用绿"强化资源多效利用，围绕"活绿"激发林业发展动力。

（一）"光头村"变成"森林村"

安徽省林长制改革选择以安庆为试点。安庆是安徽省重点林区之一，山林火灾频发，最严重的大龙山森林火灾，2014 年一天之内竟然发生 16 处火情。杨亭村，位于大龙山北麓，自从林长制改革以来，既解决了森林火灾的难题，又绿化了村庄，这其中的奥秘是什么？

昔日的杨亭村被称为"光头村"，村里的山被称为"白山坡"，山头上遍布大大小小的坟墓，远看，白花花的一片。当地有冬至祭祀烧纸钱的习俗，因此火灾频发。

I. Promoting Forest Long-term Governance by Forest Chief Scheme in Anqing

Forest Chief Scheme is a good example of the Anhui mode of eco-civilization. Forest Chief Scheme refers to the principal leaders of party committees and governments at five levels – provincial, municipal, county, township, and village – are in charge of the protection and development of forest resources, so that mountains are managed, lands are afforested, trees are protected, and responsibilities are shouldered, ensuring that each mountain, forest, and tree is taken care of by designated people.

Anhui has identified the "five greens" as the five major tasks of forest chiefs: By "protecting the green", strengthening the maintenance and restoration of forestry ecology; by "increasing the green", promoting urban and rural afforestation, and increasing greenery coverage, by "managing the green", preventing and controlling forest disasters; by "using the green", enhancing the multi-effects utilization of resources; by "activating the green", stimulating the driving force of forestry development.

i. "Bald Village" into "Forest Village"

Forest Chief Scheme in Anhui chose Anqing as the trial reform. Anqing is one of the main forest areas in Anhui Province. In the past forest fires happened

杨亭村的党委书记杨江勤成为安庆村级林长，当时的他感到很茫然，不知道该怎么干。全村有 33 个村民组，共 3374 人。他算了又算，总算安排妥当了：他自己为总负责人，全村划分 6 大网格，33 个村民组队长为网格长，另设 5 处护林卡点、7 处视频管控点，与 12 名护林员一起织成了森林防火的安全网。

防火的任务完成了，杨书记长舒了一口气，哪知道更难的任务在等着他。安庆市搞了一个林业智慧平台，根据杨亭村现状，要求该村每年植树不能少于5000 棵，杨书记觉得压力很大。他请教专家、征求群众意见，制定了护绿、增绿的行动方案。具体地说，山顶"戴帽子"，加大公益林、防护林保护力度；山腰"系带子"，大力种植茶树、杨梅等经济林；山脚"穿靴子"，栽种银杏、红枫、红梅等观赏树种，让乡村田园四季有景。

人不负青山，青山定不负人。经过补植增绿，昔日的光头村变成森林村。山绿了，景美了，生态好了，经济效益也来了。杨亭村发挥林业资源优势，连续举办郁金香花展、采茶踏青、杨梅采摘节等活动，并结合民俗年味，举办美食文化、书画展览等节庆活动，把"花旅"、"茶旅"、"果旅"、"文旅"和"康旅"有机结合。全村每年累计接待游客超过 20 万人次，旅游经济收益突破 500万元。杨亭村还被评为"国家森林乡村""全国生态文化村"和"中国最美休闲乡村"。

阳春三月，杨书记来到了村里的秀园景区，几十万株郁金香竞相绽放，很是壮观。漫步花海，他不由地停下脚步，细细观赏，拿出手机拍照。他发个朋友圈，写道："我现在理解了'绿水青山就是金山银山'这句话的真正含义，绿水青山给我们带来的不仅仅是物质的收益，还有精神的收获。花美了，景美了，我们的幸福感更强了，在家门口就找到了'诗与远方'。"很快，他收到了几十条点赞，还有人评论："你说到了我们的心坎上。"杨书记笑了，望着争奇斗艳的郁金香花海，幸福地笑了。

frequently. In 2014, forest fires in Dalongshan Mountain hit the record of 16 times within a single day. Nowadays, Yangting Village, located at the northern foot of Dalongshan Mountain, has not only solved the problem of forest fire prevention but also realized the afforestation since the reform of Forest Chief Scheme. What is the mystery?

The former Yangting Village was called " bald village", and the mountain around it was named "white hillside". The top of the mountain was covered with large or small graves, looking white from a distance. There was a local custom of burning joss paper in mourning the ancestors at the winter solstice, so fires occurred frequently.

Yang Jiangqin, the Party Secretary of the Yangting Village, was appointed as village forest chief in Anqing, and at that time he felt confused and had no idea about the way to do. He figured out that there were 33 village groups with a total of 3,374 villagers. He calculated again and again and finally arranged it properly. He was the general person in charge. The village was divided into six large grids with 33 villager group captains for the grid leaders. In addition, 5 forest protection points, and 7 video control points, and 12 forest rangers were set up to form the safety net for forest fire prevention.

Secretary Yang was relieved after he finished the task of fire prevention. However, he didn't expect there were more difficult tasks he had to face. Anqing City built a smart forestry platform, and it was required to plant no less than 5,000 trees every year according to the current situation of Yangting Village. Secretary Yang felt under great pressure. He consulted experts, solicited opinions from locals, and formulated the plan to "protect the green" and "increase the green". Specifically, the village took some measures as follows: "wearing a hat" for the mountaintop by protecting public forests and shelter forests, "tying a belt" for the mountainside by vigorously planting tea trees, bayberries, and other economic forests, "wearing boots" for the mountain foot by planting ginkgo, red maple, red plum, and other ornamental trees. Thus, the rural scenery in the four seasons was

杨亭村花展（杨军 摄）
Flower show in Yangting Village (Photo by Yang Jun)

（二）"荒山丘"变成"蓝莓园"

林长制除了森林防火、植树造林，还能做什么？安庆市怀宁县给了我们一个大大的惊喜！怀宁县地处江淮丘陵地带，土壤多为红壤、黄棕壤，呈酸性或微酸性，这种土壤不适合粮食作物生长。以往，因为"不知道种啥好"，不少山地被闲置多年，成为名副其实的荒地。这一切，在林长制改革后，彻底发生了改变。

早在 2004 年，安徽省农科院的一位专家对怀宁山丘土壤和自然环境进行过考察论证，发现该县十分适合蓝莓生长，并开始小范围试种。但由于技术推广难、资金保障难等多种原因，蓝莓一直没有得到大面积推广，到 2016 年全县蓝莓种植面积总计才 6000 亩。

林长制改革给小小蓝莓提供了千载难逢的发展机遇。在深入调研、专家论证的基础上，2017 年，怀宁县决定大力发展蓝莓产业，打造全国林长制改革的"怀宁样板"。

县委书记和县长担任林长，领衔全县蓝莓产业发展工作，成立了林长制办

idyllic.

If we do not fail nature, nature shall never fail us. After replanting and greening, the former "bald village" has become a forest village. The mountain turns green, the scenery becomes more beautiful, the ecology gets better, and the economic benefits are also improving. Yangting Village holds tulip exhibitions, tea picking, and bayberry picking festivals by the advantages of forestry resources. In addition, it also organizes festival activities such as food culture, calligraphy, and painting exhibitions in combination with the folk customs of the Spring Festival. "Flowers tour", "tea tour", "fruit tour", "culture tour", and "health tour" are all integrated well. The total number of tourists in the village is more than 200,000 each year, and the tourism income exceeds RMB 5 million. Furthermore, Yangting Village was awarded the title of National Forest Village, National Ecological Culture Village, and China's Most Beautiful Leisure Village.

In sunny lunar March, Secretary Yang came to the Xiuyuan scenic spot in the village. Hundreds of thousands of tulips were blooming, which was very spectacular. Wandering in the sea of flowers, he couldn't help stopping, watching carefully, and taking pictures by his mobile phone. He posted a message to his WeChat Moments: "I now understand the true meaning of 'Lucid waters and lush mountains are invaluable assets.' Lucid waters and lush mountains bring us not only material benefits but also spiritual gains. The flowers are so beautiful and the scenery is stunning. We're feeling much happier. 'Poetry and distance' is found right at our doorstep." Soon, he received dozens of "likes", and one commented: "You touch my heart." Secretary Yang smiled happily, looking at the sea of splendid tulips.

ii. "Barren Hill" into "Blueberry Farm"

What can Forest Chief Scheme do besides forest fire prevention and afforestation? Huaining County of Anqing City gives us a big surprise. Huaining

公室，中心工作是蓝莓产业的发展。怀宁县和安徽农业大学联合建立了皖西南综合实验站，组建蓝莓科技特派团，派遣专门技术人员到田间地头，"把脉问诊"送服务，帮助解决蓝莓灰霉病、根腐病等技术难题。怀宁县制定蓝莓产业发展规划，强化财政金融保险等扶持政策，解决蓝莓产业的资金难问题。在林长制改革的春风下，2017年怀宁县蓝莓种植就扩大到2.5万亩，从此进入了发展的快车道。2023年，全县蓝莓种植面积达8.5万亩，成为长三角最大的县级蓝莓种植区。

怀宁县蓝莓园（檀志扬 刘亮 摄）
Blueberry farm in Huaining County (Photo by Tan Zhiyang and Liu Liang)

怀宁县、乡、村三级林长们一起谋划，成立蓝乡供应链管理公司，通过"五统一"模式，即统一品牌、统一分选、统一包装、统一定价、统一销售，打造"怀宁蓝莓"区域公用品牌。目前，"怀宁蓝莓"获批国家地理标志证明商标、被纳入全国名特优新农产品名录。

林长制改革以来，怀宁县一张蓝图绘到底，一任接着一任干，坚定不移打造"一县一业"（蓝莓）全产业链，逐步实现由"卖原料"向"卖加工品"转变。

County is located in the hilly area, where the soil is mostly red, and yellow-brown, which is acidic or slightly acidic. This kind of soil is not suitable for crop growth. In the past, because villagers had no idea about what to plant, numerous hilly land was left idle for many years and became a veritable wasteland. But all have changed completely after the reform of Forest Chief Scheme.

As early as 2004, an expert from the Anhui Academy of Agricultural Sciences inspected the natural environment and the soil of Huaining Hill and found that the county was very suitable for blueberry growth. So he began a small-scale trial. However, blueberry planting was limited due to technical difficulties, financial constraints, and other factors. In 2016, the total area of blueberry planting in Huaining County was only 6,000 mu.

Forest Chief Scheme provided a rare development opportunity for blueberries. In 2017, based on in-depth investigation and expert testimony, Huaining County decided to vigorously develop the blueberry industry and create the Huaining mode of Forest Chief Scheme all over the country.

The Party Secretary of the County and County Chief acted as forest chiefs, leading the development of the blueberry industry in the county. The office of Forest Chief Scheme was established, and the central work was to develop the blueberry industry. Huaining County and Anhui Agricultural University jointly established the Comprehensive Experimental Station of Southwest Anhui, which organized the blueberry science and technology mission, providing field services from professional technicians to address technical issues such as blueberry gray mold and root rot. Huaining County set up policies to support the blueberry industry, addressing funding difficulties through fiscal, financial, and insurance measures. The blueberry planting in Huaining County expanded to 25,000 mu in 2017, moving into the fast lane of development under the reform of Forest Chief Scheme. In 2023, the blueberry planting area in the county reached 85,000 mu, becoming the largest county-level blueberry planting area in the Yangtze River Delta.

目前，怀宁县现有蓝莓精深加工项目 10 个，一箱箱新鲜蓝莓果经过生产线，摇身一变，成了蓝莓干、蓝莓果醋、蓝莓酒……

近年来，怀宁县、乡、村三级林长齐努力，依托蓝莓产业优势，探索出一条"蓝莓＋旅游"的发展新路子。建成了 5G 蓝莓科研基地、黄墩蓝莓小镇、蓝莓广场等蓝莓主题景区，还用蓝莓将县里的独秀山公园、海子（著名诗人）故里、马拉松生态廊道等旅游景区串珠成链，逐步构建起"春有景、夏有果、秋有游"的农文旅新格局。

小蓝莓富了一方百姓，成了农民致富的"金果果"。当地农民采取土地入股、合作发展、务工就业、生产托管、开办农家乐等方式，实现了"一地生五

小蓝莓富了一方百姓（郑金强 摄）
Small blueberry enriches locals (Photo by Zheng Jinqiang)

Forest chiefs of Huaining County, township, and village collaborated to establish the Blue Township Supply Chain Management Company which created Huaining Blueberry regional public brand through a five-unified approach: unified brand, sorting, packaging, pricing, and sales. Currently, Huaining Blueberry has obtained a national geographical indication trademark and is included in the national list of special and new agricultural products.

Since the reform of Forest Chief Scheme, one official after another in Huaining County has drawn up a sequential blueprint for the development of the blueberry industry, resolutely building the whole industry chain of One Industry (blueberry) for One County, and gradually realizing the transformation from selling "raw materials" to "processed products". Currently, Huaining County has ten blueberry further processing projects. Boxes of fresh blueberries go through the production line and change into dried blueberries, blueberry vinegar, and blueberry wine…

In recent years, forest chiefs of the county, township, and village in Huaining County worked together to explore a new development path of "blueberry + tourism" through the advantages of the blueberry industry. The 5G blueberry scientific research base, Huangdun blueberry town, Blueberry Square, and other blueberry-themed scenic spots were constructed. In addition, scenic spots such as Duxiu Mountain Park, Haizi (a famous poet) Hometown, and Marathon Ecological Corridor in the county were connected by the blueberry, gradually forming a new pattern of agricultural and cultural tourism with "scenery in spring, fruit in summer and walk tour in autumn".

A small blueberry has enriched the local people and becomes the "golden fruit" for farmers to make a fortune. Local farmers adopt land equity, cooperative development, employment, production trusteeship, and opening agritainment, realizing that "the land generates five sources of income." That is, land transfer gains "rent", capital equity gains "share", base labor gains "salary", order planting gains "sale", and eco-tourism gains "profits".

金"，即土地流转"获租金"、资金入股"变股金"、基地务工"挣薪金"、订单种植"得售金"、生态旅游"赢现金"。

小蓝莓果，圆了致富梦，怀宁县 497 名林长齐心合力绘出了一幅"莓"好"蓝"图。

（三）"林长制"变成"林长治"

为了实现林业的长治久安，安庆建立健全林长制的"六个一"体系框架，即一个责任体系、一个规划体系、一个支持林业发展政策体系、一个林业智慧平台、一个地方性法规、一个林业科技支撑体系。首先，全市建立全域覆盖的林长制责任体系，拉紧"责任链"，落实"林长治"。安庆实行月调度、季评价、年考核，严格包保、督察、调度、考核和执纪问责制度。其次，2020 年，安庆制定并正式实施全国首部林长制地方性法规，实现林长制的法制化。最后，安庆又建立了"林长＋检察长"监督机制。至此，林长制建立了可实施、可监测、可考核的指标体系，实现了林业经济保护和开发的有章可循。

"树上的鸟儿成双对，绿水青山带笑颜……"林长制改革以来，群众的获得感、幸福感越来越足了。更重要的是，老百姓真正尝到了"绿水青山就是金山银山"的甜头。

2020 年 8 月，习近平总书记再次视察安徽，充分肯定安徽林长制这一重大制度创新，并作出了重要指示，要求在全国推广。随后林长制在广东省、河北省、青海省等地落地生根。

A small blueberry turns the dream of getting rich into reality, and 497 forest chiefs in Huaining County jointly draw up a grand blueprint for a better life.

iii. "Forest Chief Scheme" into "Forest Long-term Governance"

To achieve forest long-term governance, Anqing has established the six systems of Forest Chief Scheme, namely a responsibility system, a planning system, a policy system to support forestry development, a smart forestry platform, a local law, and a forestry sci-tech support system. First of all, the city has established a comprehensive responsibility system for Forest Chief Scheme to enhance the "responsibility chain" and implement the "forest long-term governance". Anqing has carried out the monthly schedule, quarterly evaluation, and annual assessment, and strictly enforced the discipline and accountability system of guarantee, inspection, and assessment. Second, in 2020, Anqing formulated and officially implemented the first local regulation on Forest Chief Scheme in the country, realizing the legalization of Forest Chief Scheme. Since then, Anqing has established the supervision mechanism of "forest chief + procurator". Therefore, a standardized system, which can be implemented, monitored, and assessed, is applied to make the entire process a rule-based practice.

"Two birds in the trees are in pairs, while green waters and mountains look smiling…" Since the reform of Forest Chief Scheme, locals have had a greater sense of gain and happiness. More importantly, they have truly experienced the benefits of "Lucid waters and lush mountains are invaluable assets."

In August 2020, President Xi Jinping inspected Anhui again, fully recognizing the major institutional innovation of Forest Chief Scheme in Anhui, and making instructions to spread it nationwide. Consequently, Forest Chief Scheme has taken root in other provinces such as Guangdong, Hebei, and Qinghai.

二、把马鞍山打造成长三角的"白菜心"

长江是中华民族的母亲河。很长一段时间，长江水污染和生态破坏问题越来越严重，直接影响到长江生态安全。马鞍山是著名的钢铁城市，地处长江下游，横跨长江两岸，拥有长达 79 公里的长江岸线，保护长江的责任重大。

2016 年 1 月，习近平总书记在推动长江经济带发展座谈会上强调，要把修复长江生态环境摆在压倒性位置，共抓大保护，不搞大开发。马鞍山痛下决心，从水上、岸线和城市着手，保护长江生态，打造水清岸绿产业优美丽长江（马鞍山）经济带。

（一）薛家洼"蝶变"

马鞍山保护长江的行动先从防治水污染开始，薛家洼被当作突破口。薛家洼位于长江主航道的下游，万里江水奔流至此，流速放缓形成了天然避风港。这里长年有 200 多条船，四五百个渔民生活在船上，生活污水直排长江，成为水上的直接污染源。要想根治长江水污染，就必须让这些渔民上岸退捕转产。

三姑娘，大名陈兰香，是个渔民，家就在船上，过着"水上漂"的生活。上了岸，住哪儿？不捕鱼了，靠什么生活？她愁得睡不着觉。

II. Turning Ma'anshan into the "Cabbage Heart" of the Yangtze River Delta

The Yangtze River is the mother river of the Chinese nation. For a long time, the problem of water pollution and ecological damage to the Yangtze River has become more and more serious, directly affecting the ecological security of the Yangtze River. Ma'anshan City, famous for steel, situated in the lower reaches of the Yangtze River, spans both sides of the river with a 79-kilometer shoreline and bears significant responsibility for protecting the Yangtze River.

In January 2016, President Xi Jinping stressed that the restoration of the Yangtze River's ecological environment should be a major priority. He also urged to promote well-coordinated environmental conservation and avoid excessive development at the symposium on promoting the development of the Yangtze River Economic Belt. Therefore, Ma'anshan is determined to build a beautiful Yangtze River (Ma'anshan) economic belt with clear water, green banks, and excellent industry by focusing on ecological protection of the Yangtze River from water, waterfront, and city.

i. Metamorphosis of Xuejiawa

The protection of the Yangtze River in Ma'anshan started with water pollution control, and Xuejiawa was taken as a breakthrough. Xuejiawa is located in the

　　按照政府制定的政策，上了岸的三姑娘先用渔船征收补偿款 20 多万元买了一处新房，住的问题解决了。接着，她去参加了政府举办的渔民转产就业专场招聘会，成为滨江公园保洁员，还兼职做了护鱼员，收入嘛，比捕鱼时还多！她还补办了社保卡，政府给买了养老保险，这下子，她就没了后顾之忧。后来，

薛家洼今昔对比（李博 陈亚东 摄）

Comparison between the past and present in Xuejiawa (Photo by Li Bo and Chen Yadong)

lower reaches of the Yangtze River main channel, where the rushing Yangtze River slows down to form a natural haven. There were more than 200 boats here all year round and 400 to 500 fishermen living on the boats. Their domestic sewage was discharged directly into the Yangtze River, becoming a direct source of water pollution. To control the pollution of the Yangtze River, these fishermen had to go ashore and turn to other industries.

Chen Lanxiang (nickname: San Guniang, meaning the third daughter of Chen's family in Chinese), was a fisherman. She lived on a boat and led a "floating" life. Where to live after going ashore? What to live on after quitting fishing? She was so worried that she could not sleep.

According to the policy formulated by the government, at first, Chen who went ashore used more than RMB 200,000 from the compensation for fishing boats to buy a new house, so the problem of housing was solved. Then, she went to the special job fair for the relocated fishermen organized by the government, and became a cleaner in the Waterfront Park and a part-time fish protector. The income was even higher than fishing. She also reapplied for a social security card, and the government paid the pension insurance for her. Her worries were gone. Later, she and eight former fisherman sisters together opened "Ma'anshan San Guniang Labor Services Co., LTD". Their lives become more and more prosperous, and they feel better and better.

Chen Lanxiang and her sisters returned to Xuejiawa on holiday. They walked through the Poplar Forest to the Xuejiawa Ecological Park and climbed up to the viewing platform to look out. Suddenly, a long-lost shadow jumped out of the river and smiled at them, "Look, it's a porpoise!" They said excitedly to the smiling angel porpoise "Long time no see, how are you?" "The porpoise is a rare and endangered species in the Yangtze River, and we are so lucky to see it." At present, Xuejiawa is connected with the Waterfront Park and the Caishiji Cultural Park to form a waterfront landscape belt. They put up tents on the lawn along the bank of the Yangtze River for picnic and drank happily, "I never thought Xuejiawa would

她和以前的 8 个渔民姐妹们一合计，干脆抱团创业，合伙开了"马鞍山市三姑娘劳务服务有限公司"，日子越过越红火，心情格外舒畅。

趁着放假休息，三姑娘约了姐妹们一起重回薛家洼。她们穿过杨树林，来到薛家洼生态园，走上观江平台眺望。突然，水中有个久违的影子，跳出江面，向她们微笑，"快看，那是江豚！"她们兴奋地和微笑天使江豚打招呼："好久不见，你好啊！""江豚是长江珍稀濒危物种，我们看到了，太幸运了。"如今，薛家洼和滨江公园、采石矶文化公园连成了一条滨江景观带。她们在长江岸边的草坪上搭起了帐篷野餐，举杯畅饮。"真没想到薛家洼会变得这么美丽，这么干净。""更没想到的是三姑娘变成了陈总！"姐妹们一起哈哈大笑，笑声传得很远很远……

就这样，由于措施得力，马鞍山率先在全省完成了长江禁渔和渔民退捕转产，全市 1.1 万名渔民全部上岸。

从 2020 年 1 月 1 日零时起，全国开始实施长江十年禁渔计划。

（二）"一枝花"转型

马鞍山是一座滨江钢铁之城，因钢设市、因钢立市。过去，工业企业沿江而建，长江岸线成了"工业线"。不合理的布局拉大了城市与长江的距离，滨江难以近江，这既是城市的隐痛，也是长江水质的污染源。这里共有几百家污染企业，必须依法拆除或者关停。从哪家开始下手？那就先从"一枝花"马钢开始吧！计划经济时期，马钢曾被誉为"江南一枝花"。马钢旗下的耐火材料厂就在长江岸边，属于高污染企业，必须拆除。怎么办？"一枝花"能否在高水平生态保护中实现经济高质量发展？

大学毕业以后，23 岁的蒋明哲就到了马钢耐火材料厂工作。工厂里噪音大、粉尘大，干了一段时间，蒋明哲不干了，要换工作，可是父亲不同意。同马鞍

become so beautiful and clean." "More unexpectedly, San Guniang has become General Manager Chen!" The sisters laughed together…

Due to effective measures, Ma'anshan took the lead in Anhui to complete the fishing moratorium in the Yangtze River and 11,000 fishermen went ashore.

January 1, 2020, saw the 10-year fishing moratorium in the Yangtze River being implemented nationwide.

ii. Transformation of "One Flower"

Ma'anshan is a waterfront city built and thrived by steel. The Yangtze River waterfront became an "industrial line" in the past as industrial enterprises were built along its banks. The unreasonable layout increased the distance between the city and the Yangtze River, making citizens hardly get river access. It's not only the pain spot of the city but also the source of pollution in the Yangtze River. There were several hundreds of polluting enterprises which should be shut down according to the law. Which one to start from? From "One Flower" Masteel! During the planned economy, Masteel was once known as "One Flower" in the southern areas of the Yangtze River due to its contribution to the economy. Masteel Refractory Factory, located on the banks of the Yangtze River, was a highly polluting enterprise that should be dismantled. How to do? Can "One Flower" achieve high-quality economic development while maintaining high-level ecological protection?

Since graduation from college, 23-year-old Jiang Mingzhe has been working at the Masteel Refractory Factory. The factory was noisy and dusty then. After working for a few days, Jiang Mingzhe wanted to change to another job, but his father did not agree. Like many families in Ma'anshan, Jiang Mingzhe's grandfather and father once worked at Masteel. They thought, "Why can't you even suffer from this? The noise and dust is nothing. That's the way we all live."

What a dilemma! At that time the factory was relocated, a new plant was

山的很多家庭一样，蒋明哲的爷爷和父亲也都曾在马钢工作。他们认为，小娃娃怎么连这点苦都不能吃？噪音、粉尘有什么，大家不都这么过来的？

这不，正僵持着。厂子搬迁了，建设了新厂房，还上了新设备，污染问题也得到彻底解决。蒋明哲也有了新的工作岗位，在中控室里用电脑程序控制设备。周末，蒋明哲带着爷爷和父亲一起到雨山经济开发区参观新厂房。"你们不在长江岸边？"爷爷问。"我们厂搬迁了，转型升级了，和瑞泰科技公司成立新公司，改名为瑞泰马钢。"走进车间，10000多平方米的厂房，几乎见不到人影。加料、液压、拿砖，全由机械手臂代替。爷爷和父亲边看边赞叹变化太大："过去可都是我们钢铁工人在干活，如今换成了机器人，真是做梦也想不到的啊！""我们现在是从低效制造到高端智造，从钢花四溅到新花怒放。""如今还学会贫嘴了呢！你不再要换工作了吧？""不是已经说了嘛，我现在是乐开了花！"

马钢耐火材料厂没有因为环境整治而倒闭，反倒借着长江岸线整治的机会升级换代。就这样，马鞍山坚持"生态优先，绿色发展"，解决了长江岸线的一个又一个"拦路虎"，共整治"散乱污"企业719家，拆除非法码头153个、船舶修造企业34家，关闭、搬迁畜禽养殖场497家。

更可喜的是，成功转型的"一枝花"，受到了宝武集团的青睐。2019年，两家企业实施战略重组，更名为中国宝武马钢集团，一跃成为全球钢铁企业首位。

（三）矿坑"变形记"

马鞍山完成了渔民上岸，岸线整治，下一步就是城市治污。马鞍山的一些矿山经过长期大规模的粗放式开采，导致山体裸露、植被破坏、水污染严重等生态环境问题突出。马鞍山决定将矿坑生态修复列为重点工作，马钢的"钢铁

built, and new eco-friendly equipment was installed. The problem of pollution was solved completely. Jiang Mingzhe had a new position, using a computer program to control equipment in the control room. On weekends, Jiang Mingzhe took his grandfather and father to the Yushan Economic Development Zone to visit the new plant. "Isn't your plant along the banks of the Yangtze River?" asked Grandpa. "Our factory was relocated, transformed, and upgraded, and set up a new company with Ruitai Technology Company, renamed Ruitai Masteel." Walking into the workshop, there were no workers in the plant of more than 10,000 square meters. All the adding materials, hydraulics, and taking bricks, were operated by robotic arms. His grandfather and father marveled at the great changes: "In the past, it was our steel workers who were working, and now the manual work is operated by robots. It's unbelievable!" "We are now transforming from inefficient manufacturing to high-end smart manufacturing, from steel flowers splashing to my heart blooming." "Now you also learn to tell a joke! You're not going to change the job anymore, are you?" "Didn't I already say it? I burst with joy now!"

Masteel Refractory Factory did not shut down because of environmental remediation but took the opportunity to upgrade. Upholding the "prioritizing ecological conservation and pursuing green development", Ma'anshan solved one after another "obstacles" of the Yangtze River waterfront. A total of 719 "poorly managed and polluting" enterprises were rectified, 153 illegal docks and 34 ship-building enterprises were demolished, and 497 livestock and poultry farms were closed and relocated.

What's more, the successful transformation of "One Flower" was favored by the Baowu Group. In 2019, the two companies implemented reconstruction and named China Baowu Masteel, which became the first global steel enterprise in the world.

iii. Metamorphosis of Mine Pit

Ma'anshan completed the fishermen's fishing moratorium and waterfront

粮仓"——马鞍山雨山区向山镇凹山采场被作为"一号工程"。这里是华东地区最大的露天铁矿，具有百年开采史。

历经百年开采，凹山采场已经从 184 米的山峰变成 210 米深的矿坑，它宛如一个巨大的漏斗，成为城市巨大的"伤疤"。

马鞍山首先采用"企业＋高校"的模式对凹山矿坑进行生态修复。马鞍山南山矿业公司与浙江大学合作，攻克了高陡边坡复绿难题；再与合肥工业大学合作，共建矿区水环境生态修复与水资源综合利用产学研合作基地，为凹山矿坑水质管理提供了重要技术支撑。马鞍山南山矿业公司大力投资，进行生态矿区建设，曾经深到 210 米的凹山矿坑由此华丽转身变成巨大的人工湖，静卧于

马鞍山的蓝宝石——凹山湖（陈亮 摄）

Sapphire of Ma'anshan – Aoshan Lake (Photo by Chen Liang)

renovation, and the next step was to control urban pollution. Some mines in Ma'anshan had been savagely exploited for a long time, resulting in prominent eco-environmental problems such as exposed mountains, destruction of vegetation, and water pollution. Ma'anshan decided to prioritize the ecological restoration of mining pits. "Steel Granary" of Masteel, situated in Aoshan Quarry, Xiangshan Town, Yushan District, Ma'anshan City, was regarded as the "No. 1 Project". It's the largest open iron mine in East China with a mining history of a hundred years. After a hundred years of mining, Aoshan Quarry turned from a peak of 184 meters high into a pit of 210 meters deep, like a giant funnel, becoming a "scar" of the city.

Ma'anshan initiated to adopt the mode of "enterprise + university" to restore the Aoshan pit. The Nanshan Mining Company of Ma'anshan collaborated with Zhejiang University to overcome the challenge of greening steep slopes. In collaboration with the Hefei University of Technology, the company established an industry-university-research cooperation base for water environment restoration and comprehensive utilization of water resources in the mining area, providing crucial technical support for managing the water quality of Aoshan pit. Nanshan Mining Company of Ma'anshan vigorously invested in the construction of an ecological mining area. Once 210-meter-deep Aoshan pit thus gorgeously turns into a massive artificial lake, lying quietly in the mountains, becoming the sapphire of Ma'anshan.

How to address the funding problem for mine restoration? Ma'anshan took the action of "ecological restoration + industrial introduction". Through investment attraction, China Chemical Engineering Group was introduced to implement the Project of Three Kinds of Trees. Three kinds of trees are Maple, Eucommia, and Torreya which are all special economic forests with highly added value. Ma'anshan planted these trees on the hillside of Aoshan Lake and achieved self-sustenance through the integration of agriculture, industry, and service sectors into a complete industrial chain development mode. Nowadays, the Aoshan Geological Culture Park, with its grand scale and beautiful scenery, has become an internet-

群山之中，成了马鞍山的蓝宝石。

矿山修复需要钱怎么办？马鞍山采用"生态修复 + 产业导入"的方式解决了资金问题。通过招商引资，引入中国化学工程集团，实施"三棵树"项目。"三棵树"是指元宝枫、杜仲、山桐子这三种树木，它们都属于附加值高的特种经济林树种。马鞍山在凹山湖畔山坡上种植"三棵树"，通过三产融合，打造全产业链的发展模式，实现自我"造血"。如今，建成的凹山地质文化公园，规模宏大，风景秀丽，成为网红打卡地。

马鞍山以"谁修复，谁受益"持续推动矿山生态修复。国安采石场变成了矿山主题乐园，丁山矿变成了景观花园……一个个矿坑完成了变形记，变废为宝。截至 2021 年，马鞍山共治理矿山 400 余座，治理面积达 1050 多公顷。

2020 年 8 月，习近平总书记亲临马鞍山考察，对马鞍山长江岸线综合整治、生态环境保护修复等工作给予肯定，作出"把马鞍山打造成长三角'白菜心'"的重要指示。这个重要指示有深意，就是建设人与自然和谐共生的现代化。如今，薛家洼完成了从"滨江不见江"到"城市生态客厅"的美丽蝶变，"一枝花"完成了从"散乱污"到"绿色城市钢厂"的绿色转型，凹山矿坑完成了从城市的"伤疤"到"蓝宝石"的变形。马鞍山通过水上、岸边、城市的生态修复，成为高颜值的"白菜心"，护送一江碧水向东流。

famous site.

Ma'anshan continues to promote the ecological restoration of mines with the principle of "whoever repairs, whoever benefits". Guoan quarry turns into a mine theme park, and Dingshan mine turns into a landscape garden... One by one, the mining pits have completed their metamorphosis from waste to treasure. By 2021, Ma'anshan had restored more than 400 mines with the area of more than 1,050 hectares.

In August 2020, President Xi Jinping inspected Ma'anshan and affirmed the comprehensive renovation of the Yangtze River waterfronts, as well as ecological environment protection and restoration. He made the instruction of "making Ma'anshan the 'Cabbage Heart' in the Yangtze River Delta", which has a profound meaning, that is, to build a modernization of harmony between humanity and nature. Nowadays, Xuejiawa has completed a dramatic transformation from "a river inaccessible even close to waterfronts" to "an ecological living room for citizens"; "One Flower" has completed the green transformation from a "poorly managed and polluting" enterprise to a green urban steel plant; Aoshan pit has completed the metamorphosis from the city's "scar" to the "sapphire". Ma'anshan has become a "Cabbage Heart" with a beautiful appearance through the ecological restoration of water, shore, and city, accompanying the clear water of the Yangtze River to the east.

三、让巢湖成为合肥的最好名片

　　从英国泰晤士河到中国太湖，从日本琵琶湖到中国巢湖，大河大湖的治理始终是一道世界性难题。巢湖是中国的第五大淡水湖，其面积是日本琵琶湖的3倍，要治理好这样一个大湖，难上加难。合肥人发扬"钉钉子"精神，一锤接着一锤敲，步步为营，久久为功，解决了巢湖治理的一个又一个难题，走出了一条大湖治理的新路径。

（一）蓝藻攻坚战

　　蓝藻曾经是巢湖的顽疾，每当夏季来临，蓝藻厚厚地铺满了湖面，浓重得如同绿漆，在太阳的暴晒下散发恶臭。合肥人在和蓝藻作斗争的过程中，逐渐形成了系统的治理方案，渔民退捕转产，岸边的村民搬迁，岸线整治，巢湖岸边的农田减少使用化学肥料，还专门成立了专业的打捞队。

　　2021年5月1日，孟凡周早早地上岗了。他本是巢湖岸边的打鱼人，后来他转行成为一名治藻人，如今已有8个年头。他开始是在蓝藻打捞平台工作，现在在深井控藻平台。深井有70多米深，能够把漂浮在水面的蓝藻吸进去，藻壁受高压压破气囊，失去活性，就不会再上浮和繁殖产生异味了。深井控藻平台每天可以处理近10万立方米的藻水，处理能力较原先的打捞平台提高了30

III. The Best Business Card of Hefei: Chaohu Lake

From the Thames River in the UK to Taihu Lake in China, and from Biwa Lake in Japan to Chaohu Lake in China, the governance of massive rivers and lakes has always been a worldwide problem. Chaohu Lake is the fifth largest freshwater lake in China, and its area is three times that of Japan's Biwa Lake. It is much more difficult to control such a vast lake. Hefei upholds the spirit of perseverance, steadily and successfully tackling the Chaohu Lake problem one after another, forging a new path for massive lake control.

i. Tough Battle Against Blue-Green Algae

Blue-green algae used to be a persistent problem in Chaohu Lake. When summer came, the lake was densely covered with the blue-green algae, like green paint, emitting a fetid odor in the sun. In the process of fighting against blue-green algae, Hefei gradually formed a systematic scheme, fishermen stopped fishing and turned to other industries, villagers on the shore were relocated, and the waterfronts were renovated. In addition, chemical fertilizer was reduced on farmland along the banks of Chaohu Lake. Furthermore, a professional salvage team was also established.

On May 1, 2021, Meng Fanzhou went to work early. He was originally a fisherman on the shore of Chaohu Lake but later had been an algae killer for

多倍。

　　孟凡周巡查的时候，看见了安徽省本土企业生产的捞藻新利器——"磁捕船"，这艘船能在湖中跟踪蓝藻，喝进去蓝藻水，吐出来清水。更神奇的是，仅需90秒它就能把藻泥分离出来。这艘磁捕船除配套一艘藻泥运输船外，还带了一个好帮手——可以遥控操作的吸藻平台。它像一艘无人艇，能深入河湾、浅滩等大船到不了的水域，将藻水通过管道输送至磁捕船进行分离处理。这样一套磁捕船设备，每天可产生藻泥近90吨；藻泥被运送到后端处理厂制作成肥料后，再供应给苗圃基地，实现了废物利用。

安徽省本土企业生产的蓝藻磁捕船（王闽 摄）

Magnetic salvage boat produced by local enterprise in Anhui (Photo by Wang Min)

　　整个夏天，孟凡周都吃住在湖边，白天头顶烈日高温，晚上忍受着蚊虫的叮咬。年复一年在湖边作业，孟凡周被晒得黝黑，但看到治理有成效，他内心充满自豪。

　　据统计，像孟凡周这样的治藻人，2021年夏天合肥共有27462人，他们累计出动各类打捞船只1600船次、快艇734船次、推流器122台、汽油泵82

eight years. Initially, he worked on a blue-green algae salvage platform and then transferred to a deep well control algae platform. The well was more than 70 meters deep and sucked in algae floating on the surface of the water. The algae wall was crushed by high pressure and lost its activity. So the algae could not float up and produce a peculiar smell. The well handled nearly 100,000 cubic meters of algae-infested water per day. The treatment capacity exceeded the original salvage platform by more than 30 times.

When Meng Fanzhou patrolled, he saw a new cutting-edge tool to salvage algae produced by local enterprises in Anhui Province – a magnetic salvage boat. It tracked algae in the lake, sucked algae water, and vomited clear water. More amazingly, it took only 90 seconds to separate the algae mud. In addition to the algae sludge transportation ship, it was equipped with a good helper – algae suction platforms that was operated remotely. It was like an unmanned boat that could go deep into the bay, shoal, and other waters that large ships could not reach, and transported the algae-infested water to the magnetic salvage boat through a pipeline for treatment. Such a set of magnetic salvage ship equipment could produce nearly 90 tons of algae sludge per day. Algae sludge was transported to the back-end processing plant to be made into fertilizer, and then supplied to the nursery base, realizing the utilization of waste.

In the whole summer, Meng Fanzhou lived by the lake suffering from the scorching sun in the daytime and the bite of mosquitoes at night. Year after year, working by the lake, Meng Fanzhou was sunburned. But he was full of pride when seeing that the treatment was effective.

According to statistics, there were 27,462 algae killers like Meng Fanzhou in Hefei in the summer of 2021. They mobilized 1,600 salvage vessels of various kinds, 734 speedboats, 122 pushers, and 82 gasoline pumps… To control algae, Hefei constantly enriched their "management toolbox", and displayed "18 martial arts": algae water separation port, tornado algae extractor, amphibious digger, drone…as long as they were effective, all were used together.

台……为了治藻，合肥人不断丰富他们的"治理工具箱"，"十八般武艺"大展身手：藻水分离港、龙卷风取藻器、水陆两用挖机、航拍无人机……新办法、老办法、洋办法、土办法，只要管用，一起上。

2021年和2022年，巢湖连续两年未发生重度水华[①]，实现了期盼已久的夏天无蓝藻异味！

（二）湿地串起翡翠项链

湿地被称为"地球之肾"，能够调节水资源、净化水质和维持生态平衡。近年来，合肥以十五里河、南淝河、兆河等37条入湖河流入湖口为重点，规划建设10处湿地，打造一道环巢湖"翡翠项链"，让湿地成为入湖河水的"过滤器"，为保护巢湖铸造一道绿色环保屏障。2022年环巢湖十大湿地全面建成，合肥荣获"国际湿地城市"称号。其中，十八联圩湿地是十大湿地中面积最大、投资最多，也是最难建设的。

十八联圩因有大大小小共18个圩区而得名。所谓圩区是指四周环水、地势较低、依靠堤防保护方能从事生产、生活的地区。早些年，十八联圩主要是养殖鱼塘，渔民为了养鱼，长期投喂饲料以及使用一些化学药物，圩区内数百口鱼塘沉积着氮磷元素严重超标的高污染底泥，如何处理这些污染的底泥是湿地修复工程面临的一大难题。

十八联圩湿地修复开始时，以前的养殖渔场场长李家政就主动加入了工程队，成为一名管理人员。为了解决污染底泥，他们想出新点子，那就是"生态渗滤岛"。具体来说，就是用工程桩将底泥固定，控制底泥中污染物，以免其释放的危险，再种植池杉、垂柳等乔灌木。这些植物既可以吸收底泥中的氮磷元

---

① 水华指一些水域受到污染而产生富营养化，导致蓝藻大量繁殖、集聚的现象。

In 2021 and 2022, there was no severe algae blooms[1] for two consecutive years in Chaohu Lake. A long-awaited summer without algae odor was coming!

ii. Wetlands Strung with an Emerald Necklace

Wetlands are known as the "kidney of the earth", which can regulate water resources, purify water quality and maintain ecological balance. In recent years, Hefei focused on the mouths of 37 rivers entering the lake, such as the Shiwulihe River, the Nanfeihe River, and the Zhaohe River, and planned to build ten wetlands to form an "emerald necklace" around Chaohu Lake, so that the wetlands became a "filter" for rivers entering the lake, creating a green environmental protection belt for Chaohu Lake. In 2022, ten wetlands around Chaohu Lake were fully completed, and Hefei won the title of International Wetland City. Among ten wetlands, 18 Lianwei is the largest area, the highest investment, and the most challenging to build.

The name of 18 Lianwei came from the fact that there were 18 Lianwei of various sizes. The so-called "Lianwei" referred to the area surrounded by water with low terrain, where production and life depended mainly on the dike protection. In earlier years, 18 Lianwei was mainly fish farming ponds. For a long time, feeding stuff and some chemical drugs were used for fish farming. As a result, hundreds of fish ponds were heavily deposited by polluted sediments with excessive nitrogen and phosphorus elements exceeding the standard. How to deal with these polluted sediments was a problem in wetland restoration project.

When the restoration of the 18 Lianwei wetlands began, Li Jiazheng, the former director of the fish farm, took the initiative to join the engineering team as

---

[1] Algae bloom refers to a phenomenon in which large numbers of blue-green algae breed and gather in some water areas due to eutrophication caused by pollution.

素，也可以为鸟类提供栖息地。岛与岛之间的水域，则栽种了荷花、睡莲等挺水植物、浮叶植物和沉水植物，净化水质。

2020年，湿地建成过半，却遭遇了一场百年不遇的洪水。看着辛苦两年的成果被淹没在一片洪水中，李家政和同事们欲哭无泪：怎么办？还要继续建下去吗？

洪水过后，习近平总书记来到了十八联圩，提出了建设"生态蓄洪区"。这是李家政第一次听说"生态蓄洪区"的概念，细想想，他豁然开朗：也就是说，洪水来袭时，充当蓄洪"大水缸"，保护合肥市主城区；平日里，充当生态"净化器"，净化水质。

难题解决了，李家政他们撸起袖子加油干，调整了湿地的规划建设方案，尤其是在生态植物的选择上，更偏向耐水植物。建成了近自然人工湿地，形成了"水下有草、水中有鱼、水上有鸟"的美丽的生态画面。

湿地建成后，李家政每天都会查看湿地内植物生长和水质净化情况。令他

十八联圩生态湿地美如画（陈振 摄）

Beautiful 18 Lianwei (Photo by Chen Zhen)

a management personnel. To address the issue of polluted sediment, they proposed an innovative solution called "ecological percolation island". Specifically, this approach involved fixing the sediment with engineering piles to control pollutants so as to avoid the danger of release, followed by planting arbor shrubs such as pond fir and weeping willows, etc. These plants absorbed nitrogen and phosphorus from the sediment and also provided a habitat for birds. The waters among the islands were purified by planting water-supporting plants such as lotus, water lilies, and other floating and submerged plants.

In 2020, wetlands were half built but hit by a once-in-a-century flood. Facing the hard work of two years destroyed in a flood, Li Jiazheng and his colleagues felt heartbroken. What to do? Still, keep on building?

After the flood, President Xi Jinping came to 18 Lianwei, and put forward the construction of an "ecological flood storage area". It was the first time that Li Jiazheng had heard of it. Thinking deeply, he was suddenly enlightened. That is to say, when the flood came, it acted as a big water tank to protect the main urban area of Hefei. On normal days, it served as an ecological "purifier" to purify water.

With the problem solved, Li Jiazheng and his team rolled up their sleeves to work harder, and adjusted wetlands planning and construction scheme, especially in the choice of ecological plants, more preferable to water-resistant plants. The artificial like-nature wetlands were completed, forming a beautiful ecological picture of "grass, fish, and birds".

After wetlands were completed, Li Jiazheng checked the plants and the water quality every day. To his delight, there were more and more birds and bird watchers. Furthermore, special bird-watching sites were built. Far away, he saw Qian Maosong, who had set up a tripod and put up the camera lens. "Li, come here quickly. Today, I have a picture of a white stork, which is a national first-class protected bird." "Qian, yesterday, I saw the picture of the little swan on People's Daily Online you took. It's beautiful!" "I am so flattered. Wetlands are so pleasant that they attract birds to come. Yu Lei's research team has found 258 species

十八联圩迎来东方白鹳（王孜礼 摄）

The white stork in 18 Lianwei (Photo by Wang Zili)

欣喜的是，这里的鸟越来越多，观鸟人也越来越多，还有了专门的观鸟点。远远地，他看见了钱茂松，他已经架好了三脚架、支起了"大炮筒"。"老李，快过来，我今天拍到了东方白鹳，这可是国家一级保护鸟类。"

"老钱，我昨天还在人民网上看到你拍的小天鹅，很好看！""你过奖了，湿地环境好，鸟儿来投票，虞磊的调查小组已经在湿地发现鸟类258种。""我在这里生活了近30年了，从过去的养殖渔场变成今天的湿地，变化真大，真是沧海桑田！""老李，现如今，这里真是水清、岸绿、鱼跃、鸟欢，你留给子孙后代的是一块生态福地，你可是一位大功臣！"听到这儿，李家政笑了，沐浴在清晨的阳光中，笑得很开心！

（三）大湖名城

合肥市统筹抓好防洪治理、人居环境整治，确保国考断面水质稳定达标、

of birds here." "I have lived here for nearly 30 years, from the past fish farm to today's wetland, What great changes!" "Li, nowadays, the water is clear, the shore is green, the fish are swimming, and the birds are singing. What you're leaving for future generations is an ecological paradise. You're truly great!" Hearing this, Li Jiazheng smiled happily in the morning sunlight!

iii. Famous Lake City

Hefei makes overall plans for flood control and improvement of the living environment to ensure that the water quality of the national surface water assessment section is stable and meets the standard and that the water quality of Chaohu Lake is continuously improved. The problems of Chaohu Lake lie on the shore. To this end, Hefei has taken measures to clean up the water pollution sources of Chaohu Lake. At present, 27 urban sewage treatment plants have been built in the whole city, and main rivers such as Nan Feihe River, Paihe River, and Shiwulihe River have been continuously renovated. Green production has been carried out in the first-class water environment protection zone, chemical fertilizer and pesticide reduction demonstration zone has been established. The Chaohu Lake ecological dredging pilot project has been implemented, and blue-green algae emergency prevention and control have been strengthened. Therefore, the average water quality of Chaohu Lake has improved from inferior class V in 2015 to class IV and even reached class III at one point.

Eight hundred miles Chaohu Lake is covered with a vast expanse of hazy mist. Many ecological landmarks around Chaohu Lake have become internet-famous sites that citizens rush to visit and take snapshots. Here lies the first national forest park that has been restored from farmland to forest through ecological restoration in China – Hefei Binhu National Forest Park. Here lies Luogang Park, the largest city park in China and even in the world, which was

巢湖水环境质量得到持续改善。巢湖问题在湖里，根子却在岸上。为此，合肥对入巢湖水源实施治理，目前，全市共建成城市污水处理厂 27 座，持续整治南淝河、派河、十五里河等重点河流，在水环境一级保护区开展绿色生产，建立化肥农药减量示范区，实施巢湖生态清淤试点工程，强化蓝藻应急防控。如今，巢湖平均水质已由 2015 年的劣 V 类转为 IV 类，并一度达到 III 类。

八百里巢湖，烟波浩渺。环巢湖许多生态地标成为市民争相游览拍摄的网红打卡地。这里有中国首个退耕还林并经生态修复而成的国家级森林公园——合肥滨湖国家森林公园，这里有由骆岗机场改建的国内乃至世界最大的城市中央公园——骆岗公园，这里有各具特色、各呈风情的环巢湖 12 大古镇①，这里有

合肥滨湖国家森林公园（程兆 摄）
Hefei Binhu National Forest Park (Photo by Cheng Zhao)

---

① 12 个古镇依次为：长临河、中庙、黄麓、烔炀、柘皋、中垾、散兵、槐林、盛桥、白山、同大、三河。

rebuilt from Luogang Airport. Here lie the 12 ancient towns[①]surrounding Chaohu Lake, and each boasts its unique characteristics and exudes a captivating charm. Moreover, Here are the most beautiful villages around Chaohu Lake, Wangqiao Village, Hongjiatuan Ancient Village, and Sangua Community. This extraordinary destination is the renowned Golden Peacock and Bantang Hot Spring Resort as well as Fuchashan Mountain, Sidingshan Mountain, and Yinpingshan Mountain. Furthermore, the Anhui Provincial Art Museum awaits tourists alongside the Science and Technology Museum, Innovation Pavilion, and Celebrity Museum… Nowadays, this area has become a poetic habitat that everyone yearns for. More and more people come here to start a business and settle down. With a series of landmark buildings emerging from the ground and a modern metropolis rising on the shore of Chaohu Lake, Hefei finally boasts Famous Lake City.

In June 2021, the Chaohu Lake Basin Governance was selected as the national Shan-Shui Initiative, and in 2022, Shan-Shui Initiative in China including the Chaohu Lake Basin Governance, was selected as the ten World Restoration Flagships by the United Nations. The governance of Chaohu Lake has made remarkable achievements, and Chaohu Lake has become the best business card of Hefei.

The time has come for us to review the names of these diligent individuals: Secretary Yang Jiangqin in Yangting Village, Chen Lanxiang in Xuejiawa, Jiang Mingzhe in Masteel, "algae killer" Meng Fanzhou, Li Jiazheng in 18 Lianwei. They represent millions of hard-working people. Because of their extraordinary courage in face of difficulties, wisdom in solving problems, and perseverance in overcoming difficulties, they have created a beautiful picture of harmony between humanity and nature: "forest village" Yangting Village, "urban ecological living

---

① The 12 ancient towns are Changlinhe, Zhongmiao, Huanglu, Tongyang, Zhegao, Zhonghan, Sanbing, Huailin, Shengqiao, Baishan, Tongda and Sanhe.

环巢湖最美乡村——汪桥村、洪家疃古村落、三瓜公社，这里有著名的金孔雀和半汤温泉度假村，这里有浮槎山、四顶山、银屏山。另外，这里还有安徽省美术馆、科技馆、创新馆、名人馆……如今这里成为人人向往的诗意栖居地，越来越多的人来这里创业定居。一座座标志性建筑拔地而起，一个现代化大城市崛起在巢湖之滨，合肥人终于自豪地喊出了"大湖名城"。

2021年6月，巢湖流域治理入选国家"山水工程"。2022年，包括巢湖流域治理在内的"中国山水工程"入选联合国十大"世界生态恢复旗舰项目"。巢湖治理成就斐然，成为合肥最好的名片！

让我们重温这些辛勤劳动者的名字：杨亭村的杨江勤，薛家洼的三姑娘，马钢的蒋明哲，治藻人孟凡周，十八联圩的李家政。他们代表着千千万万辛勤的劳动者，因为他们面对困难时非凡的勇气，解决难题时的聪明智慧，以及克服困难时的坚持不懈，才创造了人与自然和谐共生的美好画面：森林村杨亭村、"城市生态客厅"薛家洼、"蓝宝石"凹山湖、大美巢湖、环巢湖十大湿地……

人与自然和谐共生是中国式现代化的重要特征，主要表现在三个方面：一是在理念上，我们坚持"绿水青山就是金山银山"。安庆实施的林长制，既保护森林资源，预防森林火灾，又发展了蓝莓特色林业经济，让绿水青山转化成金山银山。二是在道路和路径选择上，我们坚持生态优先、绿色发展。马鞍山积极探索出资源型城市高质量发展的新路子，在发展中保护，在保护中发展。三是在方法上，我们强调系统观念，坚持山水林田湖草一体化保护和系统治理。治理巢湖，合肥人不仅治理水上的蓝藻，在岸边建设环巢湖十大湿地，同时，还从源头治理城市的污水。

这就是中国式现代化，我们愿意和各国人民一起在现代化的道路上阔步前行，共同建设地球美好家园。

room" Xuejiawa, "sapphire" Aoshan Lake, the beauty of Chaohu Lake, ten wetlands around Chaohu Lake…

Harmony between humanity and nature is an important feature of Chinese modernization, which is mainly manifested in three aspects. First, in terms of concept, we adhere to "Lucid waters and lush mountains are invaluable assets." Forest Chief Scheme implemented by Anqing protects forest resources, prevents forest fires, and develops a blueberry-featured forestry economy, turning lucid waters and lush mountains into invaluable assets. Second, in the selection of paths, we adhere to "prioritizing ecological conservation and pursuing green development". Ma'anshan actively explores a new way of high-quality development of resources-based cities, protecting in development and developing in protection. Third, in the way of method, we stress the holistic approach. We persist in the concept that "Mountains, rivers, forests, farmlands, and lakes are a community of life." To govern Chaohu Lake, Hefei not only treated blue-green algae and built ten wetlands around Chaohu Lake but also controlled pollution source in the city.

Chinese modernization is a grand endeavor, as we stand ready to stride forward on the path to modernization, hand in hand with people of all countries, and jointly build a better homeland for our planet.

第四章

徽风皖韵绽芳华

安徽历史悠久、内蕴丰厚，淮河文化、皖江文化、徽州文化既博大精深又别具一格，红色文化得天独厚，是我们推进文化自信自强、铸就文化新辉煌的精神财富。新时代，安徽是如何探索具有自身特色的文化发展之路，让徽风皖韵绽放时代芳华的呢？

这里有"再芬黄梅"坚持守正创新，让优秀传统文化与现代生活完美交汇，前途更加光明响亮；这里有公共文化事业繁荣兴盛，让群众够得着、用得上，不断满足人民群众日益增长的精神文化需求；这里有黄山文旅融合，让旅游更有魅力、文化更有活力，提升旅游品质、助力文化广泛传播……

Chapter 4

Anhui Culture Blooming in the New Era

With a long history and rich connotations, Anhui has profound and unique cultural deposits, which include Huaihe Culture, Wanjiang Culture, Huizhou Culture, and exceptional red culture by nature. It is spiritual wealth for us to build cultural confidence and strength, and secure new successes in developing socialist culture. In the new era, how does Anhui explore a path of cultural development with its own characteristics to achieve the blooming of Anhui culture?

Here, Zaifen Huangmei has been upholding fundamental principles and breaking new ground, which gives the fine traditional Chinese culture a brighter future through the perfect combination with modern life. Public cultural programs are prosperous and thriving, which makes public cultural services accessible and inclusive to the people, meeting the increasing spiritual and cultural needs of the people. Huangshan City improves the quality of tourism and promotes the widespread of culture through the integration of culture and tourism, which makes tourism more attractive and culture more vibrant. From these stories, you will learn about some practices of Anhui to build cultural confidence and secure successes in developing socialist culture.

一、守正创新："黄梅飘香"彰显文化自信

　　夜幕降临，华灯初上，坐落于安庆菱湖之滨的中国黄梅戏非物质文化遗产传承基地——再芬黄梅公馆传出了悠扬婉转的曲调，"树上的鸟儿成双对，绿水青山带笑颜……"台上演员一丝不苟，一招一式娴熟流畅，唱腔优美动听、节奏分明、软糯婉转；台下观众聚精会神，仿佛置身其中，与剧中的董永和七仙女一起经历人间悲喜。

　　黄梅戏，中国五大戏曲剧种之一。怎样让年轻人爱上它？如何推动黄梅戏在新时代实现创造性转化、创新性发展？从艺 30 余年的韩再芬作为国家级非物质文化遗产代表性项目传承人，创立"再芬黄梅"①。如今，"再芬黄梅"成为中国戏曲界的领先品牌，谱写着中国优秀传统文化在新时代焕发光芒的锦绣华章。

---

　　① "再芬黄梅"是中国著名黄梅戏表演艺术团体。2005 年 12 月，安庆市黄梅戏二团更名为安庆再芬黄梅艺术剧院，韩再芬任院长，这是改革开放以来中国戏剧界第一家以个人命名的剧院。"再芬黄梅"在艺术传承、创新，人才培养各方面，积极发挥领军作用，形成"再芬黄梅"品牌，旗下有再芬黄梅公馆、再芬黄梅艺术剧院、再芬黄梅基金会、再芬黄梅股份公司等主要机构。

I. Upholding Fundamental Principles and Breaking New Ground: The Blooming of Huangmei Opera Demonstrates Cultural Confidence

The streetlights glow as evening descends. "Two birds in the trees are in pairs; Green waters and mountains look smiling," the melodious tunes come out from Zaifen Huangmei [①] Mansion, which is located on the shore of Anqing Linghu Lake. Zaifen Huangmei Mansion is a state-level intangible cultural heritage base for preserving and handing down Huangmei Opera. On the stage, the actors with beautiful singing and clear rhythm are meticulous and skillful. Off the stage, the audience is immersed in the story of *Dong Yong and the Seventh Daughter of the Emperor in Heaven*, as if experiencing their sorrow and joy.

Huangmei Opera is one of the five major operas in China. How to get young people to love it? How to push it for creative transformation and development

---

① Zaifen Huangmei: A famous Huangmei opera art troupe in China. In December 2005, the Second Troupe of Anqing Huangmei Opera changed its name to Anqing Zaifen Huangmei Art Theater. With Han Zaifen as the dean, this is the first theater named after an individual since the reform and opening-up in China. Zaifen Huangmei actively plays a leading role in artistic inheritance, innovation, training talents, and other aspects to form the brand Zaifen Huangmei. Its major institutions include Zaifen Huangmei Mansion, Zaifen Huangmei Art Theater, Zaifen Huangmei Foundation, Zaifen Huangmei Joint Stock Company, etc.

国家级非物质文化遗产：黄梅戏《女驸马》（视觉新闻中心 摄）

National intangible cultural heritage: Huangmei Opera, *the Emperor's Female Son-in-law* (Photo by Visual News Center)

（一）传承，后继有人满芬芳

戏剧传承，基础是人的传承。多年来，"再芬黄梅"将培养人才当作传承发展的重任，根据演员的艺术特色、性格特征、成长经历等，采用"传帮带"、定制演出平台等个性化培养方式，培育少儿艺术团、成立青年团，推出"今日头牌"青年名角个人专场项目，激励青年演员及早成名成才。从少儿艺术团到青年团，再到中生代，"再芬黄梅"梯队式表演人才建设系统日趋完善，同时，建立起一支编、导、音、美门类齐全的创作人才队伍和现代管理人才队伍，为黄

in the new era? As a representative inheritor of the state-level intangible cultural heritage, Han Zaifen, who has been engaged in Huangmei Opera for more than thirty years, founded Zaifen Huangmei, which has become the leading brand of Chinese opera, writing a splendid chapter of China's fine traditional culture shining brightly in the new era.

i. Inheritance: Cultivating Talents

The foundation of inheriting traditional Chinese opera is to cultivate talents. Over the years, Zaifen Huangmei has been regarding the cultivation of talents as an important task. Based on the actor's artistic characteristics, growth experience,

梅戏的发展提供源源不断、随叫随到的动力支撑。

韩再芬为即将登台的小演员指导说戏（程兆　摄）

Han Zaifen is coaching the young actors who are going on stage (Photo by Cheng Zhao)

2020 年，韩再芬正式担任安庆师范大学黄梅剧艺术学院院长，"再芬黄梅"和安庆师范大学的校企合作全面展开。"再芬黄梅"安排高水平、舞台表演经验丰富的专业老师为艺术学院学生授课，将实践融入教学。2022 年 6 月，安庆师范大学黄梅剧艺术学院表演专业成为全国唯一的黄梅戏方向国家级一流本科专业，开创了文艺院团与高校合作的新模式和新维度。

丢下一粒籽，发了一颗芽。2023 年 3 月 24 日晚，黄山学院大学生活动中心大礼堂热闹非凡、掌声不断，这里是"再芬黄梅"2023 校园大舞台"徽风皖韵进高校"的第 8 站。进校园，"再芬黄梅"已坚持了 5 年。不仅在省内高校，还先后到广东、内蒙古、贵州等部分高校演出，为学生提供了零距离接触安徽优秀传统戏曲文化的条件和机会，在年轻人心里种下优秀传统文化的种子，培育出对传统文化热爱的萌芽。

etc., Zaifen Huangmei cultivated children and youth groups by personalized cultivation ways in which beloved aging stars reprised classic roles and passed the torch to younger successors. In order to motivate young performers to become famous and successful as early as possible, Zaifen Huangmei launched Today's Star, a personalized program for young famous performers. From children to youth, and to middle-aged, the system of performance talent was increasingly perfect in Zaifen Huangmei. Meanwhile, a team of professional creators and modern management talents with complete categories of composing, directing, opera music, and opera stage performance art, had been established to provide constant support for the development of Huangmei Opera.

In 2020, Han Zaifen was appointed as the dean of the Huangmei Opera Art School of Anqing Normal University, and the school-enterprise cooperation between them was fully launched. Zaifen Huangmei delegated professional teachers with rich experience in stage performance to teach students of art school, integrating practice into teaching. In June 2022, the performance major of Huangmei Opera Art School of Anqing Normal University became the only national first-class undergraduate major in the direction of Huangmei Opera, creating a new mode of cooperation between art troupes and universities.

How to get college students to be interested in Huangmei Opera? On the evening of March 24, 2023, constant applause came out from the student center in Huangshan University, which was the event of Fine Traditional Anhui Culture into Colleges and Universities. This was the eighth campus performance of Zaifen Huangmei in 2023. Zaifen Huangmei has been performing on campus for five years, not only in Anhui but also in Guangdong, Inner Mongolia, Guizhou, etc., providing college students with opportunities for direct contact with fine traditional Anhui opera culture.

（二）创新，小荷才露尖尖角

　　戏剧传承，关键是在创新中发展。近年来，"再芬黄梅"在传承好传统剧目的同时，创作出反映时代主题的优秀剧目：《鸭儿嫂》以贫困户为原型，讲述了普通农村女性张满秀养殖鸭子带领全村人脱贫致富，过上小康生活的新风貌；《邓稼先》生动展现了以邓稼先为代表的老一辈科学家们为实现强国梦，不畏艰苦、无私奉献的精神；《不朽的骄杨》纪念杨开慧烈士诞辰120周年……"再芬黄梅"紧扣时代脉搏，贴近百姓生活，在创新中雕琢精品，让黄梅戏这一传统艺术闪烁着时代光芒，焕发出生机和活力。

全省脱贫攻坚题材优秀剧目黄梅戏《鸭儿嫂》（吴文兵 摄）
Excellent piece of Huangmei Opera, *the Duck Breeder*, based on true stories of poverty alleviation in Anhui (Photo by Wu Wenbing)

ii. Innovation: Being Always on the Way

The key to inheriting opera is development through innovation. In recent years, besides performing traditional plays, Zaifen Huangmei also created excellent pieces reflecting the themes of the times. Based on true stories of poverty alleviation, *the Duck Breeder* told the story of an ordinary rural woman, Zhang Manxiu, who led fellow villagers out of poverty to a comfortable life. *Deng Jiaxian* eulogized the patriotism of the elder scientists who committed themselves to building a strong country and contributing to national rejuvenation. *Immortal Heroine Yang Kaihui* commemorated the 120th anniversary of the birth of Yang Kaihui, the revolutionary martyr. Firmly grasping the pulse of the times, Zaifen Huangmei created these performances in a way that was close to people's lives and let Huangmei Opera shine in the modern era.

The internet supplied a broad stage for inheriting and developing Huangmei Opera. Zaifen Huangmei elaborately developed an art communication platform that met the requirements of the market and showed the characteristics of the times. As early as 2016, it launched the first global webcast *New Year Huangmei Opera Gala* attracting audience from over 60 countries. Since then, it has been trying to explore new platforms and modes of communication to spread the art of Huangmei Opera on a wider scale, growing from a single media outlet to a multi-media joint broadcast. The broadcast content had expanded from the theme performance to Cloud Theater, Cloud Classroom, and Cloud Arena. The number of clicks increased from "100,000 + " to "1,000,000 + ", opening up a new channel for Huangmei Opera to interact with the audience. On July 23, 2022, the regular live broadcast of *Zaifen Huangmei Mansion · Watching Opera* was launched, which immediately sparked the network, with 8 network platforms such as Anqing App, Tiktok, Xinhua Cloud, and Phoenix Net synchronously broadcasting. The cumulative total number of online viewers exceeded 2.35 million, which was an

网络为黄梅戏的传承发展拓展了无比宽阔的舞台空间，"再芬黄梅"精心构建适应市场要求和时代特点的艺术传播平台。早在 2016 年，"再芬黄梅"首次推出"再芬黄梅新年戏曲联欢晚会"，通过全球网络直播，吸引了 60 多个国家的观众观看。此后，不断尝试探索新的平台与传播模式，更大范围传播黄梅戏艺术，从单一媒体发展到多家媒体联合直播，展播内容从主题演出扩展到"云剧场""云课堂""云赛场"，点击量从"10 万 +"增加到"100 万 +"，打通了黄梅戏与观众互动的新渠道。2022 年 7 月 23 日，常态化现场直播的《再芬黄梅公馆·看戏》一经推出，立刻引爆网络，"安庆"App、抖音、新华云、凤凰网等 8 个网络平台同步直播，在线观众累计突破 235 万，盛况空前。

"再芬黄梅"探索"戏曲 + 网络 + 漫画"多元组合、跨界融合模式，大胆尝试将传统文化与年轻人的视角相结合，通过与腾讯动漫、爱奇艺漫画等网络平台合作，推出国风连载漫画《女驸马》。漫画以韩再芬版《女驸马》为蓝本，运用现代制作技术和表现手法来演绎传统戏曲，首次将黄梅戏的种子植入二次元世界，以"戏曲 + 漫画"的跨界组合，激发年轻人对黄梅戏、对传统文化的兴趣和认同感，赢得年轻观众的支持，培育年轻态"粉丝群"。

传统戏曲数字化是实现戏曲保护与传承、观演与传播的必由之路。至今，黄梅戏已经累积了大量的音频、音像资料，"再芬黄梅"对其进行现代技术处理与抢救性保护。同时，韩再芬主编的《黄梅小镇——中国黄梅戏富媒体数字读本》，以多元化的表现手法（动画、音频、微视频、游戏等），建立起交互式的阅读体验，全方位、立体化地展现黄梅戏的艺术魅力，让黄梅戏在新时代焕发新光彩。

（三）以戏为魂，彰显文化自信

2010 年、2018 年，韩再芬的表演艺术史和她所代表的黄梅戏艺术形式作为

unprecedented event.

Zaifen Huangmei explored the multiple combination and cross-border integration mode of "opera + network + comics". It attempted boldly to combine traditional culture with the preference of young people and launched the national-style comic series, *the Emperor's Female Son-in-law*, through cooperation with online platforms such as Tencent Animation and iQiyi Comics. Based on Han Zaifen's version of *the Emperor's Female Son-in-Law*, the comic series utilized modern production techniques and presentation methods to interpret traditional opera. In order to win the support of young audiences and cultivate young fans, for the first time, Huangmei Opera was implanted in a two-dimensional world with the crossover combination of opera and comics to arouse young people's sense of identity and interest in Huangmei opera and traditional culture.

The digitization of traditional Chinese opera was necessary to realize protection, inheritance, performance viewing, and transmission. Up to now, Huangmei Opera has accumulated a large number of audio and video materials, which were treated and protected with modern technology by Zaifen Huangmei. At the same time, the book, *Huangmei Town – Chinese Huangmei Opera Rich Media Digital Reader*, edited by Han Zaifen, used diversified expression techniques (animation, audio, micro video, games, etc.) to establish an interactive reading experience, showing the artistic charm of Huangmei Opera in an all-round way, and making Huangmei Opera shine brilliantly in the new era.

iii. Showing Cultural Confidence: Using the Essence of Huangmei Opera to Nurture the Spirit

In 2010 and 2018, Han Zaifen's art history of performance and Huangmei Opera Art were twice recorded, collected, and permanently preserved by the US Library of Congress as classics from different cultures around the world. She became the second Chinese theatrical artist to be listed in the program after Mei

世界不同文化的经典两度被美国国会图书馆记录、收藏和永久保存。她成为继梅兰芳先生之后中国第二位被该项目收录的中国戏剧表演艺术家。这标志着韩再芬作为中国黄梅戏的代表性传承者，其艺术造诣已获得世界性的认可，中国黄梅戏已走向世界。

"再芬黄梅"先后赴美国、俄罗斯、加拿大、奥地利等地进行文化交流活动，热情的美国观众把黄梅戏形容为"最美的中国乡村音乐"。2017 年 7 月，"再芬黄梅"访演多伦多时，加拿大总理亲自发来贺信，加拿大国会联邦议员谭耕说，"这种戏曲文化非常有亲和力，老少皆宜，群众喜闻乐见，是一个非常好的促进文化了解互信的方式"。黄梅戏经典剧目《天仙配》和《女驸马》在传统唱腔基础上，增加曲调种类，并且引进西洋乐器及其配器手法，体现了文化的包容、兼收并蓄。中国的文化自信在这种真实、立体和全面的交流展示中不断深刻、不断具体，在兼收并蓄中坚定文化自觉和文化自信，不断铸就中华文化新辉煌。

守正与创新，是"再芬黄梅"永恒的主题。在做好人才传承的基础上，"再芬黄梅"以戏为魂，不断加强内容形式创新，发掘文化表现新方式、开拓文化发展新市场，推动中华优秀传统文化融入当代文明，焕发中华优秀传统文化的生机活力。中华优秀传统文化蕴含着中国式现代化的文化根脉，赋予了现代化以"中国式"的特点与时代烙印。中国式现代化离不开中华优秀传统文化的滋养，文化自信的底气首先来自于此。黄梅戏在新时代不断开枝散叶，正是文化自信的体现。

Lanfang. This indicated that Han Zaifen, as a representative inheritor of Huangmei Opera, had gained worldwide recognition for her artistic attainments, and Huangmei Opera of China had gone global.

Zaifen Huangmei had been to the United States, Russia, Canada, Austria, and other places to carry out cultural exchanges. Huangmei Opera was described as the most beautiful Chinese country music by Americans. During a visit to Toronto in July 2017, the Prime Minister of Canada sent a personal letter of congratulation, and Tan Geng, a member of the Canadian Parliament, said, "This kind of traditional Chinese opera is popular with the young and the old, and it is a very good way to promote cultural understanding and mutual trust." Based on traditional singing, the classic Huangmei Opera works, *Marriage of a Fairy Princess* and *the Emperor's Female Son-in-law*, increased the variety of tunes and incorporated western musical instruments and their orchestration into the opera, showing openness and inclusiveness of Chinese culture. Chinese cultural confidence is increasingly profound and concrete through exchanges and demonstrations in a real and comprehensive way. We should raise cultural awareness and have greater confidence in our own culture to continuously add new luster to Chinese culture.

Zaifen Huangmei has been upholding fundamental principles and breaking new ground. Based on cultivating inheritors of Huangmei Opera, Zaifen Huangmei has been continuously adding further modern innovations and opening new markets to promote the integration of fine traditional Chinese culture with contemporary civilization. The fine traditional Chinese culture blooms new vitality again in the new era. The fine traditional Chinese culture is the cultural root of Chinese modernization, providing the modernization with the characteristics of "Chinese style" and a vivid mark of the times. The cultural confidence first comes from the fine traditional Chinese culture, which nourishes Chinese modernization. And the blooming of Huangmei Opera in the new era just demonstrates cultural confidence.

二、繁荣兴盛：公共文化服务"火出圈"

　　如何发挥公共文化事业的社会效益，满足人民群众日益增长的精神文化需求？近年来，安徽省公共文化场馆越来越潮，公共文化服务越来越贴心，公共文化产品和活动越来越丰富……这极大地提升了群众的获得感和幸福感，用心托举起人民群众"稳稳的幸福"。

（一）公共文化场馆越来越潮

　　听说合肥科技馆新馆要开馆了，正在进行压力测试，市民刘女士赶紧在公众号上预约，周六上午带着孩子们当了一次"体验官"。远远望去，新馆的造型很别致，就像楼梯，寓意不断攀登科学高峰的向上力量，被市民亲切地称为"智慧盒子"。出示预约码，不用花一分钱，孩子们迫不及待地跑了进去。

　　新馆占地面积约75亩。从自然到科学再到技术，1000余件展品特色鲜明。11个常设展厅，其中自然展厅是新馆的一大特色，弥补了合肥市过去没有自然博物馆的不足。孩子们感叹，新馆好大啊！根本逛不完！

II. Prosperous and Thriving Cultural Programs: Public Cultural Services Spark in Anhui

How to give full play to the social benefits of public cultural programs and meet the increasing spiritual and cultural needs of the people? In recent years, Anhui has launched more public cultural projects to benefit the people and accelerate the development of the public cultural industry. With much trendier public cultural venues, more and more attentive public cultural services, and abundant public cultural products and activities, people are increasingly feeling more satisfied and happier.

i. Public Cultural Venues Are Much Trendier

It was reported that the new Hefei Science and Technology Museum was about to open for visits. There would be a soft opening to the public before the official opening and then the final adjustments would be made to exhibits and devices at the museum. Ms Liu made a reservation on the Official Account and took the children to visit on Saturday morning. From a distance, the entire museum was shaped like consecutive steps, implying the upward force to climb toward the peaks of science. It was affectionately known as the "smart box" by Hefei citizens. Just showing the reservation code, Liu didn't spend a penny. Eagerly, the kids ran in to have a wonderful tour.

合肥市科技馆新馆（徐旻昊 摄）
The new Hefei Science and Technology Museum (Photo by Xu Minhao)

刘女士和孩子们被前面传来的阵阵笑声吸引，跑去一看原来是有人通过一键"呼叫"黑猩猩，在体验和黑猩猩赛跑。他们又来到"能量"展厅，这里有一面陈列着"元素周期表"的墙壁。当与墙壁前的多媒体屏幕互动时，墙面便会发出鲜艳的光芒，点击多媒体屏幕上对应的选项，就能播放科普视频，演示化学反应时的现象。除此之外，还有很多互动性展项，是新馆展品最重要的特色之一。这些众多新颖的互动展项，让孩子们直呼新奇又有趣，在体验中感受到了科学的奥秘。

新馆内还有诸多科技元素，如可控核聚变、量子纠缠、语音识别等先进科技在不同展厅皆有体现。飞翔球幕影院的观影感受更加立体沉浸，观众可体验

The new museum had a total floor space of about 50,000 square meters. From nature to science to technology, there were 11 permanent exhibition halls, displaying nearly 1,000 distinctive exhibits. Among them, the nature exhibition hall was a major highlight of the new museum, for there was no natural museum in the past. The kids were so excited and exclaimed, "It is so large that we can't finish in one day!"

As they walked around, a burst of laughter caught their attention. It turned out that someone was experiencing a race with the chimp by one button "call". They moved on to the Energy Hall, which had a wall displaying the periodic table of chemical elements. When visitors interacted with the multimedia screen in front of the wall, the wall glowed in vibrant colors. By clicking on the corresponding option on the multimedia screen, you could play a science video that demonstrated the phenomena during a chemical reaction. In addition, there were many interactive exhibits, which were the most important features of the new museum. These interactive exhibits were so novel that the kids couldn't help saying "What a fantastic experience of science mystery!"

The new museum was full of scientific and technological elements. There were many advanced technologies, such as controlled nuclear fusion, quantum entanglement, and speech recognition, which were displayed in different exhibition halls. There was also a dome theater with a viewing angle of up to 162 degrees which provided a three-dimensional and immersive viewing experience. The audience could experience the technical movements with the seamless integration of live action, such as flying, shuttling, rapid descent, and climbing. Manifesting the scientific quality of Hefei was another feature of the new museum.

On the second and third floors of the museum, there were public rest areas in the form of large steps. Liu and her kids, who were tired from walking, sat here on the ground. It was said that in the future, the new museum would hold scientific shows and other performances on the grand steps so that citizens could enjoy a visual feast while taking a break. After a short rest, they continued to move

到拟真感极高的飞越、穿梭、速降、爬升等技术动作。尽显合肥的"科里科气",是新馆的又一特色。

馆内 2 层至 3 层以大台阶的形式设置了公共休息区。走累了,刘女士和孩子们在此席地而坐。据说,未来新馆或在大台阶上开展科学秀等表演,让市民们休息之余还能享受到视觉盛宴。短暂的休整之后,他们继续前行,来到了青少年创新教育的科普活动室。原来,新馆除了 1 层至 4 层的特色展厅,还有地下一层,承载教育活动、特效影院、会议交流等功能。

近年来,随着安徽公共文化场馆建设步伐不断加快,在安徽创新馆内穿越量子隧道,在安徽博物院里探索历史文化,在巢湖之畔打卡安徽美术馆,在合肥市图书馆新馆畅游书海,随时来一场说走就走的 citywalk(城市漫步)已成为现实。未来,安徽省百戏城、安徽省文化馆新馆、安徽省非物质文化遗产展示馆也将成为文化新地标。空间设置多元,功能多样,玩法新颖,越来越潮的免费开放公共文化场馆不断拨动老百姓的心,更好地满足了群众日益多元的文化需求。

(二)公共文化服务越来越贴心

王大爷如今 68 岁,退休前是位中学历史教师,特别喜欢旅游。"退休后,趁还能走得动,我和老伴经常旅游,去了很多地方。因为我是教历史的,每到一个城市,博物馆是我们必去的地方。"但是,2022 年冬天,王大爷下楼时不小心踩空,腿骨折了。"本来我和老伴还想着去泗县隋唐大运河博物馆看看。大运河是我特别感兴趣的一个研究内容,虽然退休了,我还是特别关注关于大运河的最新研究动向,尤其是国家提出'大运河文化带'及'大运河国家文化公园'战略以后。2022 年 7 月,我去看过扬州的中国大运河博物馆,然后打算去看看我们泗县的隋唐大运河博物馆。可是腿摔了,出门就特别不方便。后来听说有个'安徽文化云'平台,是我们安徽省为更好满足人民群众对于文化服务的需求,

forward and came to the science activity rooms for teenagers. It turned out that in addition to the special exhibition halls from the first to fourth floors, the new museum also had an underground floor, undertaking a multifunctional complex that integrated educational activities, special visual effects cinema, and conference halls.

In recent years, with the vigorous construction of public cultural venues in Anhui, walking through the quantum tunnel in Anhui Innovation Pavilion, exploring history and culture in Anhui Museum, appreciating the artworks in Anhui Art Museum on the shore of Chaohu Lake, wandering in the ocean of books in Hefei Central Library, the citizens will be able to enjoy a scientific and cultural city walk without traveling far at any time. In the future, with the completion of Anhui Plays Hall, the new Cultural Center of Anhui Province, and Anhui Intangible Cultural Heritage Exhibition Hall, many cultural landmarks will mushroom. With diverse space settings, multiple functions, novel projects, more and more fashionable public cultural venues which are open for free continue to inspire the people and better meet the increasingly diverse cultural needs of the people.

ii. Public Cultural Services Are More and More Attentive

Uncle Wang is 68 years old and likes traveling very much. Before retirement, he was a middle school history teacher. "After retirement, my wife and I often go traveling while we are still nimble on our legs and feet. We have been to many places. Maybe for I have ever taught history in a middle school, every time we travel to a city, we are bound to visit the local museum." However, he accidentally broke his leg when walking down the stairs last winter. "Before my leg was broken, we made a travel plan to the Sui-Tang Grand Canal Museum in Sixian County, Suzhou City of Anhui Province. The Grand Canal is my favorite

积极探索'互联网＋公共文化服务'的成果，2019年7月就建成了，是全国首个。这个'安徽文化云'平台可不得了啊，覆盖了全省360个公共图书馆、博物馆、文化馆、美术馆等公共文化场馆。我只要在'安徽文化云'微信公众号或者网站轻轻这么一点，泗县隋唐大运河博物馆的视频就出来了。刚刚摔了那会儿，可把我闷坏了。现在好了，在家吹着空调，想去哪儿就点哪儿，太方便了！"

和王大爷不同，李大妈家在农村，孩子们已成家立业，因不习惯城市生活，老伴去世后就一个人在老家。大妈喜欢庐剧，得益于安徽省文化惠民工程"送戏进万村"，村里经常有演出。"在家门口就能看到这么好看的戏，党和政府的惠民政策是真好啊，让我们老百姓从心底感到高兴！"李大妈开心地说。孩子们还教她使用智能手机，通过"安徽文化云"、抖音等平台随时观看自己喜欢的节目。

乡村村晚：安徽省颍上县鲁口镇庆"双节"（沈云鹏 摄）
Spring Festival Gala in village: Lukou Town, Yingshang County, Anhui Province is celebrating the Mid-Autumn Festival and the National Day (Photo by Shen Yunpeng)

research content. Although I have retired, I still pay special attention to the latest research on the Grand Canal, especially after the strategy for the construction of the Grand Canal Cultural Belt and National Cultural Park was proposed. In July 2022, I visited the Grand Canal Museum of China in Yangzhou, and then I planned to visit the Sui-Tang Grand Canal Museum in Sixian County. But it's not easy to go out with a broken leg. Later someone told me that there was a digital cloud platform called Anhui Culture Cloud, as one achievement of Anhui Province actively exploring 'Internet + public cultural services' to better meet the people's needs for cultural services. It was completed in July 2019, and it was the first one in our country. The Anhui Culture Cloud platform is very good, covering 360 public libraries, museums, cultural centers, art galleries, and other public cultural venues of Anhui Province. By clicking on the WeChat Official Account or website of Anhui Culture Cloud, I may enjoy watching the video of the Sui-Tang Grand Canal Museum in Sixian County. At first, I was bored when my leg was hurt. But now I may go anywhere, just clicking on the website. It's so convenient!" said Wang.

Unlike Uncle Wang, Aunt Li lives in a rural area. Her children have already got married and established their careers in a city. Because she is not used to city life, she lives alone in the countryside after her husband passed away. Li likes Lu Opera very much and often enjoys watching performances in her village, thanks to the project of delivering dramas and plays to the countryside – a part of various public-interest cultural programs of Anhui Province. "It's amazing that we enjoy such brilliant plays at my doorstep. The policies designed to benefit the people are so good that we're happy from the bottom of our hearts," says Li happily. Her children also taught her to use a smartphone. She may watch her favorite programs at any time through platforms such as Anhui Culture Cloud or TikTok.

Building the Anhui Culture Cloud platform, promoting the construction of public digital cultural services in Anhui Province as a whole, and carrying out public-interest cultural programs of delivering dramas and plays to the countryside,

不管是建立"安徽文化云"平台，统筹推进全省公共数字文化服务建设，还是文化惠民工程"送戏进万村"，都是公共文化服务越来越贴心，不断提质增效的体现。

（三）公共文化产品和活动越来越丰富

携杖来追柳外凉，

画桥南畔倚胡床。

月明船笛参差起，

风定池莲自在香。

……

刚刚下班的小王来到"半亩方塘"阅读空间，接在此上暑期托管班的儿子。看到孩子端坐在小板凳上，在托管班老师的带领下正摇头晃脑地诵读古诗《纳凉》，不禁心生安慰。"社区专门招募了大学生，还有部分文化文艺工作者、科普专家、退休干部，免费为孩子们提供托管看护、兴趣培养，还辅导作业。在这里既'托'又'管'还有'教'，孩子放在这里我很放心。"小王说。

"半亩方塘"是一个城市阅读空间，位于合肥市包河区。自2017年12月试运营至今，"半亩方塘"不仅为辖区群众阅读增添了好去处，更成为政府开展更多接地气、有温度的文化惠民服务的一个重要载体。馆店一体，即图书馆和书店融为一体的运营模式，让顾客把书店变成自家书房、共享书房，实现了"由买书到借书""由个人阅读到共享阅读"的重大转变，让阅读变得更加方便，满足市民多元化、个性化的需求，提高了公共文化资源的利用率。阅读空间还可以举办读书会、艺术展，开展书法培训之类的文化活动。到了寒暑假，为解决放假家里的"神兽"无处安放、家长工作忙没空带娃的问题，阅读空间又可以变身为托管班，"半亩方塘"就是一个例子。阅读空间集合了多种功能，推进了

all show that public cultural services of Anhui are more and more attentive and increasingly efficient.

iii. Public Cultural Products and Activities Are Increasingly Abundant

Taking a cane to the willow tree to enjoy the cool
Lying on a deck chair by the south of Huaqiao bridge
The sound of flutes from boats ringing on the quiet moonlit night
The evening breeze wafting the smell of blooming lotus in the pool

…

The orderly recitation comes out far away. Ms Wang just gets off work and hurries up to pick up her son who is in daycare classes at Banmu Fangtang reading space in summer vacation. Seeing her son sitting on a small bench and reciting the ancient poem, *Enjoying the Cool*, with the daycare teacher in the reading space, she feels comforted. "The community provides the service of free babysitting, cultivation of interest, and tutoring homework for the kids who are in daycare, by especially recruiting college students, as well as some cultural, literary and artistic workers, science popularization experts, and retired officials. Here, my son may enjoy careful daycare service and also learn some knowledge. I don't need to worry at all. I feel very satisfied," says Wang.

Being located in Baohe District, Hefei City, Banmu Fangtang is one of the city reading spaces. Since its trial operation in December 2017, it has not only offered a good place for promoting reading among the people under the jurisdiction but also become an important carrier of the government to launch more down-to-earth and warm-hearted cultural programs to benefit the people. The reading space adopts the mode of Library and Bookstore Integration, which turns the bookstore into a shared study, making readers feel at home. It has realized the major transformation from buying books to borrowing books and from personal reading

基本公共文化服务的均等化，丰富了公共文化产品供给，更好地满足了现代人对公共文化服务的需求。

安徽省含山县"创梦空间"城市悦书房：志愿者在"知民俗 迎端午"活动中教孩子们绘团扇
（欧宗涛 摄）

A volunteer is teaching children to draw fans during the Dragon Boat Festival in an urban reading space in Hanshan County, Anhui Province (Photo by Ou Zongtao)

除城市阅读空间外，安徽积极推进农家书屋建设，广泛开展非遗进校园、非遗购物节、乡村村晚、广场舞比赛等丰富多彩的群众文化活动，让百姓得到真实惠，引领文化惠民走向"文化悦民"。

公共文化是社会稳定、和谐、健康发展并形成社会凝聚力的基本因素。公共文化事业繁荣兴盛是满足人民对美好生活新期待的必然要求，是中国式现代化的题中应有之义。公共文化场馆越来越潮，公共文化服务越来越贴心，公共文化产品和活动越来越丰富，是安徽公共文化服务"火出圈"的必由之路。

to shared reading, making reading more convenient, meeting the diversified and personalized needs of citizens, and improving the utilization rate of public cultural resources. Reading space is not only a place to read books, but also a venue for holding reading clubs, art exhibitions, and cultural activities such as calligraphy training. Or even it can be transformed into a daycare class. When parents are busy with work and have no time for their naughty kids during the winter and summer vacations, reading space will be transformed into a daycare class which solves the parents' biggest problem. Banmu Fangtang is a case in point. Reading space integrates many functions, promotes equalization of basic public cultural services, enriches the supply of public cultural service products, and better meets the needs of people for public cultural services in the new era.

In addition to urban reading spaces, Anhui actively promotes the construction of rural libraries and extensively carries out cultural activities with rich content and diverse forms, such as intangible cultural heritage into the campus, intangible cultural heritage shopping festival, village Spring Festival galas, square dance competition, generating substantive benefits for the people and leads the public cultural programs from facilitating the people to pleasing the people.

Public culture is the basic factor for social stability, harmony, sound development, and formation of social cohesion. The prosperity and development of public cultural undertakings is of vital importance to meet people's new expectations for a better life and is the proper meaning of Chinese modernization. So, providing much trendier public cultural venues, more and more attentive public cultural services, and increasingly abundant public cultural products and activities is the path that the public cultural services must take to spark in Anhui Province.

三、迎客天下：黄山"文旅融合"谱华章

　　黄山位于神奇的北纬 30 度线，是 1990 年被联合国教科文组织列为《世界遗产名录》的世界文化与自然双重遗产。这里有奇松、怪石、云海、温泉、冬

黄山云海（水从泽 摄）
A swathe of thick cloud above the Huangshan Mountain (Photo by Shui Congze)

III. Welcoming the World: Huangshan City Writes a Splendid Chapter with Integration of Culture and Tourism

Huangshan Mountain is located in the magical 30 degrees north latitude. In 1990, it was added to *the World Heritage List* as a double heritage both in culture and nature. Here, there are wondrous pines, strange rocks, sea of clouds, hot springs, and winter snow, displaying unique magnificent scenery to the world. Huangshan City is the birthplace of Hui Culture. Huizhou architecture with white walls and black tiles, Huizhou art with amazing wonder, Xin'an Medicine with consolidating vital base and supplementing primordial, and Xin'an Painting School with ethereal artistic conception, present unparalleled beauty of this place. In this ancient and delicately beautiful land, how does Huangshan City give full play to mixed cultural and natural heritage to achieve the perfect integration of natural landscape and culture, with more attractive tourism and more vibrant culture? Let's explore the mystery together.

i. Guarding the Guest-Greeting Pine Makes Tourism More Attractive

The Guest-Greeting Pine is one of Huangshan Mountain's most famous and iconic trees. It is named as such because it stands on the only way to the mountain

雪，风景独秀天下。黄山市是徽文化的发祥地，粉墙黛瓦的徽派建筑、巧夺天工的徽州艺术、固本培元的新安医学、意境空灵的新安画派，铸就了这方水土的绝代芳华。在这片古朴灵秀的土地上，黄山市如何发挥世界文化与自然"双遗产"的山水人文优势，让"景"与"文"完美融合，旅游更有魅力、文化更有活力？我们一起寻找黄山迎客天下的答案。

（一）守护好迎客松，让旅游更有魅力

迎客松，黄山奇松之首，因生长于黄山进山必经之路，一侧枝丫斜空而出，酷似张开手臂迎接远道而来的客人，被世人赞颂为"迎客松"，1990 年被列入《世界遗产名录》。迎客松扎根在岩石缝里，靠着自然的能量，历经千年风霜洗

胡晓春在查看迎客松的生长情况（范柏文 摄）
Hu Xiaochun is checking the growth situation of Guest-Greeting Pine. (Photo by Fan Baiwen)

and with a long branch extending out, appearing to be greeting visitors. The pine was inscribed on *the World Heritage List* in 1990. Although the Guest-Greeting Pine takes root in the rock crevice, after a thousand years of wind and frost, it is still green, tall, and straight, like a block of green pagoda. So it is a symbol of the Chinese people's spirit of perseverance and hard work. And with its long branch extending out to welcome the world, it is also a portrayal of the Chinese people's hospitality and love of peace. In 1981, the authority of Huangshan Mountain Scenic Area set up a position of guardian to watch over the tree 24 hours a day. This practice continues to this day.

On the early morning of February 12, 2023, the Huangshan Mountain Scenic Area was stormy. It was not a suitable day for climbing. One man, however, stood under a tree, picking up his telescopes from time to time and watching over the pine carefully. The man was Hu Xiaochun, the 19th guardian of the tree. "It has been raining with wind since last night, which may cause damage to the Guest-Greeting Pine. I'm going to step up my checks to make sure that it's safe and sound," said Hu. On his shift, he checks on the tree every two hours normally in daytime all year long. He observes the bark, branches, and crown tops, keeping a daily log about the conditions of the ancient tree, and recording it in notebooks for reference to provide the panel of experts in detail. When encountering extreme weather, it is required to check the tree every 30 minutes. Every year, the authority of the scenic spot also consults experts on the tree. Besides, the Guest-Greeting Pine is equipped with high-tech equipment such as a regional small meteorological observation station and infrared anti-intrusion alarm system, which makes the protection measures of the tree more and more perfect.

Besides the Guest-Greeting Pine, there are also Xin'anjiang River with green and limpid water, Mulihong known as the village on the cloud, Tachuan with colorful autumn colors, Emerald Valley called natural oxygen bar, and the tea plantations showing its brilliant history and exclusive charm of the rich tea culture in Huangshan. The people of Huangshan City not only guard the Guest-Greeting

礼，苍翠挺拔、隽秀飘逸，是中国人坚忍顽强、奋力拼搏的象征；它长伸臂膀，向世界发出邀请，是中国人热情好客、爱好和平的写照。为加强对迎客松的保护，1981 年，黄山风景区确定了守松人制度，由专人对其进行 24 小时"护理"。

2023 年 2 月 12 日清晨，黄山风景区风雨交加。在最不适合登山的日子，有一个人却逆行而上，站在一棵树下，不时拿起望远镜，仔细观察着。这个人是迎客松第 19 任"守松人"、现任"警卫"胡晓春。"这场雨从昨晚下到现在，再加上大风，对迎客松影响很大，我要加强巡查，确保它安然无恙。"胡晓春说。白天，每隔两个小时就要进行一次例行检查，详细记录每一个枝丫、梢头，甚至树皮的细微变化，写进《迎客松日记》以备查阅，也给专家组提供详细记录。遇到恶劣天气，每隔半个小时就要进行一次巡护。每年景区还会对迎客松进行专家会诊，并在迎客松四周配备了区域小型气象观测站、红外线防侵入报警系统等高科技设备，使迎客松的保护措施越来越完善。

黄山不仅有迎客松，还有一汪青水的新安江、被称为"云端上的村落"的木梨硔、拥有五彩斑斓秋色的塔川、天然氧吧"翡翠谷"、彰显黄山茶文化辉煌历史和独特魅力的茶园……黄山人民不只是守护迎客松，而是像保护自己的眼睛一样，用实际行动精心呵护着这里的一草一木一山一水：在国内首创景点"轮休"制度，尽可能发挥生态系统自我修复能力，莲花峰、天都峰等主要景点每 3 ~ 5 年封闭轮休一次；设定最大承载量，实行"分时实名预约"游览，最大限度减少旅游活动对生态景观带来的影响；开启全国首个跨省流域生态补偿的"新安江实践"，让新安江成为全国水质最好的河流之一……2023 年 7 月，黄山风景区第二次入选 IUCN 绿色名录①。黄山对山水草木的守护获得世界认可。

---

① IUCN 绿色名录：世界自然保护联盟绿色名录（Green List of Protected and Conserved Areas，简称 GLPCA）是世界自然保护联盟（International Union for Conservation of Nature，简称 IUCN）为促进以自然保护地为基础的生物多样性保护而制定的一项全球计划。绿色名录旨在认可和增强全球自然保护地有效和公正管理的能力，并维持其保护成效，实现生物多样性保护和确保人类与自然的可持续发展。

Pine but also protect and cherish every hill, every river, every tree, and every blade of grass in Huangshan Mountain with practical actions, just like protecting their own eyes. To allow nature to rest and self-repair, Huangshan has adopted a rotational closure system for several famous attractions, a practice initiated by Huangshan Mountain Scenic Area, such as Lotus Peak and Tiandu Peak which are closed 3~5 years in turns. The scenic zone also sets up the maximum capacity to curb the number of tourists by implementing the reservation system of real-name and scheduled times. It will stop selling tickets once the number of visitors reaches the upper limit of the zone's capacity to stop the human disturbance to the ecological landscape as much as possible. Practice on the Xin'anjiang River's Eco-compensation Mechanism is the first nationwide cross-provincial ecological mechanism, making Xin'anjiang River one of the rivers with the best water quality in China. In July 2023, Huangshan Scenic Area was selected for the IUCN Green List [1] for the second time. Huangshan has won worldwide recognition for its protection of landscapes and vegetation.

The Guest-Greeting Pine is more of a kind of belief and cultural inheritance than a tree. From the huge iron painting in the Great Hall of the People to the creative fireworks at the opening ceremony of the Beijing Winter Olympic Games, the Guest-Greeting Pine has gradually become a symbol and a unique mark of Chinese culture, and a business card showing China. Owing to the guardian's scrupulous care, the Guest-Greeting Pine is full of vitality. Owing to the people's preservation, Huangshan Mountain is full of vigor. A splendid Huangshan Mountain everywhere beloved, is making tourism more attractive.

---

① IUCN Green List: The IUCN Green List of Protected and Conserved Areas (GLPCA) is a global program developed by the International Union for Conservation of Nature (IUCN) to promote biodiversity conservation based on protected areas. The Green List aims to recognize and enhance the ability of the world to manage nature reserves effectively and impartially and maintain its protective effectiveness to achieve biodiversity conservation and ensure the sustainable development of human beings and nature.

迎客松不单单是一棵树，更是一种信念和文化传承。从人民大会堂接待厅门外的铁画到北京冬奥会开幕式上的创意焰火，迎客松渐渐成为一个中华文化符号和独特标识，一张展示中国的名片。迎客松，因守松人的呵护而生机勃勃；黄山，因人民的呵护而绚烂多彩。秀美黄山，处处都是你爱的样子，让旅游更有魅力。

（二）保护好古村落，让文化更有活力

《卧虎藏龙》中李慕白牵马走过宏村画桥的一幕一直在小希的记忆里挥之不去。多年以后，小希终于来到心心念念的地方。远远望去，坐落于南湖中间的画桥像一条玉带横在水面，层层叠叠的徽派建筑和周围的景色完美融合，犹如一幅水墨画。沿着青石路，走在画桥上，阵阵清凉的晨风吹过，两岸湖面上绿荷摇曳，惬意无比。站在画桥的最高点，白墙黑瓦马头墙尽收眼底，徽派建筑的布局巧妙、层次分明一目了然。移步换景，精妙绝伦，真不愧是"中国画里乡村"，小希感叹道。

走过画桥，随着人群进村，村里的青石巷纵横阡陌。傍晚的宏村，霞光万丈。月沼旁的灯光亮起来，天上人间融为一体。看了承志堂①，吃了臭鳜鱼、徽州毛豆腐等传说中的美食，兜兜转转之后，小希打算回去休息。听到旁边的人喊"快点快点，演出要开始了！"小希出于好奇，跟着一起去了，原来是《宏村·阿菊》的大型实景文化演出。

看完演出，小希回了民宿。宏村的民宿也颇具特色，主要是由徽州传统民居、传统村落改造而成。宏村始终坚持"保护为主、抢救第一，科学开发，永

---

① 承志堂：清末盐商汪定贵在1855年前后建造，至今保存完好。内有大量精美绝伦的木雕、砖雕、石雕，较为集中完整地展现了古徽州三雕艺术的特色和技艺，被誉为"民间故宫"。

ii. Protecting Ancient Villages Makes Culture More Vibrant

In the world-famous movie *Crouching Tiger, Hidden Dragon*, the scene of Li Mubai walking along the Hua Bridge of Hongcun Village with his horse had been lingering in Lucy's memory. After many years, she finally came to the place which she had been dreaming of. From a distance, the Hua Bridge on Nanhu Lake looked like a jade belt across the water. A fine mixture of layered Hui-style architecture with the surrounding landscape was just like an ink painting. Along the bluestone road, walking on the bridge, she felt very comfortable with the cool morning breeze blowing and the green lotus swaying on both sides of the lake. Standing at the highest point of the bridge, white walls, black tiles, and horse-head gables were in full view, and the ingenious layout of Hui-style architecture was clear at a glance. The scenery would change while walking, which was so impressive that Lucy couldn't help exclaiming that Hongcun Village was well deserved the name "a village in the Chinese painting".

Walking through the Hua Bridge, Lucy went into the village with the crowd. The bluestone roads of the village crisscrossed. At dusk, the beautiful view of the sunset glow shined upon Hongcun Village. With the lights near the Moon Pond lighting up, the scenery was more enchanting, just like in heaven. After sightseeing Chengzhi Hall [1] and eating the legendary local delicacy such as preserved mandarin fish and Huizhou hairy tofu, she wanted to go back for rest. Suddenly, someone said loudly "Hurry up, hurry up! The show is about to start!" Out of curiosity, Lucy went along. It turned out to be a large-scale live cultural

---

[1] Chengzhi Hall was built in 1855 by Wang Dinggui, a rich salt merchant of the late Qing Dynasty. It is well-preserved to this day, among which there are countless exquisite brick carvings, wood carvings, and stone carvings, showing the characteristics and skills of the art of Three Carvings in ancient Huizhou in a relatively concentrated and complete way. So, Chengzhi Hall is known as the Folk Palace Museum.

皖美跨越
GREAT LEAPS BETTER ANHUI

画里乡村：宏村（许家栋 摄）

A village in the Chinese painting: Hongcun Village (Photo by Xu Jiadong)

140

performance of *Hongcun Women*.

After watching the performance, she went back to the homestay. The homestays of Hongcun also had their own characteristics, which were mainly transformed from Huizhou-style traditional buildings and villages. Under the guiding principle of giving priority to both preservation and restoration, and pursuing scientific development and sustainable utilization, Hongcun Village developed many unique high-end ancient residential inns by improving the protection mechanism, actively promoting the reform of the property rights transfer of ancient dwellings, and absorbing social capital.

"Hey, you are back! Where have you been today?" said Ms Zhao warmly, the boss of the homestay,

Lucy was still immersed in the performance. "I just watched the large-scale live cultural performance. How fantastic! The women of Huizhou are so virtuous that they keep the households and educate the children well. The Huizhou-style houses with white walls, dark tiles, and horse-head gables are very beautiful in the show."

"Yes, you are right. Huangshan City has always attached great importance to the inheritance and innovation of Hui culture. Since 2009, it has been seeking a unique path with its characteristics to inherit Hui culture through performance programs in tourism. Now, it has created *Rhythm of Anhui*, *Hongcun Women*, and *Huangshan Mountain Reflection*: *Marriage of a Fairy Princess*, which are very popular. But don't underestimate these shows, in which Huizhou opera, Huizhou history and culture, folk customs, intangible cultural heritage, and other traditional culture of Huizhou, are integrated," explained Zhao.

"Indeed, it was my first time to have an intimate contact with Hui Culture and I fell in love with it unconsciously. This is a unique way to pass on and develop culture. By the way, I find that there are many homestays in Hongcun Village. Will you worry about the business? " asked Lucy.

"Of course not. And now, because the ancient buildings are well preserved, more than 100,000 students come to sketch from nature every year. We have strong

续利用"原则，健全保护机制，积极推进古民居产权流转改革，吸纳社会资本，开发出一批独具特色的高端古民居客栈。

"回来了！今天去哪儿玩了？"民宿老板赵姐和小希热情地打招呼。

小希还沉浸在演出里，应声答道："刚刚看了《宏村·阿菊》，太好看了！徽州女人真是贤惠，又会持家又会教育孩子。粉墙黛瓦马头墙的徽派建筑在里面好漂亮！"

"是的，黄山一直很重视徽文化的传承和创新，从2009年就开始琢磨怎么通过旅游演艺来传承徽文化。现在，已经打造了《徽韵》《宏村·阿菊》《黄山映象之天仙配》，可受欢迎了！你可别小看这些节目，这些演出把徽剧、徽州历史文化、民俗风情、非物质文化遗产等各种徽州传统文化都给融到一块儿了。"

"确实是，第一次这么直接地感受徽文化，不知不觉就陷进去了，这种文化传承和发展的方式真是绝了！大姐，我看这边民宿挺多的，会不会抢客源啊？"小希话锋一转。

"不会的，大家各干各的。并且，现在因为古建筑保护得好，每年光来写生的学生就十几万人，我们的民宿、餐饮经营都不缺客源。有人说去年，整个黄山的民宿收入有15个亿呢！"赵姐开心地说。

"我今天还去了承志堂，里面的木雕保存得真好！"小希感叹。赵姐说，徽州三雕是徽文化的杰出代表，承志堂的木雕最有名。近几年来，黄山市加大徽州三雕传承力度，采取抢救性保护措施，制定保护制度和管理办法，从政策、资金等方面扶持徽州三雕非遗传承人，建立生产传习基地，以生产的方式促进保护和传承。

2000年，以西递、宏村为代表的中国皖南古村落被联合国教科文组织列入《世界文化遗产名录》，这些古村落体现了工艺精湛的徽派民居特色，特别是宏村的牛形村落和人工水系，堪称"中华一绝"。徽派民居、徽州三雕、盈盈水源千年不绝的风水智慧，再加上千余项非物质文化遗产，8000处历史文化遗存，

confidence in our homestays and catering operations. It's said that the homestays of Huangshan brought in revenue of more than RMB 1.5 billion last year," said Zhao with joy.

"I also went to Chengzhi Hall today, and the wood carvings inside are well preserved," said Lucy. "The Three Carvings in Huizhou, including carvings on stones, bricks, and wood, are the outstanding representatives of Huizhou culture. Among them, the wood carving of Chengzhi Hall is the most famous," said Zhao. In recent years, Huangshan City stepped up efforts to inherit the three carvings in Huizhou by protection measures of rescue, formulating protection systems and management methods, supporting the inheritors from the aspects of policy and funds, establishing inheritance bases, and promoting protection and inheritance by carving production.

The ancient villages in southern Anhui, represented by Xidi and Hongcun, were added to *the World Cultural Heritage List* in 2000 by UNESCO. These ancient villages embody the characteristics of Hui-style dwellings with exquisite craftsmanship. In particular, the bull-shaped villages and artificial water systems of Hongcun are unique in China. With Hui-style dwellings, the Three Carvings in Huizhou, the wisdom of fengshui spreading for thousands of years, plus more than a thousand intangible cultural heritage items, over 8,000 historical and cultural relics, and millions of ancient books and documents, the perfect combination of profound historical deposits and unique cultural relics, become the cultural foundation of Huangshan City. Huangshan City takes practical measures to protect the ancient villages, deeply explores the various values of Hui Culture, and develops it in a moderate and orderly way, which makes Hui Culture more vibrant.

iii. The Government Empowering the Integration of Culture and Tourism

Huangshan Mountain is a beautiful name card of Anhui. Relying on the

百万件文书文献，深厚的历史底蕴与独特的文化遗迹，成就了黄山迎客天下的文化底气。黄山切实加强古村落保护，深入挖掘徽文化的多种价值，适度有序发展，让文化更有活力。

（三）政府赋能，文旅融合谱华章

黄山，是安徽一张靓丽的名片。依托优美的自然景色与深厚的文化底蕴，政府高瞻远瞩，推进文化和旅游深度融合发展，建设大黄山生态型国际化世界级休闲度假旅游目的地。

夯实基础设施建设。京福高铁、黄杭高铁以及徽杭、合铜黄等高速公路纵横通达，皖浙赣周边地区唯一的国际机场——黄山屯溪国际机场坐落其中，还有集文化、旅游、度假、会议、康养于一体的生态山居。这些都为文旅高质量发展提供了保障。

培育文旅新业态。利用杭州都市圈等区域合作平台，共推黄杭世界遗产游；打造徽州天路自驾游、青山绿水康养游、徽州民宿体验游等特色主题游；建成国家级研学基地，入选全国民宿产业发展示范区。文旅相得益彰，结出累累硕果。

打造国际会客厅。1979年，邓小平登临黄山，一句"要把黄山的牌子打出去"，黄山驶向国际舞台的航向就已确定。从外长的会客厅、总理的圆桌会，到RCEP（《区域全面经济伙伴关系协定》）地方政府暨友城合作论坛、联合国教科文组织名录遗产与可持续发展黄山对话会……一系列重大外交活动，向世界展示了黄山之壮美、徽州之风情。

寻自然之美，探索文化的深度，是旅游带给我们的无穷乐趣。在中国式现代化建设的新阶段，黄山以文塑旅、以旅彰文，文旅融合创造丰富的旅游供给，满足人民群众对美好生活多方面、多样化、多角度需求。

beautiful natural scenery and profound cultural deposits, the government of Huangshan City takes a broad and long-term view to promote the in-depth integration of culture and tourism, and builds Huangshan Mountain into an ecological, international, and world-class destination for leisure tourism.

Strengthening infrastructure construction. Well-developed expressways provide convenient access to the Huangshan Scenic Area. The high-speed railways of Beijing–Fuzhou and Huangshan–Hangzhou, and the expressways of Anhui–Hangzhou and Hefei–Tongling–Huangshan are interconnected. Tunxi International Airport is currently the only international airport around Huangshan Mountain. Several ecological mountain residences integrating culture and tourism, vacation, conference, and health care are under construction. All these provide a solid guarantee for the high-quality development of its culture and tourism sector.

Fostering new business forms of culture and tourism. Huangshan City uses some regional cooperation platforms, such as the Hangzhou Metropolitan Area, to launch the Huangshan–Hangzhou World Heritage Tour, creating a series of theme tours, such as self-driving tours, health and wellness tours, Huizhou-style homestay experience tours, building the state-level research base of study tours and being selected as the national homestay industry Development Demonstration Zone. Culture and tourism complement each other, bearing fruitful results.

Striving to build Huangshan City into the meeting room for diplomatic activities and global forums. In 1979, Deng Xiaoping climbed the mountain and said Anhui should make Huangshan known to the world. The Huangshan City entered a new chapter of development shortly after. From the "Foreign Ministers' Reception Hall" and the "1+6" Roundtable, to RCEP (Regional Comprehensive Economic Partnership) Local Governments and Friendship Cities Cooperation Forum, and Huangshan Dialogue on UNESCO Sites and Sustainable Development, a series of diplomatic activities have been held in Huangshan City, which shows the splendor of Huangshan Mountain and the unique charm of Huizhou Culture to the world.

新时代，人民群众对美好生活的向往中包含了更多文化期待。中国式现代化不仅要求物质生活水平提高，人民仓廪实、衣食足，而且要求精神文化生活丰富，群众知礼节、明荣辱，是物质文明和精神文明相结合的现代化。不管是"再芬黄梅"对中华优秀传统文化的创造性转化、创新性发展，还是公共文化服务繁荣兴盛充分体现出"人的现代化"的基本内涵，抑或是黄山文旅融合促进自然资源保护和徽文化传承，都是中国式现代化在文化建设方面的生动实践。

新征程，安徽要深入贯彻习近平总书记关于建设社会主义文化强国的重要论述，坚定文化自信，秉持开放包容，做好文化铸魂、文化挖掘、文化供给、文化产业、文化传播的大文章，在建设繁荣兴盛的文化强省上展现更大作为，为建设现代化美好安徽提供精神动力和文化支撑。

To find the beauty of nature and explore the depth of culture is the infinite pleasure that tourism brings us. In the new stage of Chinese modernization, Huangshan City enhances the capacity of culture and tourism product supply by encouraging positive interplay between culture and tourism and advancing deeper integration to meet the diversified needs of the people for a better life.

In the new era, the people's new aspirations for a better life contain more expectations for culture. Chinese modernization should not only promote comprehensive material abundance which makes the people enjoy a higher standard of living, but also provide cultural-ethical progress which makes people enjoy a rich spiritual and cultural life. Chinese modernization is a combination of material and spiritual civilization. Zaifen Huangmei demonstrates the creative transformation and innovative development of the fine traditional Chinese culture. The sparking of public cultural services fully embodies the basic connotation of "modernization of the people". The integration of culture and tourism in Huangshan City promotes the protection of natural resources and the inheritance of Hui Culture. All three cases are the vivid practice of Chinese modernization in cultural construction.

On the new journey, Anhui should thoroughly implement President Xi Jinping's important elaboration on building a country with a strong socialist culture. We should have greater confidence in our own culture, and adhere to the approaches of openness and inclusiveness. We should make greater breakthroughs in nurturing the people's spirit with culture, exploring the value of cultures, increasing cultural supply, developing cultural industries, and speeding up cultural transmission. We should make bolder moves in building a province with a prosperous and thriving culture to provide spiritual motivation and cultural support for building a modern and beautiful Anhui.

许家栋 摄
Photo by Xu Jiadong

第五章
幸福安居贵治理

在中国式现代化的进程中，我们坚持把实现人民对美好生活的向往作为现代化建设的出发点和落脚点。美好生活的重点在"美好"，新发展阶段需要以治理体系和治理能力的现代化来推动实现。治理涉及生活的方方面面，宏大而抽象，只有落到生活的细微处，方能感知它内在的东西。安徽省是怎样实现"美好"的呢？

这里有合肥市庐阳区"1+4+N"智慧养老，共建共享老年友好型社会，老有所养、老有所依、老有所乐在这里实现；这里有桐城市"六尺巷工作法"，中华优秀传统文化"和"的理念融入社区治理在这里实现；这里有黄山市西溪南镇的"五微"行动，宜居宜业和美乡村建设在这里实现 …… 一个个鲜活的故事浓缩成沉甸甸的民生。安徽省将群众关心关注的每一个细节变成触手可及的生活场景，用心用情用力解决好人民群众的急难愁盼问题，让安徽更美好。

Chapter 5

Governance for a Better Life

In the process of Chinese modernization, the immutable goal of our modernization drive is to meet the people's aspirations for a better life. A better life focuses on "better", which is realized through the modernization of the governance system and the capacity during the new stage of development. The content of governance, grand and abstract, covers diverse aspects of our lives. Only when it comes to the subtleties of life, can we perceive what is inside. How does Anhui Province achieve a better life?

Here is "1+4+N" Smart Elderly Care in Luyang District, Hefei City, where the elder-friendly society is built and shared, and we have achieved to ensure people's access to elderly care, elderly support and elderly happiness. Here is Six-Foot-Alley Working Method in Tongcheng City, where the concept of "harmony" in the fine traditional Chinese culture is integrated into the community governance. Here is Five-Micro-Action in Xixinan Town, Huangshan City, where we have achieved the building of a beautiful and harmonious countryside that is desirable to live and work in…These vivid stories are condensed into one important word "livelihood". In Anhui, each subtlety that the people are concerned about has become the routine life that really happens. We have urged efforts to solve the urgent problems and worries of the people. In the new era, Anhui will become much better.

一、幸福老年：庐阳区"1+4+N"智慧养老托起最美夕阳红

老年是人的生命的重要阶段，是仍然可以有作为、有进步、有快乐的重要人生阶段。"日常生活有人照料，生病了能享受专业医疗，环境越来越舒适。"这是老年人对晚年生活的朴素梦想。位于合肥市区中北部的"首善之区"庐阳区探索智慧养老模式的脚步从未停歇，新时代新征程上，我们期待在老年开启人生新阶段是我们美好的愿景，也是庐阳区一直努力的方向。

庐阳区逍遥津公园美景（赵明 摄）

Beautiful Scenery of Xiaoyaojin Park in Luyang District (Photo by Zhao Ming)

I. Happy Old Age: Smart Elderly Care in Luyang Holding up the Most Beautiful "Sunset Glow"

Old age is an important stage of human life, when elders are still able to be productive, progressive, and happy. "We can be taken care of in our daily life; professional medical care is available when we are sick; and the environment becomes more and more comfortable." It is a simple dream for the elderly. Located in the north-central Hefei City, Luyang District, the model of governance, has never stopped exploring the mode of Smart Elderly Care. On the new journey of the new era, we anticipate that it is our better vision to embark on a new phase in old age, which is also the goal for Luyang to strive for.

i. "1+4+N" Smart Elderly Care Solving the Difficulties of the Elderly Care

Let's care about the trouble of Grandma Wang in Huilongqiao Community, Sanxiaokou Street, Luyang District. Grandma Wang, who is still healthy, is over eighty years old. However, she is not nimble on her feet, feeling unable to do lots of things easily on her own. It is a dilemma for her to leave her hometown to settle in her daughter's home in another city, or ask her married daughter to return to find another job. Full of anxiety, Grandma Wang says, "My daughter is so busy that she

（一）"1+4+N" 智慧养老破解养老之难

先来关注一下庐阳区三孝口街道回龙桥社区王奶奶的烦心事。原本身体还算硬朗的王奶奶年过 80 了，腿脚不方便，感觉很多事情已力不从心。自己离开生活了一辈子的家乡去女儿所在的城市养老或让成家的女儿回家乡另谋职业，都是两难的选择。王奶奶忧心忡忡地说："远在省外的女儿工作繁忙，难得有空回家看看。我不知道今后的日子要怎么过啊？"

像王奶奶这样有烦心事的，在庐阳区又何止她一个。据 2023 年的官方数据显示，庐阳区 60 岁以上老年人约 8.93 万，占比约 17.5%，已步入老龄化社会，人口老龄化、高龄化、空巢化趋势不断加快。快速老龄化背后是每个人的感同身受：人人都会变老，如何破解养老之难？

近年来，庐阳区不断完善养老服务体系，打造了走在安徽省前列的"1+4+N"智慧养老服务"庐阳模式"。

"1"指的是 1 个养老大数据平台。在庐阳区养老大数据中心，大屏幕上清晰显示出养老服务设施分布图、养老机构入住老人监测、养老助餐、家庭养老床位等信息。这里的平台负责人说："近年来，如何获取老人真实诉求、跟踪老人满意度、关注老人身心健康等是政府迫切需要解决的问题。依托大数据，可以对各类老年人的服务需要进行统计分析，为政府精准施策提供迅速、可靠、翔实的数据支撑。"

"4"指的是对庐阳区养老机构、社区养老服务站点、居家养老服务质量及为老人提供的康养系列服务的切实管理和监督。简而言之，就是实现居家、社区、机构、康养全方位监管。三孝口街道搭建了智慧社区网格服务管理平台，街道网格化服务管理中心负责人说："只要打开'智慧庐阳'App，就可以实时查看辖区范围内的各种情况。"

rarely spares time to come back home. How can I live alone in the future?"

Similar to Grandma Wang who has such trouble, there are still so many in Luyang District. The official data in 2023 showed that the number of elders aged 60 or above surpassed about 89,300, accounting for 17.5% in Luyang District, which entered the aging society. The trend of population aging, high aging, and empty nest continues to exacerbate the problem. Behind the phenomenon of the rapid aging, everyone has empathy: All of us will get old, and how to solve the difficulties of the elderly care?

In recent years, Luyang District has continued to improve the elderly care service system, creating the Luyang mode of "1+4+N" Smart Elderly Care which is leading in Anhui Province.

"1" refers to one big data platform for the elderly care. In the big data centre for the elderly care in Luyang District, the screen clearly shows such information as the distribution map of the elderly service facilities, the institutions monitoring the elderly condition, assisted meals, and elderly care beds. The person in charge of the platform said, "In recent years, it is an urgent need for the government to solve these problems, for example, how to collect the real demands of the elderly, follow up the elderly feedback, pay close attention to the elderly physical and mental health, etc. Supported by big data, the service demands for all kinds of the elderly can be statistically analyzed, which provides rapid, reliable, and informative data for the government's precise policymaking."

"4" refers to the effective management and supervision of the elderly care institutions, community-based elderly care service sites, the quality of home-based elderly care, and a series of healthcare services in Luyang District. In short, it is to realize all-around supervision for home, community, institution, and healthcare. In Sanxiaokou Street, a smart platform for community grid service management was built. The person in charge of it said, "Just open Smart Luyang App on the mobile phone, you can check a variety of situations within the community in real time."

"N" provides flexible and diversified elderly care services nearby, such as

　　"N"就是为附近老人提供文体活动、医疗护理、居家照护、日常用餐、心理咨询等一应俱全、灵活多样的养老服务。这是社区"嵌入式"养老①模式的创新举措，实现了老年人"在家门口养老"的愿望，这是"一碗汤的距离"的美好景象。

庐阳区养老服务指导中心智慧信息平台（程兆　摄）
Smart Information Platform in Luyang Elderly Care Guiding Center (Photo by Cheng Zhao)

（二）助医更好呵护老年人身体健康

　　老年人的健康管理是智慧养老模式的关键问题之一，助医更好呵护老年人的身体健康。看看以下两个场景，您的忧愁是否会减少很多呢？

---

　　①　"嵌入式"养老就是养老机构与社区有机融合，以社区为载体，以资源嵌入、功能嵌入和多元运作方式嵌入为理念，在社区内嵌入一个市场化运营的养老机构。

recreational and sports activities, medical care, home-based care, daily meals, psychological counselling, and so on. This is an innovative measure of the "embedded"[①] mode for the elderly in the community, realizing the desire for elderly care at the doorstep, which is the beautiful scene within "the distance of a bowl of hot soup".

ii. Assisted Medical Service Caring About the Elderly Health

Health management for the elderly is one of the key issues in Smart Elderly Care, and assisted medical service focuses on their health. Two typical examples about assisted medical service are as follows.

Lenian Luyang Nursing Home, publically constructed and privately operated, is a community "embedded" nursing home built by the People's Government of Luyang District, integrating intelligence, information technology, and digitization. Grandpa Zhao, 82-year-old, wearing presbyopic glasses, is leisurely reading the newspaper, and lies on the bed to rest for a while when he feels tired. The smart mattress implanted on the bed uploads his heart rate, respiratory rate and other body sign data to the Smart Elderly Care service platform, monitoring his health all the time. Grandpa Zhao cheerfully says, "How lucky I can still enjoy high-tech services at my old age!" The real fact reveals many objects here reach the Intelligent Internet of Things. His room is equipped with a blood pressure meter, blood glucose meter, temperature control, smart mattress, smart beeper, and smart robot, and so on, which can monitor his physical condition and room environment 24 hours a day. The staff can use mobile terminals to access the real-time health

① "Embedded" elderly care is that the elderly care institutions and the community are organically integrated, and the elderly care institution with market-oriented operation is embedded in the community, using the community as the carrier, and with the concepts of embedded resources, embedded functions and embedded operation of diversified modes.

　　乐年庐阳记忆院是由庐阳区政府打造的公建民营社区"嵌入式"养老院，是集智能化、信息化、数字化于一体的社区养老机构。82 岁的赵爷爷戴着老花镜悠闲地看着报纸，感觉累了就躺床上休息一会儿，植入床内的智能床垫则将他的心率和呼吸频率等生命体征数据上传到"智慧养老"服务平台，时刻守护他的健康。赵爷爷乐呵呵地说："没想到我这把年纪还能享受到高科技的服务。"原来，这里的许多物件都实现了"智慧物联"。老人房间配备的血压仪、血糖仪、温度调控、智能床垫、智能呼叫器、智能机器人等设备，可 24 小时监测他的身体状况及房间环境。工作人员使用移动终端就能获取每位入住老人的实时健康数据，需要提供的看护服务一目了然。

　　再来看看庐阳区新建的四季青老年公寓。这家公寓依托安徽庐州医院的优质医疗资源，探索出一种医养结合的养老服务新模式。在这里，使用适老化设计，不仅为自理老人提供舒适宽敞、优雅温馨的养老居所，又为因年迈或疾病生活不能自理的老人提供悉心的医务护理、生活照料和健康膳食。86 岁的钱奶奶刚刚入住这里，她说："以前在家买个吸氧机，不仅贵而且氧气纯度也达不到专业标准。现在，在老年公寓里有医生照护，医疗器械也多，比在家省心多了。"

（三）助餐暖胃又暖心

　　在庐阳区，居家养老是老年人主要的养老方式之一。民以食为天，"吃饭难"是首先要解决的问题，也是事关民生的大事。

　　庐阳区三孝口街道地处老城区，辖区部分老人处于空巢、独居状态，烧菜做饭对其来说是件困难事。每天中午或晚上饭点的时候，三孝口街道回龙桥社区食堂便热闹非凡，时不时传来欢乐的笑声。这是三孝口街道按照打造 10 分钟老年就餐圈的服务理念，让辖区老年人真切享受"舌尖上的幸福"。看看这里的

data of each elder, and care services in need are obvious at a glance.

Now take a look at the newly-built Sijiqing Nursing Home in Luyang District. It relies on the high-quality medical resources of Anhui Luzhou Hospital to explore a new mode of combining medical services with healthcare services for the elderly. Here is elder-friendly design. For the elderly who can take care of themselves, it provides a comfortable and elegant residence. For the elderly who is unfit or disabled, it provides attentive medical care, life care, and healthy food.

Grandma Qian, 86-year-old, who just moved here, says, "In the past, it was expensive to buy an oxygen machine at home, and the purity of oxygen was not up to professional standard. But now, in the nursing home, the doctor can take care of me, and there are many types of medical equipment. I think I am less worried here."

iii. Assisted Meals Warming Stomach and Heart

In Luyang District, home-based elderly care is one of the main ways for the elderly care. Food is the most basic necessity of the people. Therefore, the food problem must be the first to be solved, which is a matter of great importance involving the people's livelihood.

Sanxiaokou Street in Luyang District lies in the city's area, where some elders are empty nesters or live alone. Cooking at home is a great trouble for them. Every day, at meal time at noon or in the evening, the community cafeteria in Huilongqiao is bustling, and from time to time there comes out joyful laughter. This is the service concept of creating a 10-minute dining circle for the elderly in Sanxiaokou Street, so that the elderly in the community can truly taste a bite of happiness. What delicious dishes here: braised fish, pork rib soup, stir-fried broccoli, scrambled egg with tomato, sliced pork with green pepper, etc. These dishes include not only meat but also vegetables, with balanced nutrition. The waitress in the cafeteria says, "Such catering enterprises as Liuhongsheng, Zhengxiaowan, and

菜品，有红烧鱼、排骨炖汤、清炒西兰花、西红柿炒鸡蛋、青椒肉丝……荤素搭配，营养均衡。食堂大姐说："我们还有刘鸿盛、蒸小皖、九久夕阳红等餐饮企业参与助餐服务。"街道61岁的孙大爷是这里的常客，他兴奋地说："我一个人做饭特别不方便。在这里，一个荤菜、一个荤伴素、一个素菜、一个汤、一份米饭，价格有优惠①，只需要8元钱，吃得饱、有营养，口味好，很适合我们老年人的饮食需求。"只要步行10分钟，不用下厨房也能吃上热乎可口的饭菜，成为孙大爷津津乐道的事。社区工作人员说："我们建设智慧助餐服务系统，与银行、企业合作，以庐阳区智慧养老信息平台为依托，通过刷脸支付消费、后台系统归集服务信息，实现助餐服务更方便、更快捷、更安全。"原本的"吃饭

庐阳区养老服务指导中心老年食堂（袁兵 摄）
The Cafeteria of Luyang Elderly Care Guiding Center (Photo by Yuan Bing)

---

① 安徽省各级政府财政有老年助餐服务的建设补贴、运营补贴以及就餐补贴等。

Jiujiu Xiyanghong also contribute to assisted meals." Grandpa Sun, 61-year-old, is a regular customer here. He says excitedly, "It is particularly inconvenient for me to cook by myself. Here, I ordered a portion of meat, vegetables, soup, and rice, for only RMB 8. It is so cheap.[①] It tastes good, full of nutrition. All in all, it is suitable for us!" Grandpa Sun told everyone he knew delightedly. The community staff says, "We build smart assisted meal service systems and cooperate with banks and enterprises. Assisted meals have become more convenient, faster, and safer, through face scan payment and collecting information with the backstage management system. The food problem is no longer a worrying thing. Assisted meals make the elderly enjoy a flavor of happiness near their home.

iv. Culture and Recreation Making the Elderly Life Colorful as Well

There is a famous saying of Kant, the founder of German classical philosopher and thinker: Be as happy as a young man in old age! Youth, like a lark, has his morning songs. Old age, like a nightingale, should have his nocturnes. Many elders are not satisfied with "care for the elderly" and "dependence for the elderly". They are eager to learn and have fun in their old age. "1+4+N" Smart Elderly Care has never ignored their spiritual world. Culture and recreation make the elderly life colorful as well.

There are more than 20 interest teams such as calligraphy, dancing, Tai-chi, and gas volleyball in Sanxiaokou Street, which make the elderly have more fun with a wider range of venues and more regular activities. Therefore, they have a stronger sense of belonging. Grandma Zhang, 62 years old, says, "Now we have a regular place to learn and study. We can come here and study together. It's close to

---

① In Anhui Province, government finances at all levels include construction subsidies, operating subsidies, and meal subsidies for assisted meals for the elderly.

难"问题不再是烦恼事了，老年助餐服务让老年人在家门口吃出幸福味道。

（四）文化娱乐让老年生活也精彩

德国古典哲学创始人、思想家康德曾说："老年时像青年一样高高兴兴吧！青年，好比百灵鸟，有它的晨歌；老年，好比夜莺，应该有他的夜曲。"许多老人对养老生活的需求已不仅仅满足于老有所养、老有所依，还渴望实现老有所学、老有所乐。庐阳区"1+4+N"智慧养老模式没有忽视老年人的精神世界，文化娱乐让老年生活也精彩。

三孝口街道辖区有书法、舞蹈、太极、气排球等 20 余个兴趣活动队伍，使老有所乐的场地覆盖面更广，活动更有规律，老人的归属感也更强。辖区 62 岁的张奶奶说："现在有了固定的学习活动场所，以后就能来这里和大家一起学习了，离家还近，大家一起学习氛围也好，可以相互交流，同时我们还建立了微信群，方便线上讨论交流。"

在庐阳区养老服务指导中心，老人们兴致高昂地学习凤阳花鼓和旗袍走秀；在社区阅读空间，热爱阅读的大爷大妈们在书海里遨游；在社区老年大学，老人们可以根据自己的爱好选择班次学习……在庐阳区，聚焦老年群体的需求，他们不仅得到了味蕾上的享受，更实现了精神上的愉悦。65 岁的李奶奶风趣地说："我们虽然已是风霜满面，而岁月留下的却是七彩斑斓。"

老有所养、老有所依、老有所乐，是人们共同的美好心愿。中国式现代化是人的现代化，建设中国式现代化的道路上，老年人不能缺位。新时代庐阳区积极应对人口老龄化工作，努力实现老年人朴素的梦想，老年人获得感、幸福感、安全感显著提升。在"1+4+N"智慧养老模式的带动下，庐阳区将智慧养老进行到底，托起最美夕阳红，让老年人拥有幸福美满的晚年。

home, and the atmosphere of learning together is great. We can communicate with each other. At the same time, we have a WeChat group for online communication."

In Luyang Elderly Care Guiding Center, the elders are in high spirits to learn Fengyang flower-drum dance and Qipao show; in the community reading space, the elders who love reading are wandering in the sea of books; in the community seniors university, the elders can choose classes suited to their hobbies. Luyang attaches great importance to the needs of the elderly, so the elders not only have joy on taste buds, but also get pleasure in mind. Grandma Li, 65 years old, says happily, "Although we are weather-beaten, the rest of our life is colorful."

It is the common hope for people to have "care for the elderly", "dependence for the elderly", and "fun for the elderly". Chinese modernization is closely related to the modernization of "human beings", so the elderly cannot be absent on the path to Chinese modernization. In the new era, Luyang District actively responds to the aging of the population, strives to realize the simple dream of the elderly, and significantly improves the sense of gain, happiness, and security of the elderly. Driven by "1+4+N" Smart Elderly Care, Luyang will carry it through to the end, holding up the most beautiful sunset glow, so as to build a happy life for the elderly.

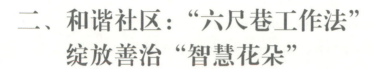

二、和谐社区："六尺巷工作法"
绽放善治"智慧花朵"

在皖西南的一座小城，有这样一个小巷，从巷头到巷尾不过百米长，既没有飘着京韵的北京胡同那般蜿蜒深邃，也没有福州市的三坊七巷那么繁华热闹。就这样普普通通的小巷背后却有一个饱含人生智慧的故事，以及因这个故事而得名的社区治理工作法。这座小城就是有着"桐城派""国家历史文化名城""平安中国建设示范县"等诸多美誉的安徽桐城，小巷就是坐落在市中心的六尺巷。

桐城六尺巷（李博 摄）
Six-Foot-Alley in Tongcheng City (Photo by Li Bo)

II. Harmonious Community: Six-Foot-Alley Working Method Blossoming out into "Wisdom Flowers" of Good Governance

In a small city in the southwest of Anhui Province, there is such an alley, which is only one hundred meters long from one side to the other. The alley is not as sinuous and deep as Beijing Hutong with rhyme of Beijing opera, and not as flourishing and bustling as Sanfangqixiang (the historical and cultural block) in Fuzhou City. However, behind this ordinary alley, there is a story implying life wisdom and the community governance named after it. This small city is Tongcheng City in Anhui Province, with many reputations of Tongcheng School of Literature, National Famous Historical and Cultural City, Peaceful China Initiative Demonstration County, and so on, and the alley is Six-Foot-Alley in the city center.

i. The Story of Six-Foot-Alley Enjoying Historical Reputation

Along the Longmian River which runs through the city, strolling around this small city full of the fragrance of literature, we will find that a story is hidden in every step, and a memory is carried in every place. Meanwhile, we feel that this small city has the quality of modernization nowadays. China's fine traditional

（一）六尺巷的故事传美谈

沿着横穿市区的龙眠河畔，在翰墨飘香中漫步于这座小城，我们会发现，每一步都深藏着一个故事，每一处都承载着一段记忆；同时也会感受到如今的这个小城充满了现代化的浓浓气息。中华优秀传统文化无处不在，在潜移默化中已经融入当今老百姓的生活，焕发出新的生机活力。

从六尺巷的巷头，远眺小巷，全长约100米、宽约2米（合六尺）。据史

张英的题诗（叶红艳 摄）
The Poem by Zhang Ying (Photo by Ye Hongyan)

culture is found around the city, which is integrated into people's lives with new vitality.

From the entrance, as far as we can see from eyesight, the alley is with a total length of roughly 100 metres and a width of about 2 metres (about six feet). According to historical records, the south of the alley is Zhang's residence, and the north is Wu's. As we are walking in the alley, a series of pictures in front of our eyes pass through. During the reign of Emperor Kangxi in Qing Dynasty, one of his ministers, Zhang Ying, received a letter from his family in his hometown of Tongcheng City. From the letter, Zhang learned that his family quarreled with their neighbor Wu, who intended to occupy the narrow space between their houses. Zhang's family wrote the letter hoping that Zhang could force the Wu family to give up their demand for his power. However, Zhang wrote a poem back, "Writing a letter from home, miles away, just for a wall. Why not give up three feet? Looking at the ten-thousand-mile-long Great Wall. Long gone is its builder Emperor Qin Shihuang." His reply enlightened the family members. They suddenly realized what mattered was the close relationship with their neighbors. They decided to move three feet back for their neighbor. In return, the Wu's was deeply touched by their comity and also gave up about three feet backward in building their wall. As a result, a Six-Foot-Alley appeared between the walls of two families. Six-Foot-Alley thereby got its name, becoming a beautiful story today.

ii. Six-Foot-Alley Working Method Creating the Brand

"There are two walls in my house, roughly one hundred meters long; walk in the middle of virtue and righteousness and stand on both sides with comity." This sweet song is named *Six-Foot-Alley*, which the locals are familiar with. It was broadcast in the Spring Festival Gala, making this small alley popular. Accompanied by the song, we will explore the Six-Foot-Alley Working Method

料记载，巷南为文华殿大学士张英的旧宅，巷北为吴氏宅。行走在六尺小巷中，一幅幅画面在我们眼前"穿越"。清康熙年间，有个名叫张英的官员，他老家桐城的官邸与吴家为邻，两家院落之间有个空地，供双方出入使用。后来吴家要建新房，想占这个空地，张家人不同意。双方争执不下，将官司打到当地县衙。张家人一气之下写封加急信送给张英，要求他出面解决。张英看了信后，认为应该谦让邻里，他在给家里的回信中写了四句话："一纸书来只为墙，让他三尺又何妨？长城万里今犹在，不见当年秦始皇。"家人阅罢，明白其中含义，主动让出三尺空地。吴家见状，深受感动，也主动让出三尺房基地，两家握手言和，各让三尺而成的六尺巷从此美名远扬。

（二）"六尺巷工作法"创品牌

"我家两堵墙，前后百米长；德义中间走，礼让站两旁……"这首悦耳动听的歌曲是桐城当地人都熟悉的《六尺巷》，曾亮相央视春晚，唱火了这条小巷。伴着歌声，我们来探寻一下与小巷故事结下不解之缘的"六尺巷工作法"，了解它创立品牌的发展历程。

让我们先把视线转向毗邻桐城经济开发区的"千年古镇"孔城镇，这里是"六尺巷工作法"的发源地——桐城法院孔城法庭。走进孔城法庭，映入眼帘的是六尺巷法治文化长廊和六尺巷文化墙，"法安天下 德润人心"八个大字镶嵌在长廊入口，显现出浓郁的法院文化气韵。2015 年，为提升案件办理效率，更好地解决老百姓矛盾纠纷，桐城法院提出"六尺巷工作法"，率先在孔城法庭试点运行。"六尺巷工作法"具体表现为"听、辨、劝、借、让、和"六步走法则，该工作法调解的核心为"劝"，而"劝"的核心在于以基本事实为依据，以法律规定为准绳。随后，该工作法在全市推广，同时设立 260 余家"六尺巷调解工作室"。"六尺巷工作法"在桐城大地落地生根。

which possesses an indissoluble bond with the story, and have an understanding of the development of its brand creation.

First let's turn our attention to the Millennium Old Town, Kongcheng Town, adjacent to Tongcheng Economic Development Zone. Kongcheng court is the birthplace of Six-Foot-Alley Working Method. When we enter it, Six-Foot-Alley rule of law culture corridor and Six-Foot-Alley cultural wall come into view. Eight Chinese characters meaning "Law can stabilize things in the world, and morality can nourish people's hearts" are inlaid at the entrance of the corridor, showing a strong court culture. In 2015, in order to improve the efficiency of case handling and better solve the people's disputes, Six-Foot-Alley Working Method was first tested and operated in Kongcheng court. The specific principles of the method consist of six steps "listening, analyzing, mediating, borrowing, conceding and reconciling". Its core is "mediating". As for the core of "mediating", we should regard the fact as the basis, and the law as the criterion. Subsequently, the working method was popularized in the whole city, and more than 260 Six-Foot-Alley Mediation Offices were set up. Hence, Six-Foot-Alley Working Method took root in Tongcheng City.

Zhang Yun, residential committee director of Six-Foot-Alley community, said, "The story of Six-Foot-Alley embodies the virtue of modesty, which is also in line with the relevant rights and interests of neighbor relationship and public areas in the Civil Code of the People's Republic of China." He has been engaged in community work for more than 20 years. When dealing with the contradictions among residents, he often cites the story of Six-Foot-Alley for mediation. Six-Foot-Alley community where Zhang Yun works now was founded in the 1950s. It lies in the city's old area, with more than 2,200 permanent residents. The community has set up a volunteer service organization called Delinshe, which skillfully uses the Six-Foot-Alley Working Method and effectively applies the connotation of modesty and courtesy from the well-known Six-Foot-Alley to the mediation of civil disputes.

　　文昌街道六尺巷社区社居委主任张耘说："六尺巷的故事体现了谦让的美德，这与我国《民法典》中针对邻里关系、公共区域的相关权益规定也是相符的。"他从事社区工作 20 余年，在处理居民之间的矛盾时，经常会引用六尺巷的故事来进行调解。张耘所在的六尺巷社区成立于 20 世纪 50 年代，位于老城区，常住居民 2200 余户。社区成立了"德邻社"志愿服务组织，巧用"六尺巷工作法"，把家喻户晓的六尺巷谦和礼让的内涵有效运用到民事纠纷调解中。

　　这里有一个张耘运用"六尺巷工作法"调解纠纷的典型案例。[①] 辖区内某企业破产后，因年久失修，部分院墙垮塌，周边居民有意无意地占用了少量土地。前不久，该厂区转让给了一家企业，企业在勘测土地时发现了这个问题，遂与居民交涉，但个别居民表示自己已经住了 10 来年了，拒绝返还，企业开工日期不得已一延再延。张耘得知情况后，找来企业负责人和居民代表，搬出桐城人童叟皆知的故事——六尺巷的故事，充分运用"六尺巷工作法"。先通过事实证明个别居民的确存在侵权行为，再劝说企业负责人"强者先让"，最终促使双方达成一致。这位企业负责人说："六尺巷的故事让我心生触动，考虑到老百姓动迁不便等实际困难，我们决定对被占土地'让三尺'。"企业开工后，又面临着安装空调外机可能会干扰居民生活的问题。这时，有一位居民代表说："人家企业能让步，我们也能做得到的。"这样，此前"先让"的企业得到了周边居民的"后让"，双方互相理解，问题迎刃而解。

（三）"六尺巷工作法"见成效

　　张耘社区调解的典型案例是"六尺巷工作法"在民事纠纷调解实践的一个

---

　　① 素材来源：《从优秀传统文化中汲取社会治理智慧——安徽桐城探索建立新时代"六尺巷工作法"》，腾讯网，https://new.qq.com/rain/a/20230511A021M800。

Here is a typical case that Zhang Yun adopted Six-Foot-Alley Working Method to mediate disputes. [1] After the bankruptcy of an enterprise in this community, the wall partially collapsed due to no maintenance for years, and the surrounding residents occupied a small amount of land. Not long ago, the factory was transferred to another enterprise. The enterprise found this problem when surveying the land, and negotiated with the residents. But some residents said they had lived for more than ten years, refusing to return it, so the project had to be delayed again and again. After Zhang Yun got the news, he called for the enterprise's director and the residents' representatives, told the story of Six-Foot-Alley known to the locals, and made full use of six-step principle. First, Zhang told the residents they did have infringement acts, and then persuaded the enterprise's director, the stronger side, to concede first, and finally made the two sides reach an agreement. The enterprise's director said, "The story of Six-Foot-Alley touched me. Considering their practical difficulties in relocation, we decided to concede about three feet from the occupied land." After the enterprise started work, it was faced with the problem of installing air conditioners, which might interfere with the lives of the residents. At this time, a resident representative said, "The enterprise can concede, and we can do the same thing as well." In this case, both sides reached a mutual understanding, and the problems were solved smoothly.

iii. Six-Foot-Alley Working Method Proving Effective

The typical case of Zhang Yun's community mediation is the epitome of Six-Foot-Alley Working Method in the mediation practice of civil disputes. The story of Six-Foot-Alley has been passed down from generation to generation in

---

[1] Source: *Absorbing Social Governance Wisdom from China's Fine Traditional Culture – the Exploration of Six-Foot-Alley Working Method in Anhui, Tongcheng in the New Era*, Tencent News, https://new.qq.com/rain/a/20230511A021M800.

六尺巷调解庭（李博 摄）
Six-Foot-Alley Mediation Court (Photo by Li Bo)

缩影。六尺巷的故事在桐城代代相传、生生不息，滋润着这片土地的根和魂。"六尺巷工作法"绽放出基层善治"智慧花朵"，让社区成为居民最放心、最安心的港湾。我们在佩服和赞美古人智慧的同时，也陷入沉思："六尺巷工作法"为什么能闯出成功的善治之路？

其一，"和"文化的魅力。"懿德流芳"是张英高尚品格的最高褒奖，他的高尚品格影响着子子孙孙。张泽国（桐城市博物馆原馆长、张英后人）说："六尺巷里面的一砖一瓦都闪耀着我们祖先品质的光辉，是实实在在的历史文化遗存。"张英的谦和礼让不仅成为邻里之间和睦相处的典范，更是中华民族和谐理念的充分体现，彰显了"和"文化的魅力。"六尺巷工作法"是中华优秀传统文化——"和"文化的生动案例。

其二，"小故事"里有"大智慧"。六尺巷里蕴含了人生智慧，"宰相肚里能撑船""海纳百川、有容乃大""退一步海阔天空"等包含着解决纷争的中国智慧、

Tongcheng City, nourishing the root and the soul of this land. Six-Foot-Alley Working Method blossoms out into "wisdom flowers" of good governance at the primary level, making the community become the most reliable and comfortable harbor for residents. While admiring and praising the wisdom of the ancients, we are in deep thought: Why can Six-Foot-Alley Working Method open up the successful road of good governance?

First, it is owing to the charm of "harmony" culture. The praise "Virtue leaving a good reputation" is the highest for Zhang Ying's noble character, which has an impact on his offsprings. Zhang Zeguo (former curator of Tongcheng Museum and descendant of Zhang Ying) said, "Every brick and tile in Six-Foot-Alley shines with the brilliance of our ancestors' quality, which belongs to a real historical and cultural heritage." Zhang Ying's modesty and comity become a model of harmonious relationships among neighbors, and also a full embodiment of the concept of "harmony", highlighting its charm. Six-Foot-Alley Working Method is a vivid case of "harmony" culture of China's fine traditional culture.

Second, there is great wisdom in small stories. The story of Six-Foot-Alley implies the life wisdom, "A prime minister can hold a boat in his stomach." (A person's mind is broad enough.) "The sea is vast for it embraces so many rivers." "It is to take a step further back to see broader in the horizon." All of these contain Chinese wisdom and Chinese solutions to solve disputes. Social governance is a systematic project, and China's fine traditional culture is an important "source and fount". We should make full use of its valuable resources, and explore future-oriented theoretical and institutional innovation. Six-Foot-Alley Working Method, with the system of source governance, multi-governing mode, and harmonious share, is modern primary-level governance with regional characteristics and rich connotations.

Third, it is based on law. As Zhao Wangyou, deputy director of Tongcheng Judicial Bureau, said, "Six-Foot-Alley Working Method shouldn't act as a peacemaker with no rules, but it is reasonable based on law-abiding, and then

中国方案。社会治理是一个系统工程，优秀传统文化则是重要的源头活水。我们要充分运用中华优秀传统文化的宝贵资源，探索面向未来的理论和制度创新。以源头治理、多元共治、和谐共享为体系的"六尺巷工作法"是极具地域特色、富有内涵的现代基层治理模式。

其三，以法律为依据。正如桐城市司法局副局长赵旺友所说："'六尺巷工作法'不是无原则地做和事佬，而是在守法的基础上明理，在明理的基础上礼让。"为此，桐城市在基层调解中引入律师参与，让律师提供有针对性的法律意见，为调解划出一条平衡线。

看看今日的桐城，从政法单位到公共场所，从邻里小矛盾到诉讼大纠纷，"六尺巷工作法"无处不在，将社区治理与中华优秀传统文化融合起来，把为人处世的智慧转换到基层善治，朝着和谐社区的目标前进，走出了基层善治好路子。"六尺巷工作法"体现了新时代桐城人的精神追求和使命担当，所取得的成绩斐然：全市矛盾纠纷、警情数和发案数逐年下降，调解成功率、群众安全感和幸福指数逐年上升。在2023年全国两会上，带有"桐城元素"的"六尺巷调解法"出现在最高人民法院的工作报告之中。

中国式现代化深深植根于中华优秀传统文化。中华优秀传统文化为我国国家制度和国家治理体系发展提供了丰富的思想资源，为新时代推进国家治理现代化提供了有益启示。在中国式现代化新征程上，六尺巷故事被赋予了新的时代内涵。"六尺巷工作法"充分发挥了"文都"蕴含的智慧，让其"金字招牌"展现新颜，绽放善治"智慧花朵"。

follows the principle of comity." Therefore, lawyers get involved in primary-level mediation, so that they can offer targeted legal opinions, and draw a balance line for mediation.

Take a look at today's Tongcheng City, from legal units to public places, from neighborhood contradictions to litigation disputes. Six-Foot-Alley Working Method is widely adopted. It integrates community governance with China's fine traditional culture, transforms the wisdom of how to conduct oneself to good primary-level governance, and moves towards the goal of harmonious community, so as to open up the successful path of good primary-level governance. It reflects the spiritual pursuit, missions, and responsibilities of Tongcheng City in the new era, and has achieved remarkable results: The number of conflicts and disputes, police reports, and incidence of criminal offenses in the city has decreased year by year, and the success rate of mediation, the sense of security and happiness index of the masses have increased year by year. During the 2023 National Two Sessions, Six-Foot-Alley Mediation Law with Tongcheng characteristics appeared in the work report of the Supreme People's Court.

Chinese modernization is deeply rooted in China's fine traditional culture, providing rich ideological resources for the development of China's national system and national governance system. What's more, it gives beneficial enlightenment for advancing the modernization of national governance in the new era. On the new journey of Chinese modernization, the story of Six-Foot-Alley is endowed with new connotations of the times. Six-Foot-Alley Working Method gives full play to the wisdom in the "Cultural City" Tongcheng, takes on its new look, and blossoms out into "wisdom flowers" of good governance.

三、和美乡村："五微"行动
助力西溪南小镇治理

在黄山徽州区，有一个千年历史的古村落，位于黄山南麓、丰乐河畔，绿水青山与白墙黛瓦相映成趣，如凝固在青绿山水间的水墨画，这就是西溪南镇，入选"全国最美特色小镇50强"，被称为一座与世界对话的小镇。去过小镇的人一定会流连忘返于那里醉人的风景，脑子里也会有个大大的疑问：传统古村落难治理，那么，西溪南镇有什么独特的治理之道才成为如今和美乡村的模样？西溪南镇在特色小镇治理中焕发出勃勃生机，一个个创意的金点子落在"原生态"土壤里，生根发芽、开花结果。其中，"五微"行动是最突出的。

（一）"微"治理探原因

如诗如画的西溪南镇，曾经也经历过乡村治理的艰难。古村落存在人口多、街巷多、生活垃圾多以及污水排放等问题，所以村容村貌一度成为村庄治理之痛。这些问题是农业农村现代化以及农民群众对美好生活向往的一大障碍。有位村民说："现在的网红景点其实是过去淤泥堵塞的臭水沟改造的呢！"可见，乡村人居环境的治理有多重要。

"五微"行动是西溪南镇和美乡村治理的重要途径之一，具体而言，就是

III. Beautiful and Harmonious Countryside: Five-Micro-Action Advancing the Governance of Xixinan Town

In Huizhou District of Huangshan City, there is an ancient village with a thousand-year-old history, located in the southern foothill of Huangshan Mountain and on the riverside of Fengle. Clear waters and green mountains, white walls and tiles form a delightful contrast, just like paintings in the beautiful landscape. This is Xixinan Town, one of China's most beautiful top 50 towns, the town in dialogue with the world, etc. People who have been to the town definitely linger in the fascinating scenery here, and there emerges a big question in their mind: Traditional ancient villages are difficult to govern, so what is the unique governance for making today's beautiful and harmonious countryside? With the featured governance, Xixinan Town glows with vitality, and every creative golden idea falls in the soil of "natural ecology", takes root, and bears fruit. Among them, Five-Micro-Action is the most prominent.

i. "Micro" Governance Exploring the Reasons

The picturesque Xixinan Town once suffered the difficulties of rural governance. The ancient villages had such problems as a large population, many

西溪南生态湿地（潘祯祥 摄）
Xixinan Ecology Wetland (Photo by Pan Zhenxiang)

"微改造"提升、"微景区"培育、"微创意"运营、"微循环"发展、"微奉献"治理，达到"微改造、精提升"的效果。"五微"行动鲜明的特征在于"微"，那么，西溪南镇为什么选择"微"治理方式呢？

传统村落是活着的历史，活化利用、以用促保，方能激发传统村落保护发展的内生动力。西溪南镇是拥有1200多年历史的古村落，有皖南保存最完好的枫杨林天然湿地及众多明清时期的古建筑。古村落原汁原味的模样、原生态

streets and lanes, more household garbage and sewage discharge, so the village's appearance became the pain spot of rural governance. These problems remain a large obstacle to the modernization of agriculture and rural areas, and the villagers' aspiration for a better life. A villager said, "The current popular scenic spots are actually the renovation of the stinking ditch blocked by silt in the past!" It can be seen how important the governance of the rural living environment is.

Five-Micro-Action is one of the important ways to govern the beautiful and harmonious villages in Xixinan Town. Specifically, it includes Micro Transformation, Micro Scenic Spot, Micro Creativity, Micro Cycle, and Micro Contribution, so as to achieve the effect of "micro transformation and refined upgrade". The distinctive feature of Five-Micro-Action focuses on "micro". Why does Xixinan Town choose the "micro" governance?

Traditional villages are living history. Only by activating the existing resources and protecting them through utilization, can we stimulate the driving force of the protection and development for traditional villages. Xixinan Town is an ancient village with a history of more than 1200 years. It has the best preserved natural wetland of Chinese wingnut in southern Anhui, and many ancient buildings in Ming and Qing Dynasties. The natural appearance of the ancient village and the original ecological scene are definitely the charm of Xixinan Town. Fan Changhong[1], the Party Secretary of Xixinan Town said, "Without the original ecology, the transformation of the town is impossible." During the construction of featured towns, Xixinan Town has given its satisfying answer − protecting the ancient villages and avoiding the demolition and construction on a large scale. In accordance with the integration of ecology, production, and life, it always puts ecological conservation in the first place. Not only the waters and wetlands around, but also the villages and valuable ancient residences are well protected. Fang

---

[1] Source: "Xixinan: Beauty of Creativity in Mountains and Waters," *Huangshan Daily*, http://www.hsdaily.cn/html/2018-08/13/content_1_4.htm.

的场景，正是西溪南镇的魅力所在。西溪南镇党委书记范长虹说："失去原生态，小镇建设就无从谈起。"[1]在探索特色小镇建设中，西溪南镇交出了自己的答卷——保护好古村落，对大拆大建说"不"，按照生态、生产、生活融合思路，始终将生态呵护放在首位，不仅是村落周边水系、湿地，而且村落每一幢有价值的古民居都得到了很好的保护。徽州区农业农村局副局长方华平认为，由于不适合大规模开发，因此在美丽乡村及和美乡村建设中，我们从细微处着手，进行保护性开发利用。[2]

（二）"五微"行动争"微改造和精提升"

对于宜居宜业和美乡村来说，建设是基础，治理是关键。改善农村人居环境事关广大农民根本福祉。西溪南镇和美乡村的治理从"五微"行动入手，整治农村人居环境，保留村落徽州的独特风格，力求最小干预、最好效果，以小切口实现大目标。

"微改造"提升让乡村有品质。西溪南镇在"微改造"提升上，将村内庭院、道路沿线、村口节点等微缩空间作为改造重点；鼓励农户发展"庭院经济"，将美丽庭院创建融入农家乐和民宿改造提升当中。西溪南镇枫杨林湿地景区的"客厅人家"[3]是本地居民郑先生精心打造出来的美丽庭院。庭院里花草、池水、山石交相映衬，似有一种世外桃源般的景色。郑先生说："当时做这个民宿的时候，我们就想着把院子好好利用起来，让游客能在院子里用餐，那时候的院子

① 素材来源：《西溪南：美在创意山水间》，《黄山日报》，http://www.hsdaily.cn/html/2018-08/13/content_1_4.htm。

② 素材来源：《古村复苏添动力》，中安在线，http://ah.anhuinews.com/gdxw/202304/t20230412_6789760.html。

③ 《徽州区西溪南镇："小美"庭院点亮"大美"乡村》，中新网安徽，http://www.ah.chinanews.com.cn/news/2022/1027/310786.shtml。

Huaping[1], deputy director of Agricultural and Rural Bureau of Huizhou District, thinks it is not suitable for large-scale development, so they start from the precise details and carry out protective development in building beautiful and harmonious villages.

ii. Five-Micro-Action Striving for Micro Transformation and Refined Upgrade

For a beautiful and harmonious countryside that is desirable to live and work in, construction is the foundation and governance is the key. Rural living environment upgrade is closely related to the well-being of villagers. The beautiful and harmonious countryside governance of Xixinan Town starts with Five-Micro-Action, improves the rural living environment, and retains the unique style of Huizhou Village, so as to strive for the best results with the minimum transformation and achieve the big goal through micro actions.

Micro Transformation enhances the quality of the countryside. As for the Micro Transformation of Xixinan Town, the miniature space, such as the courtyard in the village, the area along the road, and the village entrance, is taken as the focus of transformation. Villagers are encouraged to develop the "courtyard economy", integrating beautiful courtyards into the transformation of agritainment and homestay. "Guest Lounge"[2] in Chinese Wingnut Wetland Scenic Spot in Xixinan Town is a beautiful courtyard, which was carefully made by Mr. Zheng, a local resident. The flowers, water, and rocks in the courtyard enhance each other's beauty, like a dream place of idyllic beauty. Mr. Zheng said, "When we designed this homestay, we thought we should make good use of the yard, so that tourists could have dinner in the yard.

---

[1] Source: *Revitalization of Traditional Villages Enhancing Driving Force*. Zhong'an Online, http://ah.anhuinews.com/gdxw/202304/t20230412_6789760.html.

[2] Source: *Xixinan in Huizhou District: Beautiful Courtyard Making the Countryside Attractive*. China News Service Anhui, http://www.ah.chinanews.com.cn/news/2022/1027/310786.shtml.

可不像现在这么漂亮，就只是大石板地面配上几个盆栽，相对来说太单调。"后来，刚好遇到镇妇联来宣传美丽庭院创建活动，郑先生就借着这个机会对院子进行了"微改造"，院子变得有品质了，还被评为"省级美丽庭院"。"客厅人家"只是整个西溪南镇美丽庭院当中的一隅之景，常来西溪南镇，你就会发现这里处处皆景。

"微景区"培育让乡村更美丽。西溪南镇有很多美丽的小村庄，都是各有特色的"微景区"。西溪南村历史上有着"歙邑首富"的称号，至今保留明代建筑 10 多处，清代民居 100 多幢。凭借着独特的自然风貌历史底蕴，西溪南村也成为不少游客专程打卡点。为了更好满足游客体验需求，村里每天还安排专人，对小花园、小游园等"微景区"进行维护保养。西溪南村小曹说："我们村庄有很多的古建筑需要保护，从细微处着手保护好。"

"微创意"运营让乡村有活力。西溪南镇坚持"古镇旅游 + 创意产业"双轮驱动，引进创意人才，打造与世界对话的创意小镇。梦溪·方会设计师交流中心位于西溪南镇上村村口，背靠新徽式村落。走进梦溪·方会，清新自然的内部装饰让人眼前一亮，设计师工作室、大堂书吧、咖啡厅、客房、餐厅、高速网络应有尽有。老板李松是一名资深建筑设计师，在深圳打拼 20 多年，第一次到西溪南镇就被这里的美景深深折服，举家搬迁到此。[1] 李松说："一直谈诗和远方会疲乏的，我们要打造一个有别于一般民宿，让人耳目一新的设计师交流平台，来承接北上广深的设计师团队和活动，让设计师们到这儿既能度假又能工作。"一个又一个像李松这样的设计师入驻，盘活了闲置资源，也把西溪南镇变成了创意的"硅谷"，创意产业在这里枝繁叶茂。

"微循环"发展让乡村生态优。坑上村位于丰乐河上游，四面环山，是西溪

---

[1]　素材来源：《西溪南：美在创意山水间》，《黄山日报》，http://www.hsdaily.cn/html/2018-08/13/content_1_4.htm。

The yard at that time was not as beautiful as it is now. It was only a big stone ground with a few potted plants, which was relatively simple." Later, when the Women's Federation in the town came to promote the creation of beautiful yards, Mr. Zheng took the opportunity to improve the Micro Transformation of the yard, which enhanced the quality on the whole. Soon, it was selected as "provincial beautiful yard". "Guest Lounge" is just an epitome of the beautiful courtyard in the whole Xixinan Town. If you come here, you will find beautiful scenic spots everywhere.

Micro Scenic Spot makes the countryside more beautiful. There are many beautiful small villages in Xixinan Town, which are "micro scenic spots" with their own characteristics. Xixinan Village has the title of "the richest place in Huizhou" in history. Until now, it has preserved more than 10 buildings of Ming Dynasty and more than 100 houses of Qing Dynasty. With its unique natural scenery and historical background, Xixinan Village also becomes a destination attracting many tourists. In order to better meet the needs of tourists, the village also arranges professionals to maintain the "micro scenic spots", such as small gardens and playgrounds every day. Mr. Cao from Xixinan Village said, "There are lots of ancient buildings in our village that need to be protected. We should protect them from micro actions."

Micro Creativity makes the countryside vibrant. Xixinan Town adheres to the dual drive of "ancient town tourism + creative industry", introduces the related talents, and builds a creative town that can have a dialogue with the world. Mengxi · Fanghui Designer Exchange Center is located at the entrance of the village, against the new Hui-style village. Entering Mengxi · Fanghui, we are impressed all at once by its fresh and natural interior decoration, with various facilities of designer studios, lobby book bar, coffee shop, guest rooms, restaurants, and high-speed Internet. Li Song[1], the boss, is a senior architectural

---

[1] Source: "Xixinan Beauty of Creativity in Mountains and Waters," *Huangshan Daily*, http://hsdaily.cn/html/2018-08/13/content_1_4.html.

徽州区西溪南镇坑上村（潘成　摄）
Kengshang Village in Xixinan Town, Huizhou District (Photo by Pan Cheng)

南镇唯一的山区库区村。坑上村重点在微循环发展上下功夫，让良好的生态资源实现价值转换。早些年，生活污水排放一直是影响坑上村生态环境的难题，村民的厨余水、洗衣水等排到路上，流到沟里，或者下河洗衣，水源地生态环境无法得到充分保护。坑上村党总支第一书记鲍志国说："坑上村于 2012 年建立了污水处理系统，在村里实现污水管网全覆盖，全村 128 户居民生活污水全部经由管道运输集中在处理站处理。2019 年，我们又建设了中水回收利用系统，将经过处理后的中水提灌至山上茶园，便于村民在山上进行种植灌溉。"① 村民告

①　素材来源：《黄山坑上村：守住绿水青山　走出绿色致富路》，中安在线，http://ah.anhuinews.com/gdxw/202308/t20230808_7010473.html。

designer who had worked in Shenzhen for more than 20 years. The first time he came to Xixinan Town, he was deeply impressed by the beautiful scenery and then moved his family here. Li Song said, "Talking about romance all the time may be a bit empty, we want to create a refreshing club for designers, different from the common homestay, so as to undertake the designer teams and activities from Beijing, Shanghai, Guangzhou, and Shenzhen. Hence, designers cannot only take a vacation but also work here." One by one, designers like Li Song came here, revitalizing spare resources and turning Xixinan Town into a creative "silicon valley", where the creative industries thrived.

Micro Cycle makes the ecology of the countryside better. Situated in the upper reaches of Fengle River, surrounded by mountains, Kengshang Village is the only reservoir village in a mountainous area in Xixinan Town. Kengshang Village focuses on the micro cycle so that good ecological resources can achieve value conversion. In earlier years, sewage discharge was a problem affecting the ecological environment of Kengshang Village. The villagers' kitchen water and laundry water were discharged onto the road and flowed into the ditch, or villagers washed clothes in the river, thus the ecological environment of the water source could not be fully protected. Bao Zhiguo[1], the first secretary of General Party Branch of Kengshang Village, said, "Kengshang Village established a sewage treatment system in 2012, realizing full coverage of sewage pipe network in the village. The sewage of 128 households in the village was transported through pipes and concentrated in the treatment station. In 2019, we built a water recycling system, which pumped the treated water to the tea garden in the mountain, so that the villagers could plant and irrigate in the mountain. The villagers didn't need to irrigate through water diversion across mountains any more. "Not being sun-

---

[1] Source: *Kengshang Village in Huangshan: Protecting Clear Waters and Green Mountains and Striving for the Road to Get Rich.* Zhong'an Online, http://ah.anhuinews.com/gdxw/202308/t20230808_7010473.html.

别了翻山越岭引水浇灌的历史。"不用日晒雨淋，也避免了下河洗衣服污染水源，大家边聊天边洗衣服，说笑间，邻里关系更和谐了。"村里为杜绝村民下河洗衣服，建设了生态共享洗衣房，被村民赞为"污水处理站的好搭档"。

"微奉献"治理让乡村更和谐。西溪南镇结合"生态美超市"推广农村人居环境整治文明"积分制"。西溪南镇6个村的村民积极参与"积分制"，在人居环境整治中贡献自己的一份力量，这样，"微奉献"治理成了长效机制。在"生态美超市"里的墙壁上，写着详细的兑换规则。西溪南镇坑上村村民王大哥常去村里的"生态美超市"。王大哥说："刚开始我在地上捡塑料袋和烟头是为了换取其他的物品。现在成了我的习惯。这样做不仅仅是换取东西而是保护环境。"自从有了"积分制"，王大哥一家节约了不少生活开支，搞卫生的热情越来越高。目前，乡村出现了越来越多的"生态美超市"，在促进村民积极参与环

西溪南镇石桥村生态美超市集中兑换日（潘成 摄）
The Ecological Beauty Supermarket in Shiqiao village, Xixinan Town (Photo by Pan Cheng)

scorched and rain-drenched, we avoid the pollution of the water by washing clothes in the river. We wash clothes while chatting and laughing, and the neighborhood is more harmonious." In order to eliminate the phenomenon that the villagers wash clothes in the river, the village built an ecological shared laundry, which was praised by the villagers as "a good partner of the sewage treatment station".

Micro Contribution makes the countryside more harmonious. Combined with the Ecological Beauty Supermarket, Xixinan Town popularized a "credit system" for rural living environment upgrade. The villagers from six villages actively participated in it, contributing to the environmental protection. Hence, Micro Contribution formed a long-term mechanism. The specific exchange rules were written on the wall. Mr. Wang, who lived in Kengshang Village, came to the supermarket in the village frequently. "I picked up plastic bags and cigarette butts on the ground to exchange goods at the beginning. Now it has become my habit, protecting the environment more than exchanging something needed," said Wang. Owing to the "credit system", his family saved some expenses, and the enthusiasm for cleaning was getting higher and higher. So far, there are more and more Ecological Beauty Supermarkets scattered in the rural areas, playing a significant role in promoting villagers' participation in environmental protection.

iii. Xixinan Town Taking off in Popularity

Xixinan Town has achieved good results in Five-Micro-Action and beautiful countryside governance, and the countryside has got more and more beautiful, vibrant, and rich. What's more, Xixinan Town has become an internet-famous village, and taken off in popularity. In addition to many tourists from all over the world, there are films and documentaries shot here. The director of the youth inspirational comedy film *No Need a Word* said, "Xixinan has natural beauty, so it is an optimum place for shooting *No Need a Word*. The director was also thinking about overseas release, hoping to show Xixinan Town to the world.

境保护中起到了重要的作用。

（三）西溪南小镇"火"起来

西溪南镇"五微"行动和美乡村治理成效显著，乡村美起来、活起来、富起来。西溪南小镇成为"网红"村落，"火"起来了。除了各地纷至沓来的游客，还有电影、纪录片摄制组在此拍摄，青春励志喜剧电影《心照不宣》的导演说："西溪南是自然的美，人工雕琢的痕迹很少，拍《心照不宣》，西溪南是必选之地。"导演还表示，也考虑在海外发行，希望把西溪南镇展示给世界。

在国际化浪潮中，西溪南镇以开放包容的国际视野与世界对话，打造国际范的"乡村国际会客厅"。西溪南镇与世界旅游名村荷兰羊角村[①]签署友好交流合作备忘录，是安徽省缔结的首个国际友好村（镇），打开了"村门"，走向了世界。爱尔兰 Create One 制片公司《我们的蓝色世界》摄制组走进西溪南镇，纪录片导演表示，"这是一部关于水的纪录片，我们在世界各地拍摄人们创造的与水相处的新方式，希望可以帮助人类解决今天面临的一些最大的问题。在西溪南镇有一些解决方案，这里的人们已经学会了与水共存、和谐相处，值得世界其他地方学习"。

习近平总书记说："搞乡村振兴，不是说都大拆大建，而是要把这些别具风格的传统村落改造好。"加快建设彰显徽风皖韵的宜居宜业和美乡村，是推进安徽省农业农村现代化的"一号工程"，是建设现代化美好安徽的基础工程。乡村治理是国家治理体系的重要组成部分，治理有效是乡村振兴的重要保障。西溪南镇"五微"行动以环境"高颜值"提升农民幸福值，村容村貌焕然一新，加快了和美乡村治理的步伐，成为乡村人居环境治理的新典范。

---

① 羊角村位于荷兰西北方上艾瑟尔省，已有 700 多年历史，休闲养生旅游业发达。

In the wave of internationalization, Xixinan Town has opened up an inclusive international perspective to have a dialogue with the world and build Village International Reception. Xixinan Town and Giethoorn[①] in Netherlands, the world-famous tourist village, signed a cooperation memorandum. Xixinan Town was the first international friendly village (town) in Anhui Province, opening the door of the village and going towards the world. The filming team *Our Blue World* from Ireland's Create One Production Company visited Xixinan Town. The documentary director said, "This is a documentary about water. We have recorded new ways of living with water around the world, hoping to help solve some of the toughest problems mankind faces today. Some solutions are found in Xixinan Town. People here have learned to live with water in harmony, which is worth learning for the rest world."

President Xi Jinping said for rural revitalization, we shouldn't adopt the methods of demolition and construction on a large scale, but transform the traditional villages with a unique style well. The building of a beautiful and harmonious countryside with Hui-style (Hui refers to Anhui) is the No. 1 project for the modernization of agriculture and rural areas, and also a basic project for the modernization of better Anhui. Rural governance is an important part of the national governance system, and effective governance is an important guarantee for rural revitalization. Five-Micro-Action improves the happiness of villagers with the beauty of the environment. Xixinan Town takes on a new look and speeds up the governance of the beautiful and harmonious countryside, which becomes a new mode for the governance of the rural living environment.

As socialism with Chinese characteristics has entered a new era, the principal contradiction facing Chinese society has changed, which is between unbalanced

---

① Giethoorn is located in the nature reserve of Overijssel Province in the northwest of Netherlands. It has a history of more than 700 years, developing leisure and health tourism.

随着中国特色社会主义进入新时代，我国社会主要矛盾已经转化为人民日益增长的美好生活需要和不平衡不充分的发展之间的矛盾。社会主要矛盾的变化对国家治理体系和治理能力现代化提出了更高的要求，特别是在实现人们美好生活的需要上。在推进国家治理现代化进程中，要树立以人民为中心的发展思想，满足人民对美好生活新期待。

新时代十年巨变，安徽省一直在努力探索治理新路径，治理有效、秩序良好，更好地回应人民对美好生活的新向往新需求，为现代化美好安徽建设提供了健康环境，汇聚起了磅礴力量。每一位安徽人都感受到了实实在在的获得感、幸福感、安全感。无论是庐阳区"1+4+N"智慧养老模式，还是充满人生智慧的"六尺巷工作法"、创意金点子"五微"行动，这些都能看出我们对美好生活的向往与追求。人人参与、人人尽责的共治种子撒满整个江淮大地，每个安徽人都能在这里找到属于自己的美好"坐标"。

and inadequate development and the people's ever-growing needs for a better life. The change in the principal contradiction raises higher requirements for modernizing China's governance system and capacity, particularly in meeting people's needs for a better life. During the process of modernizing China's governance system and capacity, we should implement a people-centered philosophy of development, meeting the people's anticipation for a better life.

Great changes have taken place for ten years in the new era. Anhui Province has been trying to explore the new path of governance which is effective and in good order, better responding to the people's new yearning for a better life, providing the healthy environment, and gathering tremendous strength for the construction of a better modern Anhui. Everyone in Anhui has a real sense of gain, happiness, and security. Whether it is "1+4+N" Smart Elderly Care in Luyang District, Six-Foot-Alley Working Method with life wisdom, or Five-Micro-Action with creative golden ideas, all of these can embody our yearning and pursuit for a better life. The seeds of governance, which everyone participates in and takes responsibilities for, spread through Anhui, where all of us can find our own better life.

第六章
活力开放添新翼

开放是当代中国的鲜明标识。只有开放的中国，才会成为现代化的中国。习近平总书记两次亲临考察，深刻指明安徽改革开放的重要地位、奋进目标和方法路径，赋予安徽改革开放新高地的战略定位。安徽大力弘扬改革创新、敢为人先的小岗精神，以更大决心深化改革、以更大力度扩大开放，努力走出一条质量更高、效率更好、结构更优、活力更强、优势充分释放的发展新路。安徽已日益成为外商投资的热土，开放安徽，活力越来越足。

作为一个内陆型省份，如何通江达海、联通全球？安徽聚焦重点领域和关键环节改革攻坚突破，加快建设开放大通道大平台大通关，在更大范围、更宽领域、更深层次上扩大高水平对外开放，为经济发展注入新动力，增添新活力，拓展新空间。我们可以通过以下三个代表性故事一窥打造活力开放安徽的创新之路：建设中新苏滁高新技术产业开发区，使安徽主动融入长三角；开通中欧班列（合肥），让安徽制造更便捷地走向世界；永久举办世界制造业大会，让世界了解安徽，让安徽融入世界。

Chapter 6

Building a Vibrant and Open Anhui

Opening-up is the hallmark of contemporary China. Only an open China can become a modern China. President Xi Jinping has inspected Anhui Province twice and pointed out Anhui's important role, aims and paths, placing Anhui a new highland of reform and opening-up. Anhui vigorously carries forward the Xiaogang Spirit featuring "reform, innovation, and daring to be the first". It deepens reform with greater determination, expands opening-up with bigger efforts, and strives to find a new development path with higher quality, better efficiency, more optimized structure, stronger vitality and full release of advantages. Anhui has increasingly become a hot land for foreign investment. An open Anhui is more and more invigorated.

As an inland province, how to reach the sea and connect with the world? Anhui focuses on breakthroughs in key areas and links of reform, and accelerates the construction of open channels, platforms and customs clearance. Through efforts, it has advanced a broader agenda of opening-up across more areas and in greater depth, which injects new impetus, adds new vitality and expands new space for economic development. The following three representative stories offer a glimpse of the innovative path to building a vibrant and open Anhui: the construction of Suchu High-Tech Industrial Park reflecting Anhui's active integration into the Yangtze River Delta; China−Europe freight trains (Hefei) facilitating more made-in-Anhui exports, the World Manufacturing Convention held permanently in Hefei making Anhui better understood by the world and integrate into the world.

一、中新苏滁高新技术产业开发区：合作发展的示范点

位于安徽最东部的滁州市，有一处网红打卡地——中新苏滁高新技术产业开发区①（以下简称"园区"）鱼尾狮公园。这里既有滁州市的山水、苏州市的园林，又有新加坡的鱼尾狮等元素，有何寓意呢？原来，它象征着中新两国、苏皖两省、苏州滁州两市友好合作。那么这个园区是如何助力安徽开放发展的呢？我们先从它的起源说起。

（一）溯园区的来历

20 世纪 90 年代，中国和新加坡合作开发的苏州工业园，成功借鉴新加坡的先进办园经验，被誉为"中国改革开放重要窗口"和"国际合作成功范例"。2011 年 11 月，长三角地区②三省一市领导座谈会在合肥召开，共商区域合作发展大计。2012 年 4 月，苏州滁州两市携手合作，苏滁现代产业园（园区原名，2019 年改为现名）横空出世。10 多年来，园区充分借鉴苏州工业园区经验，乘

---

① 中新苏滁高新技术产业开发区是省际合作共建产业园，"中新"指中国、新加坡，"苏滁"指江苏省苏州市、安徽省滁州市。
② 长三角地区包括上海市、江苏省、浙江省、安徽省。

I. Suchu High-Tech Industrial Park: A Demonstration Site for Cooperative Development

In Chuzhou City, the most eastern city of Anhui Province, there is an internet-famous site – the Merlion Park in Suchu High-Tech Industrial Park [①]. The Merlion Park blends the landscape of Chuzhou City, the garden of Suzhou City, and the elements of Singapore. What does it mean? It symbolizes the friendly cooperation between China and Singapore, Jiangsu Province and Anhui Province, as well as Chuzhou City and Suzhou City. Then how does Suchu High-Tech Industrial Park (hereinafter referred to as the Park) contribute to the opening-up and development of Anhui? Let's start with its origin.

i. Tracing the History of the Park

In the 1990s, China and Singapore jointly developed the Suzhou Industrial Park. Successfully drawing on Singapore's advanced experience in running the Park, it has been hailed as a crucial platform to showcase China's opening-up and a successful example of international cooperation. In November 2011,

---

[①] It belongs to the inter-provincial co-built industrial park which involves cooperation between China and Singapore, Suzhou City in Jiangsu Province and Chuzhou City in Anhui Province.

中新苏滁高新技术产业开发区（记者部 摄）
Suchu High-Tech Industrial Park (Photo by Journalist Department)

长三角的东风，利用国内和国际两种资源、两个市场，承接国内外产业转移，将先进产业及产业群体引进园区，突出"引进来""走出去"双向开放战略，实现荒坡向新城的蝶变，成为合作发展的典范。

（二）做引来金凤凰的梧桐树

走进位于园区伟业路88号的道益精密科技（安徽）有限公司厂区，就像走进一处环境整洁、管理规范的花园。马来西亚籍总经理陈诗章彬彬有礼，向大家介绍企业的发展历程和基本情况：道益公司是滁州市首家新加坡企业，其母公司新加坡道益国际是金属和陶瓷粉末注塑成型领域最大供应商之一；他们

the regional meeting of the Yangtze River Delta^① was held in Hefei. The main leaders of three provinces and one city conducted a symposium to discuss cross-regional cooperation and development plans. In April 2012, Chuzhou and Suzhou joined hands, and thus the Park was born. In the past decade, the Park has learned experience from Suzhou Industrial Park, taken advantage of the Yangtze River Delta Integration, and made good use of the resources and markets both domestically and internationally. It has undertaken industrial transfer at home and abroad and introduced advanced industries and industrial groups into the Park. Meanwhile, it has highlighted a two-way opening strategy of "bringing in" and "going out". Now, the Park has transformed from wild-land to a modern industrial

---

① The Yangtze River Delta refers to urban agglomeration in China including Shanghai City, Jiangsu Province, Zhejiang Province and Anhui Province.

2000 年进入苏州工业园发展，对其发展模式和亲商理念十分认同。2014 年，当以打造皖版苏州工业园为目标的苏滁现代产业园递出橄榄枝时，企业欣然接受，成为首批落户园区的外资企业之一。

从规划起，园区就借鉴、复制苏州工业园区开发、建设、管理的成功经验，与苏州工业园理念和标准等实行高对接，打造品牌效应。作为苏皖两省区域合作的重点项目，园区享受省辖市管理权限，实行一站式审批，企业足不出园即可办妥所有行政事务。开展校企合作，在当地高校设有"苏滁班""定制班""光伏班"等，帮助企业招工。"对企业而言，苏州工业园里招工难度相对较大，因此选择一脉相承的苏滁现代产业园发展，是企业明智的选择。"园区一流的营商环境令陈诗章十分满意。

如今，在光亮整洁的办公区一层大厅，陈诗章颇为自豪地介绍展示台上的企业产品：精度达 0.05 毫米、各种造型和类别的精密注塑件，现成为汽车、机械、电子、医疗设备等多领域的世界知名企业产品配套的青睐组件……新加坡企业精益求精的品质也吸引了园内同行企业员工纷纷参观学习。

园区秉持"高端、品牌、外资"的理念，主攻重大项目、外资项目、品牌项目的引进，以带动行业发展，同时入驻企业也获得了更好的发展。植脂奶油的创始者维益食品公司于 2020 年 9 月签约落户园区。维益食品创建于 1945 年，是全球化的全品类奶油制造商、世界烘焙和餐饮领域的主要品牌之一，拥有混合脂奶油、植脂奶油、乳脂奶油完整的产品结构。维益食品（滁州）有限公司总投资 6800 万美元，购地 100 亩，建设维益食品奶油、酱料等产品生产项目。2023 年 1—9 月，该公司实现产值 8.9 亿元、纳税 0.54 亿元。

梧桐树高，凤凰自来。园区充分利用长三角高质量一体化战略，以及双圈互动①、左右逢源带来的区位优势，深化省际毗邻地区合作，共同探索不破行政

---

① 双圈互动：园区东依南京，西邻合肥，是联动南京经济圈和合肥都市圈的重要节点。

park, and thereby become a paradigm of cooperative development.

ii. Being the "Parasol Tree" That Attracts the "Golden Phoenix"

Walking into the factory of Dou Yee Precision Technology (Anhui) Co., Ltd. located at 88 Weiye Road in the Park, is like entering a garden with a clean environment and standardized management. Chen Shizhang, the Malaysian general manager, is politely introducing the development process and profile of the enterprise, "Dou Yee is the first Singapore enterprise in Chuzhou, with its parent company, Dou Yee International being one of the largest suppliers in the field of Metal and Ceramic Powder Injection Molding. In 2000, it entered the Suzhou Industrial Park approving of its development model and business-friendly idea. In 2014, when the Park, Anhui version of Suzhou Industrial Park, offered an invitation, Dou Yee Precision Technology gladly accepted and became one of the first foreign-funded enterprises to settle in the Park."

Since planning, the Park has fully drawn on the successful experience in the development, construction and management of Suzhou Industrial Park, and implemented the same high-level concepts and standards as Suzhou Industrial Park to create the brand effect. As a key regional cooperation project of Jiangsu and Anhui Province, the Park enjoys provincial-level management rights and a one-stop approval policy as well. The enterprises can fulfill all administrative affairs within the Park. Besides, by school-enterprise cooperation, the Park sets up Suchu Class, Custom Class and Photovoltaic Class in local colleges and universities to help enterprises recruit workers. "For enterprises, it is relatively difficult to recruit workers in Suzhou, so it is wise for enterprises to move here, the Anhui version of Suzhou Industrial Park, with better recruiting conditions." Chen Shizhang is very satisfied with the first-class business environment of the Park.

Now, in the hall of the first floor of the clean office area, Chen Shizhang is

劳士领滁州项目开工仪式（丁亚 摄）

Röchling (Chuzhou) project commencement ceremony (Photo by Ding Ya)

隶属、打破行政边界的一体化发展新模式，施行双主体①管理，共同建设，联合招商，积极为园区企业提供服务，基础设施建设日趋完善，投资环境日趋向好。园区成为全省外资项目的新兴集聚区，为区域经济发展增添了活力和动力，入驻企业在合作中也实现了优势互补、互利共赢。

---

① 双主体是指园区管委会、中新苏滁开发公司。

proudly presenting the products on the display stand: Precision injection parts of various shapes and types with an accuracy of 0.05 mm, are now becoming the popular accessory complex opponents of the products from world-famous enterprises involving automobile, machinery, electronics, medical equipment and other fields... The excellent performance has also attracted other peer companies in the Park to visit and learn.

Adhering to the concept of "high end, brand, foreign investment", the Park focuses on the introduction of related projects to drive the development of the industry, and the settled enterprises have also achieved better development. Rich Products Corporation, the founder of vegetable fat cream, signed a contract to settle in SuChu in September 2020. Built in 1945, Rich Products is one of the main brands in the baking and catering industry, and a global full-range cream manufacturer with a complete product structure of blended cream, vegetable cream, and cream. Rich Products (Chuzhou) Co., Ltd has a total investment of USD 68 million and purchases $0.67km^2$ land to construct a production project for products such as Rich's Cream and Sauce. From January to September 2023, the production base of Rich Products (Chuzhou) Co., Ltd has achieved a total output value of RMB 890 million and a tax payment of RMB 54 million.

There is a Chinese saying that if the parasol tree is tall, the golden phoenix will come. The Park makes full use of the high-quality integration strategy of the Yangtze River Delta and its location advantages brought by the mutual circle interaction.[1] It deepens inter-provincial cooperation among neighboring areas by jointly exploring a new mode of integrated development through cross-provincial management. The Park carries out dual-subject[2] management, joint construction and common investment. To provide better services for the Park enterprises, the

---

[1] The Park, located in the east of Nanjing City and west of Hefei City, is an important node linking Nanjing economic circle and Hefei metropolitan circle.

[2] The Park's management committee and China-Singapore Suchu Development Co., LTD.

（三）助企做大做强

2017 年，意特利（滁州）智能数控科技有限公司落户园区，实现了迅猛发展，从最初产值只有 2000 万元，到 2023 年产值预计可达 5 亿元，已发展成为国内高端五轴数控加工机床领先企业。总经理张伟介绍说："从上海来到滁州发展，是我们企业做的最对的决定。在企业快速发展的这几年里，我们受到了来自园区无微不至的高效服务。从资金、用工到项目申报，'保姆式'帮扶解决了我们的后顾之忧。前不久，我们与合肥知名高校合作研发、攻破一项核心技术，获得滁州市政府的 3000 万元科研奖励。公司许多高层次人才因为园区的好政策购房定居，成为了'新滁州人'。目前跟随我们而来的上下游企业已有 5 家，园区就是引才助企发展的福地。"

园区近年来吸引了长三角企业尤其是先进制造企业组团式承接、集群式入驻发展，引入项目总数超过七成来自沪苏浙；借力中新集团全球化招商平台，已引进瑞士山特维克集团、新加坡欣阳科技、美国派罗特克新材料、韩国喜星精密、南方黑芝麻等一大批国际国内知名外资企业。园区形成了以高端装备制造、新能源材料、新一代信息技术、营养健康为四大主导产业，以现代服务业为支撑的产业体系。

园区为培育企业走"专精特新"路线，链接长三角科创共同体，搭建苏大天宫科技园、灏谷科技园等科技平台孵化科技创新，启动"揭榜挂帅"创新激励政策。助推外向型企业"走出去"，组织"万企百团出海行动"活动，鼓励企业参加境内外展会、投洽会等。园区星恒电源、旭合科技等龙头企业不断攻破核心技术、扩大生产基地，纷纷"出海"进行全球化布局，跨入百亿企业行列。2021 年园区规上工业企业数达 107 家，较 2020 年增加 38 家；产值亿元以上工业企业 27 家，较 2020 年实现翻番；新增高新技术企业 17 家，为历年

Park has made its infrastructure construction gradually perfect, and the investment environment increasingly favorable. It has become an emerging gathering hub for foreign-funded projects in Anhui Province, adding vitality and impetus into regional economic development. Meanwhile, the settled enterprises and the Park have achieved mutual complementarity and win-win cooperation.

iii. Empowering Enterprises to Grow Bigger and Stronger

In 2017, YTL (Chuzhou) CNC Technology Co., Ltd. settled in the Park and realized rapid development, with an output value from RMB 20 million initially to estimated RMB 500 million in 2023. The company has developed into a leading domestic enterprise of high-end CNC five-axis machine tools. "Transferring from Shanghai to Chuzhou for development is the best decision our company has made. During the past few years of rapid development, we have received meticulous and efficient service from the Park. From funds, employment to project application, the intimate service helps solve our problems," General Manager Zhang Wei appraised, "Not long ago, we cooperated with well-known universities in Hefei to research and develop. After breaking through a core technology, we won a scientific research award of RMB 30 million from the Chuzhou government. Many senior talents of the company decided to buy houses and settle down as new Chuzhou citizens because of the good policy of the Park. At present, there are five upstream and downstream enterprises following us, and the Park is a good place to attract talents and help enterprises develop."

In recent years, the Park has attracted enterprises from the Yangtze River Delta, especially advanced manufacturing enterprises, to undertake group and cluster development, and more than 70% of the introduced projects are from Shanghai, Jiangsu and Zhejiang. By the global investment platform of the China-Singapore Suzhou Industrial Park Development Group, a large number of well-

园区企业工作车间（程兆 摄）

The workshop in the industrial park (Photo by Cheng Zhao)

known foreign and domestic enterprises have been introduced to the Park, including Sandvik Group of Switzerland, Sunningdale Precision Industries Company of Singapore, Pirotec New Materials Company of the United States, Heesung Precision of South Korea, and Nanfang Black Sesame Group Co., Ltd. of China, and so on. The Park has formed four leading industries involving high-end equipment manufacturing, new energy materials, new-generation information technology, and nutrition and health. An industrial system has taken shape supported by the modern service industry.

To cultivate enterprises, the Park supports enterprises that use special and sophisticated technologies to produce novel and unique products, links the sci-tech innovation community in the Yangtze River Delta, builds related platforms such as Su Da Tiangong Science Center and Hawku Science Park for companies to cultivate sci-tech innovation, and launches the innovation policy incentive of Open Bidding for Selecting the Best Leader of Projects. The Park promotes export-oriented enterprises to go to the outside world, launches the "Thousands of Enterprises Going Abroad" campaign, and encourages enterprises to participate in domestic and foreign exhibitions and fairs for investment and trade, etc. The leading enterprises like Phylion Battery Co., Ltd. and Solar Plus in the Park keep breaking through core technologies, expanding production bases, and conducting a global layout, with main business revenue exceeding RMB 10 billion.

In 2021, the number of up-scale industrial enterprises in the Park reached 107, with an increase of 38 compared with the previous year, and 27 industrial enterprises with an output value of more than RMB 100 million, doubling that of the previous year; increasing a record 17 new high-tech companies over the past years, with a total of 47. In 2022, the up-scale industrial added value of the Park increased by 20%, of which the value of strategic emerging industries accounted for 74.1%, and the imports and exports value of foreign trade reached USD 480 million, with a year-on-year growth of 12%. The cumulative foreign investment projects reached 62 from 13 countries, including 8 of Global Fortune

最多，累计达 47 家。2022 年园区规上工业增加值增长 20%，战略新兴产业值占规上工业比重 74.1%，外贸进出口 4.8 亿美元，增长 12%；引进外资项目增至 62 个，项目来源地涉及 13 个国家，其中世界 500 强企业 8 个，上市公司投资项目 39 个，较 2021 年增加 29 个；实现国家"专精特新"小巨人[①]、省"专精特新"冠军企业、获省科技进步奖企业 3 个"零的突破"。园区先后被评为"长三角共建省际产业合作示范园"、首批"安徽省国际交流合作基地"。园区企业的做大做强也带动了滁州乃至安徽外向型经济的飞跃发展，安徽开放的东大门越开越大。

新时代的中新苏滁高新技术产业开发区，宛如江淮大地上一颗璀璨的明珠，在长三角一体化东风的沐浴下，洋溢着更加澎湃的青春活力，正以高质量发展全力打造安徽对外开放新高地，为实现现代化美好安徽添上浓墨重彩的一笔。

---

① 专精特新"小巨人"指具有"专业化、精细化、特色化、新颖化"特征的有潜力的中小工业企业。

500 companies and 39 projects invested by listed companies, with an increase of 29 over the previous year; the Park achieved three breakthroughs from scratch, having the national Little Giants[1], the provincial Champion Enterprises, and the provincial Science and Technology Progress Award enterprises.

The Park has been awarded Inter-provincial Industrial Cooperation Demonstration Park in the Yangtze River Delta and regarded as one of the first batches of International Exchange and Cooperation Bases in Anhui Province. The enterprises in the Park are rapidly expanding and strengthening, which have subsequently advanced the development of the export-oriented economy of Chuzhou and even Anhui by leaps and bounds. Now, the eastern door of Anhui is opening wider and wider.

In the new era, Suchu High-Tech Industrial Park looks like a shining pearl in the land of Anhui. Taking advantage of the Yangtze River Delta Integration, brimming with more surging youthful vitality, the Park is making every effort to help build a new highland of Anhui's opening-up with high-quality development, which writes a splendid chapter for realizing a better, modern Anhui.

---

[1] Little Giants refer to specialized and sophisticated leading enterprises that produce new and unique products.

二、中欧班列（合肥）：新丝路上的
"钢铁驼队"

古丝绸之路驼铃声声，新丝路上汽笛长鸣。中欧班列是运行于中国与欧洲及"一带一路"共建国家间的铁路国际联运列车，被誉为"钢铁驼队"。"一带一路"倡议提出 10 年来，中欧班列作为"一带一路"的旗舰项目不断加速发展，已经成为连接亚欧大陆的重要贸易线和"一带一路"建设大动脉。中欧班列（合肥）是如何为开放安徽乃至全国作出重要贡献的呢？

（一）中欧班列（合肥）的诞生与发展

2014 年 6 月 26 日，随着一声汽笛鸣响，安徽首个国际铁路货运专列——中欧班列（合肥）从合肥北站缓缓启程，一路向西，经阿拉山口口岸驶向哈萨克斯坦阿拉木图。中欧班列（合肥）这支"钢铁驼队"自此开启了亚欧大陆的新丝路之旅。安徽为什么要开通中欧班列呢？中欧贸易往来传统的运输方式更多依赖于海运和航空运输，运输时间和运输费用一直是难以协调和解决的现实问题，尤其是对于没有出海口的内陆城市。为打破现有交通方式对进出口贸易的束缚，促进开放，安徽响应国家"一带一路"倡议开通新丝绸之路中欧铁路货运班列。

II. The China–Europe Railway Express (Hefei): The Steel Caravan on the New Silk Road

The camel bells echoed on the ancient Silk Road and the Steel Caravan sirens hoot on the new Silk Road. The China–Europe Railway Express is an international multi-modal freight train shuttling between China and Europe as well as other countries along the Belt and Road Initiative, known as the Steel Caravan. Since the Belt and Road Initiative was proposed ten years ago (2013), as a flagship project, the China–Europe Railway Express has become an important trade route linking China with the major regions of Eurasia and served as a major artery of the Belt and Road Initiative through accelerating the development. What contribution has the China–Europe Railway Express (Hefei) made to the opening-up of Anhui and China?

i. The Birth and Development of the China–Europe Railway Express (Hefei)

On June 26, 2014, with the sound of a siren, Anhui's first international freight train, the China–Europe freight train (Hefei), smoothly set off from Hefei North Railway Station and headed west to Alma-Ata, Kazakhstan via Alashankou Port. Since then, the China–Europe Railway Express (Hefei), has embarked on its New Silk Road journey across the Eurasian continent. Why did Anhui launch the

整装待发的中欧班列（合肥）（徐旻昊 摄）
A China-Europe freight train is ready to depart from Hefei (Photo by Xu Minhao)

　　一经开通，中欧班列（合肥）便以其运距短、速度快、稳定性高的特征，以及安全快捷、绿色环保、受自然环境影响小的优势，受到了广大沿线国家企业的欢迎。丹麦物流公司 DSV 称，从中国到欧洲的铁路运输时间约为海运所需时间的一半，运输成本约为空运的 1/4。中欧班列平均碳排放量为航空运输的 1/15、公路运输的 1/7。截至 2023 年 8 月底，中欧班列（合肥）已点对点通达 18 个国家，德国汉堡、芬兰赫尔辛基、匈牙利布达佩斯等 122 个国际站点城市，实现了对大部分欧亚国家的覆盖，正助力更多的"皖美制造"走向世界，同时拓展

service? The traditional transportation mode of China–EU trade relies more on sea and air transport, and the time and logistic costs have always been difficult to coordinate and solve, especially for inland cities without access to the sea. To break the shackles of the existing mode of transportation on import and export trade and promote high-level opening-up, Anhui has actively integrated into the New Silk Road and operated the China–Europe Railway Express (Hefei) in response to the Belt and Road Initiative.

Since its launch, the China–Europe Railway Express (Hefei) service has been welcomed by the enterprises of the countries along the Belt and Road Initiative because of its short transport distance, fast speed and high stability, as well as the advantages of being green and less affected by the natural environment. According to Danish logistics company DSV, the railway transport time from China to Europe is about half of the time needed for shipping, and the transportation cost is about 1/4 of air transport. Statistics show that the average carbon emission of the China–Europe freight trains is 1/15 of air transport and, 1/7 of road transport.

By the end of August 2023, the China–Europe Railway Express (Hefei) has reached 122 international station cities in 18 countries, such as Hamburg in Germany, Helsinki in Finland, Budapest in Hungary, etc., forming a network covering the major regions basically covering the entire Europe. The China–Europe Railway Express (Hefei) is helping more made-in-Anhui exports go global and expanding the inbound train resources along the Belt and Road route, thus building a two-way international trade corridor. It has become a new engine for promoting economic and trade exchanges between China and Eurasia. What are the innovative practices of the Steel Caravan from Hefei?

ii. Directional and Customized Trains Facilitating Products Export

The China–Europe Railway Express (Hefei) innovates the marketing mode of

沿线回程资源，构建了双向联通的国际贸易大通道，成为促进中欧、中亚经贸往来的新引擎。来自合肥的这支"钢铁驼队"有什么创新做法呢？

（二）定向定制班列助力产品出口

中欧班列（合肥）创新"坐商变行商"营销模式，立足合肥、服务安徽、辐射长三角，采用城际定向班列和企业定制班列两种模式，先后开辟中欧班列（合肥）"+阜阳""+芜湖""+黄山"等城际定向班列，服务范围已覆盖全省16个地市。

2021年8月，有着敏锐市场嗅觉的中欧班列（合肥）得知，黄山绿茶受全球新冠疫情影响，物流通道阻塞，外贸发展受限，中欧班列（合肥）迅速主动与黄山市茶叶企业联手，开通了安徽首趟黄山—合肥—塔什干"茶叶专列"。在茶叶集装箱装运方面，中欧班列（合肥）严格把关，费了不少心思。第一关，严选使用三年左右、密封、干净、无异味的集装箱，避免在途中因外部环境影响茶叶口感与香气。第二关，精挑细选超重型空箱。茶叶被烘干、压缩、密封后单位体积的质量变大了，唯有32.5吨的超重箱能担此"重"任。第三关，专门安排班列中间的厢位。因为若是集拼班列，火车两头的厢位是活动的。所有这些细节，于外人看似烦琐，但于中欧班列（合肥），为企业提供最优质的服务就是自己的使命。班列稳链畅链的同时，为黄山茶叶出口开辟了一条全新的陆路物流通道。在随后的两个月里黄山茶叶企业又追加了好几列，"茶叶专列"很快突破百柜大关，而这只是黄山茶走向中亚、中欧地区各国的开始。

接下来，中欧班列（合肥）还准备再整合所有黄山的茶企资源，优化路线，助企降成本，拓宽通道。受黄山"茶叶专列"的辐射带动，安徽汽车、白色家电、芯片等企业纷纷找上门来定制，"江淮号""奇瑞号""美的号""美菱号""京东方"等专列竞相出发。安徽本土企业借力"钢铁驼队""皖货皖运"，纷纷搭上亚欧的"快车"。

"passive business into active business". Serving Anhui, and radiating the Yangtze River Delta, it typically adopts two modes of inter-city directional trains and customized trains for enterprises. Intercity directional trains such as "+ Fuyang City", "+ Wuhu City", and "+ Huangshan City" have been opened successively, and the service has covered 16 cities of Anhui Province so far.

In August 2021, the China−Europe Railway Express (Hefei), with a keen sense of the market, learned that Huangshan green tea was affected by COVID-19, the logistics corridors were partially blocked, and the development of foreign trade was limited. It quickly took the initiative to join hands with Huangshan tea enterprises to open Anhui's first Huangshan−Hefei−Toshkent Tea Train.

In terms of tea container transport, the Steel Caravan from Hefei checked them very carefully and paid a lot of effort. First, they strictly selected air-tight containers that had been used for about three years, clean and odorless to avoid the taste of tea being affected by the external environment on the way. Second, they carefully selected containers for overweight goods, for the mass per unit volume became larger after tea was dried, compressed and sealed. Only 32.5-ton overweight containers could bear the volume. Third, they arranged only the middle compartments, which were safer and more stable. All these details might seem cumbersome to outsiders, but in the eye of the Steel Caravan, providing the best quality service for enterprises was their first mission. The trains have kept the goods supply chains stable and smooth and opened up a new land logistics corridor for Huangshan tea export. In the following two months, Huangshan tea enterprises added more containers, and the tea train soon hit 100 containers. And this was just the beginning of Huangshan tea going toward Central Asia and Europe by freight trains.

Now, the China−Europe Railway Express (Hefei) is ready to integrate all the Huangshan tea enterprises' resources, optimize the route, and help enterprises reduce costs and broaden their channels. Driven by Huangshan Tea Train radiation, Anhui enterprises involving automobiles, white goods, chips, etc., have come to

合肥北站物流基地（解琛 摄）
Hefei North Railway Station Logistics Base (Photo by Xie Chen)

customize special trains named JAC, Chery, Meiling, BOE, etc. departing one by one. The local enterprises choose the Steel Caravan from Hefei in succession to facilitate "Anhui goods, Anhui transport", and take the express of Eurasia.

iii. Cross-border E-commerce Trains Promoting the Close Partnership Between Sister Provinces (States)

As an ancient poem goes, distance cannot divide true friends who feel close even when they are thousands of miles apart. On July 13, 2021, under a burst of applause, the railway station in Wilhelmshaven Port in Germany ushered in a special guest. The first cross-border e-commerce special train from the China–Europe Railway Express (Hefei) is entering the station. The characteristic of cross-border e-commerce trains is "cloud pickup", which is an important link in cross-border e-commerce. The platform enterprises in both countries can make orders for cargo delivery through intelligent terminals, with smart scheduling of the special train in the background. At the same time, all tax procedures for goods can be completed backstage. It marks the opening of a new operation mode of the Digital Silk Road for the China–Europe Railway Express (Hefei). Cross-border e-commerce trains are precisely controlled through the program and fulfill point-to-point linear transportation with foreign stations, providing stable, efficient and convenient logistics guarantee for people along the route to buy global goods at their doorsteps.

Whether small household commodities or large electrical appliances, auto parts, all can be sent from Anhui to the countries along the route. The cross-border special train carried 100 twenty-foot equivalent units of high-quality goods mainly made in Hefei with a value of nearly USD 10 million to Wilhelmshaven Port, conveying goodwill and friendship. Lower Saxony which the port belongs to, has joined hands with Anhui as sister provinces (states) since 1984. It is the first time

（三）跨境电商班列助力友城往来

相知无远近，万里尚为邻。2021 年 7 月 13 日，在一阵热烈的掌声下，德国威廉港铁路场站迎来了一位特殊的客人。首趟来自中欧班列（合肥）的跨境电商专列正在进站。跨境电商专列的特色在于"云接车"，作为跨境电商重要联通环节，两国企业可通过智能终端制作货物运送订单，后台智能调度专列；同时，货品的所有税务手续也可以在后台完成，标志着中欧班列（合肥）开启了数字丝绸之路的运营新模式。跨境电商专列通过程序精准控制，与国外站点点对点线性运输，为沿线民众在家门口"买全球"提供稳定、高效、便捷的物流保障。小到家用小商品，大到电器、汽车零配件，都可以从安徽送到沿途各国。专列将载有"合肥造"的 100 标箱、货值近 1000 万美元的优质货品送达威廉港，仿佛是在传递善意与友谊。威廉港所属的下萨克森州与安徽自 1984 年起就是友好省州关系，这次是威廉港与合肥国际陆港①第一次牵手合作，两个友好城市亲上加亲，世界上没有跨越不了的距离。

这一班列的开行标志着两个友好省份首次建立铁路连接，以前货运往来主要通过海运进行。在接车仪式现场，下萨克森州州长魏尔满心期待地说，"威廉港与合肥、下萨克森州与安徽地理上虽相距甚远，但双方不断深化经贸等各领域合作，拉近两国距离。希望未来有更多的中欧班列连接合肥与威廉港"。在场的中国驻汉堡总领事杜晓晖称赞中欧班列（合肥），"将为威廉港带来新的机遇，威廉港将成为'一带一路'倡议下中欧货物运输新的桥头堡，因此将成为德国下萨克森州通往中国长三角地区的门户"。回程中，来自法国的护肤品和挪威的燕麦牛奶饮料在威廉港集结后到达合肥。自此两城开启了常态化的班列运行合

---

① 合肥国际陆港：安徽省中欧班列运营平台，2021 年被评为陆港型国家物流枢纽。

that Wilhelmshaven Port and Hefei International Land Port[①] have cooperated hand in hand, which makes the two sides become closer. There is no insurmountable distance in the world.

The train marks railway connections that have been established for the first time between sister provinces (states), with previous freight mainly by shipping. At the reception ceremony, Lower Saxony Governor Weil said with full expectations, "Although Wilhelmshaven and Hefei, Lower Saxony and Anhui are geographically far apart, the two sides continue to deepen cooperation in various fields such as economy and trade, narrowing the distance between the two countries. I hope there will be more China−Europe freight trains connecting Hefei with Wilhelmshaven in the future." Du Xiaohui, Consul General of China in Hamburg, praised the China− Europe Freight Train (Hefei) service on site, "It will bring new opportunities to Wilhelmshaven, which will become a new bridgehead for goods transportation between China and Europe under the Belt and Road Initiative, and therefore will become the gateway of Lower Saxony, Germany, to Yangtze River Delta region, China."

On the inbound train, skin care products from France and oatmeal milk drinks from Norway were shipped to Hefei after being assembled at Wilhelmshaven Port. Since then, the two cities have assumed normal cooperation by the shuttle trains. The cross-border e-commerce trains from Hefei have built a new platform for economic and trade cooperation along the Belt and Road, expanded the circle of economic and trade, and promoted international exchanges.

Over the past nine years (2014−2023), more than 3,500 China−Europe freight trains (Hefei) have departed from Hefei, with 280,000 TEUs through a combined rail-sea transport, exceeding USD 10 billion of the total trade volume of imports and exports. In the first three quarters of the year 2023, a total of 736 trips have

---

① China−Europe Freight Train (Hefei) operation platform, which was rated as a national land port logistics hub in 2021.

作。中欧班列（合肥）跨境电商班列为沿线经贸合作搭建了新平台，扩大了经贸朋友圈，助力国际友城往来。

9年来，中欧班列（合肥）累计发运超3500列，铁海联运28万标箱，进出口总贸易额超百亿美元。在2023年前三个季度，合肥累计发运736列，发运集装箱60282标箱，同比增长超20%。中欧班列（合肥）不仅促进了沿线区域经济的共同繁荣，还增进了沿线国人民的福祉，安徽的品牌车辆、宣城的机器人、马鞍山的钢铁、合肥的智能家电和笔记本电脑等优质的"皖美智造"深受沿线国家人民的欢迎；同时沿线回程带来的西班牙的红酒、比利时的巧克力、荷兰的奶制品等优质产品进入安徽百姓家，也大大提高了安徽人民的生活幸福感。

大道如砥，行者无疆。如今，中欧班列（合肥）越来越成为安徽对外开放的靓丽风景线。它将瞄准"国际物流中心、国际贸易中心、临港产业集群、国际大物流运行体系"建设目标，以更加开放、昂扬的姿态，阔步前行在"一带一路"上。"钢铁驼队"正驶向中国式现代化的新征途，为沿线国家人民带去开放安徽乃至长三角地区更多新的发展成果，在美美与共的新丝路上，越跑越快，越跑越欢。

视觉新闻中心 摄
Photo by Visual News Center

been made in Hefei with 60,282 TEUs of goods, up 20% year-on-year. The China–Europe Railway Express (Hefei) not only promotes the common prosperity of the regional economy along the Belt and Road, but also brings more benefits to the peoples. Anhui brand vehicles, Xuancheng robots, Ma'anshan steel, Hefei smart household appliances and laptops, and other high-quality made-in-Anhui exports are deeply welcomed; meanwhile, high-quality products like Spanish red wine, Belgian chocolate, Dutch dairy products, etc., brought by inbound trains into Anhui families greatly improve their sense of happiness.

The great way is broad and even, and there are no boundaries for a traveler. Nowadays, the China–Europe Railway Express (Hefei) is becoming an increasingly beautiful landscape of Anhui's opening-up. It will aim at four integrated construction of an international logistics center, an international trade center, port industry clusters, and an international logistics operation system together. With a more open, high-spirited attitude, the China–Europe Railway Express (Hefei) is actively engaged in the Belt and Road Initiative. On the new journey of Chinese modernization, the Steel Caravan from Hefei will bring more new development results of open Anhui and the Yangtze River Delta for the peoples in countries along the Belt and Road Initiative. On the New Silk Road with shared prosperity, the faster it runs, the happier it feels.

三、世界制造业大会：携手世界，共"造"美好

　　从 2018 年起，在安徽省会合肥，每年举办一次经国务院批准的重要国际会议，它就是世界制造业大会，被安徽省定为首位活动。第一届大会便吸引了 70 多个国家和地区的 4000 多位政府官员、国际组织、商协会代表和国内外优秀企业家出席。之后每届都向国内外参会嘉宾推出了新主题、新科技、新动态。大会给开放安徽起到了怎样的推动作用？给安徽的本土企业联动世界带来了怎样的深远影响？让我们先从最初落户合肥开始说起。

（一）缘起合肥

　　合肥市作为安徽省会，一直致力于打造具有国际竞争力的制造业中心。身为长三角城市群的重要节点城市之一，交通网络便捷、城市基础设施完善，为制造业的发展提供了良好的环境和条件。此外，作为全国重要的科技创新中心，合肥拥有丰富的科技资源，包括中国科技大学、合肥工业大学等知名学府，以及多个国家级实验室。这使得大会永久落户合肥有了得天独厚的基础优势。

　　大会对全省而言，更是推动制造业高质量发展不可多得的机会。习近平总书记向 2019 年世界制造业大会致贺信说，中国高度重视制造业发展，坚持创新

III. World Manufacturing Convention: Hand in Hand with the World, "Manufacturing" a Better Future Together

From 2018, in Hefei City, the provincial capital of Anhui, an important international conference approved by the State Council of the People's Republic of China was held once a year, which was called the World Manufacturing Convention, and designated as the initial activity by Anhui. The first convention attracted more than 4,000 government officials, representatives of international organizations, business associations, and outstanding domestic and foreign entrepreneurs from more than 70 countries and regions. Since then, each convention has launched new themes, new technologies, and new developments for global guests. How does the convention promote Anhui's opening-up? What far-reaching impact has it had on the local enterprises of Anhui to connect with the world? Let's start from why it settled in Hefei.

i. Why Hefei

Hefei has been committed to building a manufacturing center with international competitiveness. As one of the key node cities in the Yangtze River Delta city clusters, Hefei has a convenient transportation network and perfect urban infrastructure, which provides a good environment and fine conditions

驱动发展战略，把推动制造业高质量发展作为构建现代化经济体系的重要一环。安徽持续深入贯彻习近平总书记的重要指示，随着新发展格局加快构建和长三角一体化发展深入推进，坚定不移实施制造强省战略，特色鲜明等独特优势逐渐显现，到处呈现动能强劲之势。通过举办大会取得喜人"战果"：5 年来，累计参会嘉宾 14824 人次，签约项目共 3021 个，其中外资企业签约项目 1153 个，德国大众新能源汽车、比亚迪新能源汽车、蔚来智能电动汽车产业园等一批百亿、千亿级重大项目落地安徽，实际完成投资超万亿元，有力促进了安徽制造业高质量发展，让世界更多分享中国制造机遇。

安徽省政府副秘书长、办公厅主任孙东海在 2023 世界制造业大会新闻发布会上介绍："世界制造业大会自 2018 年首次举办以来，正逐步成为安徽乃至全国标志性、引领性、高能级的开放合作平台，具有国际影响力的制造业盛会。"下面我们以一个故事为缩影，看看安徽制造业借力大会，得到的发展机遇。

（二）情牵"江淮·大众"

早在 2017 年 6 月 1 日，在时任国务院总理李克强和时任德国总理默克尔的共同见证下，大众汽车集团与安徽江淮汽车集团股份有限公司于德国柏林正式签署协议。双方在安徽合肥共同成立合资企业大众安徽，进行新能源汽车的研发、生产和销售并提供相关移动出行服务。

2018 年首届大会，备受参会代表瞩目的，是江淮和大众合作后推出的首款车型——思皓（SOL）E20X，该车型恰好在大会召开当天正式下线。思皓基于江淮汽车先进的新能源技术框架打造，且拥有大众汽车集团的品质保障，充分体现两大汽车企业的合作成果。

for the development of the manufacturing industry. In addition, as an important sci-tech innovation center in China, Hefei has a wealth of sci-tech resources, including the University of Science and Technology of China, Hefei University of Technology, and other well-known universities, as well as a bunch of state-level laboratories. All of the above offer Hefei basic exceptional advantages to have the convention permanently settled down.

As far as the significance to Anhui is concerned, it's an unparalleled opportunity to promote the high-quality development of the manufacturing industry. In the congratulatory letter to the second convention in 2019, President Xi Jinping said that China attached great importance to the growth of the manufacturing sector, adhered to an innovation-driven development strategy, and saw promoting the high-quality development of the manufacturing sector as an important part of developing a modern economic system. Anhui sticks to implementing the important instructions in depth. Along with speeding up the construction of the new development pattern and deepening the integrated development of the Yangtze River Delta, Anhui firmly facilitates the strategy of strengthening the manufacturing province. The province's unique advantages with distinctive characteristics have gradually emerged, such as in manufacturing industries. A strong momentum is seen everywhere in Anhui. By holding the convention annually, Anhui achieved fruitful results. Through past 5 conventions, it welcomed approximately 14,824 guests, and signed a total of 3,021 projects, with 1,153 projects by foreign-funded enterprises. New Energy Vehicles of Volkswagen and BYD, Intelligent Electric Vehicle of NIO, and a number of important investment projects of up to RMB 10~100 billions landed in Anhui. The whole actual completion of the investment was more than RMB 1 trillion, which was a strong boost to the high-quality development of manufacturing industries in Anhui, thus, making the world enjoy more opportunities for Chinese manufacturing.

Sun Donghai, Deputy Secretary-general and Director of the General Office of the People's Government of Anhui Province, said at the press conference of the

2018 世界制造业大会上的江淮大众汽车 SOL E20X（范柏文 摄）

SOL E20X displayed at the World Manufacturing Convention in 2018 (Photo by Fan Baiwen)

此后几乎每届大会上，江淮汽车都带给大家不同的惊喜。2019 年第二届大会，不仅展出了江淮和大众共线生产的全新掀背式运动轿车嘉悦 A5，还推出了本届大会的"黑科技"看点之一——户外无人驾驶汽车体验，使得江淮展台成为此届大会人气最为火爆的展台之一，甚至成为许多海内外观众的"打卡胜地"，吸引了部分外国政要及代表团参观考察。通过此届大会，江淮汽车向世界完美诠释了"中国智造"。

2020 年第三届大会，受新冠疫情影响，江淮汽车在"云展区"参会。大会

2023 World Manufacturing Convention, "Since the first convention held in 2018, it has gradually become a symbolic, leading and high-powered open cooperation platform of Anhui and even the whole country, and a manufacturing feast with international influence." Here we take a story as an example, to see how the Anhui's manufacturing industries harvest development opportunities from the convention.

ii. The Joint of JAC and Volkswagen

As early as June 1, 2017, in Berlin, Germany, under mutual witness by then-Premier Li Keqiang of China and then-Chancellor Angela Merkel of Germany, Volkswagen Group and Anhui JAC Automobile Group Co. signed a formal agreement to establish a joint venture – Volkswagen Anhui in Hefei, Anhui. It would undertake the research and development, production and sales of new energy vehicles, and the provision of related mobile travel services.

What attracted the attention of the delegates at the inaugural convention in 2018, was the first model vehicle – Sihao (SOL) E20X displayed after the cooperation between JAC and Volkswagen, which was officially launched from the production line on the exact same day as the convention was held. Sihao was based on JAC's advanced new energy technology framework and had a quality guarantee by Volkswagen Group, fully reflecting the results of the cooperation between the two automobile companies.

Since then, almost every convention, the joint venture has brought different surprises to everyone. Through the second convention in 2019, it not only displayed the new hatchback sports car – Jiayue A5, which was co-produced by JAC and Volkswagen, but also introduced one of that convention's "black technology" attractions – the outdoor pilotless car driving experience. It made the joint venture become one of the most popular booths at that convention, and even became a "hot spot" for many domestic and overseas visitors, attracting some foreign dignitaries and delegations. Through that convention, the joint venture had

运用5G、虚拟现实、增强现实、大数据等现代信息技术手段，建立沉浸式3D立体"云展馆"，方便江淮汽车展示新技术、新理念、新动态，全方位体现了江淮汽车在智能网联、绿色出行等领域的最新科技成果及技术实力。

在2021年第四届大会上，大众安徽CEO葛皖镝博士致辞道："世界制造业大会将会为我们提供一个建立深度伙伴关系、探索制造业未来发展的绝佳平台。我想对安徽省政府以及合肥市政府给予的持续支持表示衷心的感谢。安徽不断拓展的汽车产业价值链为我们在江淮汽车建设一个坚实的生产制造基地提供了良机。"

在2022年第五届大会上，大众安徽承诺：在皖建立可持续、强健的新能源汽车生态系统，并积极参与合肥低碳、智慧城市建设。此外，与江淮汽车等合作伙伴共同推出智慧物流项目，将引入智能网联电动卡车车队及L4级自动驾驶穿梭巴士，在大众安徽工厂及本地供应商之间运行。

借由历届大会，江淮汽车推广了最新产品，展示了前沿科技，提高了国际影响力，扩大了销售渠道，旗下产品还成为大会官方服务保障用车。2023年第六届大会，江淮汽车再次为大会提供出行服务，为全球嘉宾提供优质出行，充分展现"中国智造"崛起的力量。

大会给大众和江淮提供了优质的平台和宝贵的商机，从一定程度上推动了合肥乃至安徽新能源汽车制造业发展，得到了省委、省政府领导的高度重视。2023年9月15日，正在德国访问的安徽省委书记韩俊前往大众汽车集团，与集团董事会成员、大众汽车集团（中国）董事长兼首席执行官贝瑞德举行会谈，并共同见证安徽省人民政府与大众汽车（中国）投资有限公司签署全面合作备忘录。这次会谈充分体现了大众汽车集团将新能源汽车制造中心落地安徽，并在合肥建立大众总部之外全球第一个新能源汽车研发、创新和部件采购中心，深度参与安徽新能源汽车产业链建设的决心，必将为安徽打造具有全球影响力的世界级新能源汽车产业集群作出重要贡献。安徽也将对大众汽车集团在安徽的发展给予大力支持，推动双方合作结出更加丰硕的成果。

perfectly illustrated "China's Intelligent Manufacturing" to the world.

At the third convention in 2020, affected by COVID-19, the joint venture participated in the "Cloud Exhibition Area". The convention utilized various means of 5G, VR, AR, Big Data, and other modern IT to establish an immersive 3D Cloud Pavilion, which facilitated the joint venture to display new technologies, new concepts, and new dynamics, and comprehensively embodied its latest sci-tech achievements and technical strength in the fields of intelligent network connection and green travel.

At the fourth convention in 2021, the CEO of Volkswagen Anhui, Dr. Ge Wandi said, "The World Manufacturing Convention will provide an excellent platform for us to establish deep partnerships and explore the future development of the manufacturing industry. I would like to express my heartfelt thanks to the People's Government of Anhui Province and the Hefei Municipal Government for their continued support. The expanding automotive value chain of Anhui provides us with a great opportunity to build a solid manufacturing base at JAC."

At the fifth convention in 2022, Volkswagen Anhui pledged to build a sustainable and robust new energy vehicle ecosystem in Anhui and to actively participate in the construction of a low-carbon, smart city in Hefei. In addition, a smart logistics program would be launched with JAC and other partners, which should introduce a fleet of smart internet-connected electric trucks and L4-class self-driving shuttle buses that can run between Volkswagen Anhui plants and local suppliers.

The joint venture has promoted its latest products, demonstrated cutting-edge technologies, increased its international influence, and expanded its sales channels through every convention, and its products have become the official service vehicles of the convention. At the sixth convention of 2023, the joint venture provided travel services for the convention again, offering high-quality trips for global guests, and fully demonstrating the rising power of China's Smart Manufacturing.

The convention has provided Volkswagen and JAC with a high-quality

（三）"皽"美未来

　　类似江淮汽车的成功案例数不胜数。安徽诸多城市纷纷亮相，通过大会助力当地经济发展：宿州市举办了 2021 年第四届大会"数字赋能智造宿州"招商对接会，EMS 智能制造、汽车零部件、成品药及原料药等 8 个生产制造项目现场集中签约，投资总额达 43 亿元；亳州市的中医药、白酒、农副产品深加工等产品深受海内外嘉宾欢迎，仅 2022 年第五届大会就引资 95 亿元；池州市在 2023 年第六届大会开始前，已"云"签约 7 个重点项目，共 65 亿元项目投资。

2023 世界制造业大会开幕式（程兆 摄）

The opening ceremony of the World Manufacturing Convention in 2023 (Photo by Cheng Zhao)

platform and valuable business opportunities and promoted the development of new energy automobile manufacturing in Hefei and even Anhui to a certain extent. It is highly valued by the leaders both of the provincial party committee and the provincial government of Anhui. On September 15, 2023, during the visit to Germany, Han Jun, Secretary of the Anhui Provincial Party Committee, went to Volkswagen Group to hold talks with Ralf Brandstaetter, who is a member of the board of directors of the group, both the chairman and CEO of Volkswagen Group (China). Together, they witnessed the signing of a comprehensive cooperation memorandum between the People's Government of Anhui Province and Volkswagen (China) Investment Co.. This meeting fully embodied Volkswagen Group's determination to place its new energy vehicle manufacturing center in Anhui, to establish the first global new energy vehicle R&D, innovation and parts procurement center in Hefei outside of Volkswagen's headquarter, and to deeply participate in the construction of Anhui's new energy vehicle industry chain, which would surely make an important contribution to the building of a world-class new energy vehicle industry cluster with global influence in Anhui. Anhui will also firmly support Volkswagen Group's development and enhance productive cooperation between the two sides.

iii. A Bright Future of Anhui

Such successful cases like the joint venture are countless. Many cities in Anhui have appeared at the convention to strengthen their local economic development: Suzhou City held "Digital-Empowered Intelligent Manufacturing, Suzhou" – a business referral of the fourth convention in 2021. The contracts of its EMS intelligent manufacturing, automotive parts and components, finished-dosage pharmaceutical products and APIs, altogether 8 manufacturing projects were signed on-site, with a total investment of RMB 4.3 billion. Bozhou City's Chinese traditional herbal medicine, liquor, and deep-processed agricultural by-

2023 年的第六届大会更加精彩纷呈，分为政府展和市场化展两大系列，以线下 10 个展馆、14 个展厅为主，同步线上云展厅全面铺开；不仅举行专题活动，还有相关业界平行论坛，笑迎国内外宾朋。9 月 20 日开幕当天上午，大会即达成"六百"合作项目[①]587 个，总投资额近 3500 亿元。

2023 世界制造业大会（周俊 摄）
The World Manufacturing Convention in 2023 (Photo by Zhou Jun)

在开幕式上，大众汽车集团（中国）董事长兼首席执行官贝瑞德通过视频连线深情说道："在安徽省强大的电动出行集群中，大众安徽是我们的大本营。大众汽车集团将在合肥成立大众汽车（中国）科技有限公司，投资约 10 亿欧元，把来自研发及采购等多个领域的 2000 名专业人才聚集到这家新公司。未来大众

---

① "六百"合作项目即安徽省商务厅牵头的"央企、民企、外企、港澳企、台企、侨企"对接活动，旨在大会上力争签约 600 个项目，投资总额超 5000 亿元，是大会成功的重要标志。

products were warmly welcomed by domestic and overseas guests. Only at the fifth convention in 2022, it attracted RMB 9.5 billion in investment. Before the sixth convention in 2023, Chizhou City had signed 7 key projects on "cloud", with a total of RMB 6.5 billion project investment.

The sixth convention in 2023 was more exciting. It's divided into two series of government and market-oriented exhibitions, with 10 offline pavilions, 14 exhibition halls, as well a synchronized online cloud pavilion comprehensively. It held not only themed events but relevant industry parallel forums, welcoming guests from around the world. On the morning of the opening day, September 20, the convention reached 587 signed projects with a total of RMB 350 billion investment of the "600 projects"[①].

At the opening ceremony, Ralf Brandstaetter delivered a speech via video link, "Volkswagen Anhui is our home base in the strong electric vehicle manufacturing cluster in Anhui Province. Volkswagen Group will establish Volkswagen (China) Technology Co., Ltd. in Hefei, investing about EUR 1 billion and bringing together 2,000 professionals from various fields such as R&D and purchasing to this new company. The Volkswagen Group will continue to invest in Anhui in the future, expanding our entities in Anhui and Hefei into a strong R&D and production base for smart internet-connection vehicles in China."

The World Manufacturing Convention is soaring in popularity, and Anhui's manufacturing industries are flourishing. On the new journey of Chinese modernization, Anhui's circle of partners is getting larger and larger by hosting a series of activities such as the convention. The province's road to openness is getting wider. Many foreign-funded enterprises choose Anhui and take root. Anhui

---

① "600 projects" means 6 hundred cooperation projects, which is run by the Anhui Provincial Department of Commerce, connecting "central enterprises, private enterprises, foreign enterprises, Hong Kong and Macao enterprises, Taiwan enterprises, and overseas Chinese enterprises", aiming to sign 600 projects, with a total investment of more than RMB 500 billion at the convention. It is an important symbol of the success of the convention.

汽车集团在安徽还将继续投入，把我们在安徽以及合肥的实体扩大为在华强大的智能网联汽车研发和生产基地。"

世界制造业大会人气高涨，安徽制造业发展欣欣向荣。在中国式现代化新征程上，安徽通过举办大会等一系列活动，开放之路越走越宽，众多外资企业选择安徽、扎根安徽，安徽的朋友圈越来越大。安徽将珍惜机会，踔厉奋发，坚持将制造业作为立省之本，加快实施制造强省等"七个强省"战略，谱写更加壮丽的篇章。让我们祝福安徽：畅游"智造世界"，开创"皖"美未来！

安徽抢抓机遇，勇毅前行，紧扣一体化和高质量两个关键词，充分利用长三角一体化的最大势能和红利，推动产业深度对接、集群发展，将中新苏滁高新技术产业开发区率先打造成长三角高质量一体化发展示范园区；充分发挥中欧班列在国际贸易中的大动脉作用，不断拓宽西向开放大通道；世界制造业大会开放平台能级不断提升，推动安徽制造业高质量发展，为中国式现代化建设奉献安徽力量，为世界的发展创造更多的安徽机遇。

下一步，安徽将牢牢把握习近平总书记"争当击楫中流的改革先锋"的要求，加快构建新发展格局，进一步扩大更高水平开放。我们将积极对标和借鉴国内外先进经验，推动中国（安徽）自由贸易试验区高质量发展；优化完善开放通道，持续拓展融入"一带一路"建设的深度和广度；深入推进高水平制度开放，提升安徽对外开放新能级，在打造改革开放新高地上走在前列，在加快建设充满活力的开放安徽上展现更大作为。

will treasure the chance, strive hard, adhere to the manufacturing industry as the fundamental of the province, and accelerate the implementation of manufacturing province together with The strategy of strengthening Anhui in 7 aspects, to write a more magnificent chapter. Let's wish Anhui manufacturing a bright and intelligent future!

Anhui seizes great opportunity and forges forward with enterprise and fortitude, focusing on the two key words of "integration" and "high-quality", making full use of the maximum potential and dividends of the integration of the Yangtze River Delta and promoting the in-depth industrial coordination and cluster development. It makes Suchu High-Tech Industrial Park the pioneer to become a demonstration for high-quality integration development of the Yangtze River Delta; it gives full play to the role of the China−Europe Railway Express (Hefei) as the main artery of international trade, constantly broadening the westward opening channels; it upgrades the open platform − World Manufacturing Convention at a higher level, boosting high-quality development of manufacturing in Anhui. The province is dedicated to the construction of Chinese modernization, creating more opportunities and benefiting the world.

In the future, Anhui will firmly "advance bravely in the torrent to be a reform pioneer" in accordance with President Xi Jinping's instructions. The province will foster a new development pattern at a faster pace, and expand opening-up at a higher level. We will learn from advanced experiences at home and abroad, promote the high-quality development of China (Anhui) Pilot Free Trade Zone, optimize and improve the open channels, and expand the depth and breadth of engagement in the Belt and Road Initiative. We will further advance high-level institutional opening-up, and enhance the new level of opening-up, thus, making more efforts to take the lead in forming a new highland of reform and opening-up, and accelerate to build a vibrant and open Anhui.

视觉新闻中心 摄
Photo by Visual News Center

第七章
党建引领写新章

　　党的二十大报告明确指出："中国式现代化，是中国共产党领导的社会主义现代化。"中国式现代化是中国共产党领导、推动、开创的现代化，党的领导直接关系中国式现代化的根本方向、前途命运、最终成败。欲筑室者，先治其基。基层党组织是有效实现党的领导的坚强战斗堡垒。基层党组织是全面推进中国式现代化的直接组织者、推动者、实施者。基层党建是新时代中国之治的有力支撑。

　　让我们一起来看看合肥市滨湖世纪社区怎样以党建为引领，做到创新城市基层治理模式，和居民一起共建共治共享新生活；安徽省金寨县的大湾村怎样以党建促乡村振兴，带领全村走上幸福富裕路；江淮汽车集团怎样以高质量党建推进企业高质量发展。

Chapter 7

Writing a New Chapter in the Construction of a Modern and Beautiful Anhui through Party Building

The report of the 20th National Congress of the CPC clearly states, Chinese modernization is socialist modernization pursued under the leadership of the Communist Party of China. Chinese modernization is a modernization which is led, promoted, and pioneered by the CPC. The Party's leadership is directly related to the fundamental direction, future, destiny, and ultimate success of Chinese modernization. To build a house, the foundation is essential. Primary-level Party organizations play a key role in ensuring the exercise of the Party's leadership. It is the direct organizer, promoter and implementer of advancing Chinese modernization on all fronts. Primary-level Party building is a strong support for governance in China in the new era.

How does Binhu Century Community in Hefei City use Party building initiatives to innovate the urban community-level governance mode and work with residents to build a life of collaboration, participation, and shared benefits? How does Dawan Village in Jinzhai County, Anhui Province use Party building initiatives to propel rural revitalization and lead the villagers to prosperity? How does JAC Group promote high-quality development of enterprise with high-quality Party building?

一、滨湖世纪社区：党建引领城市基层治理

　　早上8点，清晨的阳光挤入合肥市滨湖新区的一座小楼，这里就是合肥市包河区滨湖世纪社区中心。小楼里，步履匆匆的工作人员早已开始了一天忙碌的工作。滨湖世纪社区是怎么以党建引领基层治理，打造美好生活的呢？

滨湖世纪社区（王悠然 摄）
Binhu Century Community (Photo by Wang Youran)

I. Binhu Century Community: Intensifying Party-building Efforts in Urban Communities

At eight o'clock in the morning, a ray of sunshine brightens up a three-story building in Binhu New District, Hefei City. This is the Binhu Century Community Center in Baohe District, Hefei City. In the small building, the busy staff have already started to work.

Binhu District is located in the southeast of Hefei City. Binhu Century Community, in the center of the district, covers an area of approximately 6 square kilometers. There are many large residential areas here with a population of more than 150,000, large businesses, Party and government offices, financial service units, parks and plazas. The large population and diverse business formats have brought a series of new problems to community-level governance.

i. The Party Committee Taking the Lead

Urban Primary-level Party organizations play a key role in ensuring the exercise of the Party's leadership in cities. The Community Party Committee is the front-line headquarters of community-level governance. The Binhu Community Party Committee visited various units in this area. After thorough research and discussion, the organizational structure for the community center is reformed to

滨湖新区位于合肥市东南，其核心区域滨湖世纪社区辖区约 6 平方公里。区域内有多个超大型居住区，人口超过 15 万人，汇集了大型商业、党政机关、金融服务单位、公园广场。人口众多，业态多样，给城市基层治理带来了一系列新难题。

（一）党委当好"领头雁"

城市基层党组织是党在城市全部工作和战斗力的基础。社区党委是基层治理的一线指挥部。滨湖社区党委走访摸排了辖区内的各小区、商业企业和机关单位等，经过充分研究和讨论，以理顺服务流程为目的，改革组织架构，形成了一办七部两中心的创新模式。一个办公室是党政办公室，七个部门是党群工作部、社区建设部、智慧建设部、平安建设部、城市管理部、发展服务部和社会事务部，两个中心是网格化服务中心和党群服务中心。社区党委还有两个功能性组织：共治理事会和党建共同体（见图 7-1）。

其中的智慧建设部，又被称为大共治中心，通过新技术为民服务。近些年，我国的老龄化趋势明显，独居老人日渐增多，安全问题受到了社区党委的重视。因此，滨湖世纪社区开展了一项独居老人安全守护工作。依托电力使用实时数据，大共治中心利用 AI 技术监测异常并自动提醒工作人员，确保意外事件能够及时被发现从而高效处置，是一种全程"无感化"的智慧养老服务。2022 年春节期间，年过七旬的社区居民王叔叔家里发生电量偏低预警，这个预警信息经过大共治中心的信息平台直接发送至工作人员小张的手持终端，小张立刻电话联系了王叔叔询问情况。王叔叔事后感慨道："我当时正在上海的儿子家中过年，外出前就关闭了家里总电闸，导致用电量偏低。我接到了小张的电话非常惊讶，了解了他打电话的目的，我们全家心中都很感激也很感动。我儿子也说，有这么智能的安全守护还有这么负责的好同志，合肥滨湖世纪社区工作人员真是把

serve the purpose of providing better service and an innovative mode of "one office, seven departments and two centers" is built. "One office" represents the Party and Government Office, and "seven departments" are the Community Party and Mass Department, Community Construction Department, Smart Construction Department, Security Construction Department, Urban Management Department, Development Services Department and Social Affairs Department. "Two centers" are the Grid Service Center and the Community Party and Mass Service Center. The Community Party Committee also has two functional organizations: the Co-governance Council and the Party Building Community (see Figure 7-1).

Among them, the Smart Construction Department, also known as the Grand Co-governance Center, serves the people with new technologies. In recent years, there has been an increasing trend of aging in China, and the number of elders living alone has increased day by day. Safety issues have attracted the attention of Community Party Committees. Therefore, Binhu Century Community has launched a safety protection work for the elderly living alone. Relying on real-time data on power usage, the Grand Co-governance Center uses AI technology to monitor abnormalities and automatically inform staff to ensure that unexpected events can be discovered in time and handled efficiently. It is smart elderly care service that is "non-intrusive" throughout the process. During the Spring Festival of 2022, a low power consumption warning occurred at the home of Uncle Wang, a community resident who was over 70 years old. This warning message was sent directly to the staff Mr. Zhang through the information platform. Zhang immediately called Wang and checked what had happened. Uncle Wang later lamented, "I was celebrating the Spring Festival at my son's home in Shanghai. I turned off the main breaker before going out, which resulted in low electricity consumption. I was very surprised when I received a call from Zhang and understood the purpose of his call. Our whole family is very grateful and touched. My son also said that with such smart security guards and such responsible good comrades, the staff of Hefei Binhu Century Community serves the people wholeheartedly. My son felt relieved

全心全意为人民服务放在心上，落在实处。儿子在上海也可以放心了。"

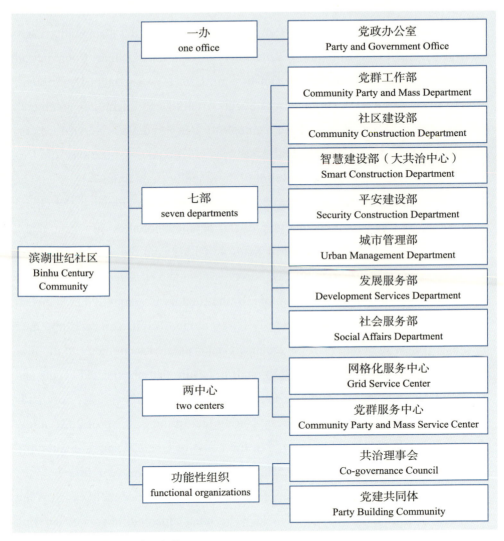

图 7-1　滨湖世纪社区组织架构图

Figure 7-1　The organizational structure diagram of Binhu Century Community

（二）党员成为居民的"贴心人"

在社区管理模式上，滨湖世纪社区党委以党建为统领科学划分社区网格，

in Shanghai."

ii. Party Members Caring Residents

In terms of community management mode, the Party Committee of Binhu Century Community used Party building initiatives to scientifically divide the community into grid and established a grid management system, dividing the jurisdiction into 8 grid areas, with one neighborhood committee responsible for each area. Besides, a Party organization was established in the neighborhood committee. Party branches were established in residential communities and commercial enterprises. In addition, a Party group was set up in the building of the community and the leader of which was elected and called the Red Butler. The four-level management mode of Party committee district, Party organization community, Party branch building, Party group realizes the goal that problems are solved, conflicts are resolved and services are provided on the front line. So why is this governance mode chosen? Because CPC members have a strong sense of identity, organizational belonging, and political responsibility. CPC members are loyal to the cause of communism and serve the people wholeheartedly. When encountering problems, CPC members do not hesitate to take the initiative to stand up, take on responsibilities, play a pioneering and exemplary role, and care residents.

In 2021, various communities in Binhu began to implement garbage classification, and each resident community faced the problem of selection of garbage sorting sites. At first, residents were reluctant to have garbage sorting stations built next to their buildings. The Party branches of each residential community in Binhu played a leading role and convened a meeting of community Party members to explain the importance of garbage sorting. The Party members expressed their support and understanding, and took the initiative to publicize it to their families and neighbors after meeting. Ms Yao, the Red Butler who lives

建立了网格化管理模式，将辖区划分为 8 个网格片区，一个居委会负责一个片区。在居委会成立党组织。在片区管理的住宅小区、商业企业等成立党支部。在小区的楼栋内成立党小组，选举党小组的组长称为"红色小管家"。社区党委－片区党组织－小区党支部－楼栋党小组的四级管理模式实现了问题在一线解决，矛盾在一线化解，服务在一线满足。那么为什么要选择这样的治理模式呢？因为共产党员有强烈的身份认同感、组织归属感、政治责任感。共产党员忠诚于共产主义事业，以全心全意为人民服务为宗旨。在遇到问题时，共产党员会毫不犹豫主动站出来，勇于担当，发挥先锋模范作用，成为居民的"贴心人"。

2021 年滨湖各小区开始实行垃圾分类，每个小区都面临垃圾分类站点的选址问题。起初，居民们都不大愿意垃圾分类站建在自家楼栋下。滨湖各小区的党支部发挥引领作用，召集小区党员开会，将垃圾分类的重要性向党员们陈述，党员们纷纷表示支持和理解，回到家后主动向家人和邻居宣传。住在社区琼林苑 8 栋的"红色小管家"姚大姐是一名有 30 多年党龄的老党员，虽然已经退休，还一直热心于公益事业。平时，哪家遇到困难，姚大姐都主动帮忙。除了上门探望 8 栋的独居老人，帮他们做家务，也会帮忙照顾邻居的孩子，她还特意学习了烘焙，常常给整栋楼的住户送自制的小蛋糕和小零食。这次垃圾分类站选在 8 栋附近，她说："垃圾分类站总是要建的，考虑季节风向、地下管道和房屋构造等方面，建在我们这栋楼下看来是最合理的选择。所以我回家就主动先做好我家人的思想工作，然后又去劝说邻居，最后主动组织了楼栋居民开会，选举了楼栋代表参加整个小区的讨论会。"小区现场讨论，经过大家民主表决，垃圾分类站点顺利建成。建成后，姚大姐还组织了好几次垃圾分类公益教学。琼林苑小区的整体卫生情况有了很大的改善，居民们纷纷向党员姚大姐竖起了大拇指。

in Building 8 of Qionglinyuan residential community, is a Party member with a Party standing of more than 30 years. Although retired, she has always been enthusiastic about public welfare undertakings. Whenever any family encounters difficulties, Ms Yao is there to help. In addition to visiting the elderly living alone in Building 8 to help them with housework and taking care of the neighbors' children, she also learned how to bake and often sent homemade cakes and snacks to neighbors. The garbage sorting station was chosen to be set up near Building 8. She said, "Garbage sorting stations have to be built recently. Considering the seasonal wind direction, underground pipes and house structure, our building seems to be the most reasonable choice. So when I got home, I took the initiative to persuade my family first, and then the neighbors. Finally, I organized a meeting for the residents of the building and elected the representative of the building to participate in the discussion meeting of the entire residential community." After the discussion, representatives of each building voted and the garbage sorting station was successfully built. After it was completed, Ms Yao held several public lectures on garbage sorting. The overall sanitary condition of Qionglinyuan was greatly improved. The residents gave a thumb up to Ms Yao.

iii. The Party and the Masses Working Together

The Party Committee of Binhu Century Community has established a Party-mass working mode: Promoting the cooperation between the government and society, exploring a multiple governance path. It actively leverages social organizations, enterprises and other resources, builds consensus and teamwork. At the beginning of each year, community residents come up with their needs, and the Party and Mass Office forms an annual service project list to find resources. Finally, the Co-governance Council and the Party Building Community implement it.

During the 2023 Spring Festival, a cultural festival called the "Our Chinese Dream – Culture Enters Ten Thousand Families" which was hosted by the

（三）党群合力手牵手

滨湖世纪社区党委建立了"政社合作，多元共治"的党群工作模式，积极撬动社会组织、企业等资源，引导各方平等交流对话，凝聚共识、群策群力。每年年初，社区居民提出需求，由党群办公室形成年度服务项目清单，协调辖区内企业和单位的资源，由共治理事会和党建共同体落实实施。

2023年春节期间，滨湖世纪社区党建共同体、共治理事会承办的"我们的中国梦——文化进万家"新春文化节就搞得红红火火。辖区内的合肥市文化馆组织书法家们挥毫泼墨，为广大居民朋友写春联、写福字，送上浓浓的新春祝福。整个活动现场翰墨飘香、热闹非凡，一个个寓意祥和的"福"字，一副副充满喜气的春联，表达了人们对新年美好生活的期盼和向往。居民赵淑梅笑呵呵地说："和印刷出来的春联相比，我更喜欢手写的春联，觉得更有年味，更加喜庆。"现场还有很多志愿者主动教授剪纸。社区居民小李说："我因为要值班，一个人留在合肥过年感觉挺孤单的，社区工作人员主动邀请我去参加活动，我学会了剪纸。你看，今年过年窗户上、门上贴的剪纸都是我自己的作品！"

通过织密党的组织"一张网"，第一时间了解群众的所想与所需，党群关系有了质的变化。现在，越来越多的党员、社会组织和热心群众参与到社区治理的全过程和各方面，下活了协商共治"一盘棋"。

社区虽小，但连着千家万户。滨湖世纪社区党委主导创新了城市基层治理模式，党员构成了城市基层治理的中坚力量，党群合力打造共建共治共享的新社区。只有织密党的组织"一张网"，才能让党建建设成效融入人民群众对美好生活的向往，才能真正实现城市治理体系和治理能力现代化。

Party Building Community and Co-governance Council was a boom. The Hefei Cultural Center organized calligraphers to write Spring Festival couplets blessing characters for residents, and sent New Year blessings. The entire event was full of fragrant calligraphy and bustling, with the word "Fu" meaning peace and harmony, and pairs of joyful Spring Festival couplets appearing, expressing people's expectations and yearning for a better life in the New Year. Resident Zhao Shumei said with a smile: "Compared with the printed Spring Festival couplets, I prefer the handwritten ones, which make me feel more festive." There were also many volunteers at the scene who took the initiative to teach paper-cutting. Li, a community resident, said, "Because I have to be on duty, I feel quite lonely away from families in Hefei during the New Year. The community staff invite me to participate in the activities. I learn paper-cutting. Look, the paper-cuts posted on the windows and doors are all by my hands!"

By weaving a "network" of the Party's organization, the people's thoughts and needs are understood at the first time, and the relationship between the Party and the mass has witnessed great changes. Now, more and more Party members, social organizations and citizens are participating in all aspects of community governance, playing a "game of chess" through consultation and social governance on collaboration.

Although the community is small, it is connected with thousands of households. The Party Committee of Binhu Century Community has taken the lead in innovating the urban primary-level governance mode. Party members constitute the backbone of urban primary-level governance. The Party and the mass work together to create a better community of collaboration, participation, and shared benefits. Only by weaving a "network" of Party organizations can the effectiveness of Party building be integrated into the people's yearning for a better life, and urban system and capacity for governance be truly modernized.

二、大湾村：党建引领乡村振兴

盛夏时节，骄阳似火，巍巍大别山中有一处热闹的小村，这里是安徽省金寨县大湾村。在这里，一幅秀美和谐的乡村新画卷正徐徐铺开。村里的茶园里，一片片碧绿鲜嫩的茶叶，在微风的吹拂下轻轻摇晃着；游客人头攒动，熙熙攘攘，给宁静的小山村带来了一股鲜活劲，村民们谈笑风生，喜迎客来；村里的图书馆里，孩子们畅游在知识的海洋。通过强化党建引领，大湾村彻底甩开以前的闭塞和贫困，不断改善乡村环境，持续探索乡村产业发展的特色道路，成为全国著名的乡村振兴示范点。

（一）基层党组织"强起来"

村级党组织是带领群众脱贫致富的核心，抓好乡村振兴离不开坚强有力的基层党组织。过去的大湾村，村民们"各人自扫门前雪，莫管他人瓦上霜"。村里的年轻壮劳力大多选择进城务工，村里就剩下了老弱妇孺，眼看着大湾村一天天破败下去。

II. Dawan Village: Party Building Propels Rural Revitalization

In midsummer, when the sun is blazing, there is a lively small village in the Dabie Mountains. This is Dawan Village in Jinzhai County, Anhui Province. Here, a new picture of a beautiful and harmonious countryside is slowly unfolding. In the tea garden of the village, green and tender tea leaves are swaying gently in the breeze; tourists are crowded and bustling, bringing a sense of vitality to the quiet mountain village. The villagers are chatting and laughing, and they are happy to welcome guests. In the village library, children are reading. By strengthening the guidance of Party building, Dawan Village has completely farewelled its previous isolation and poverty, improved its rural environment and explored a path of rural industrial development with its own characteristic. Now, Dawan becomes a nationally renowned demonstration site for rural revitalization.

i. Strengthening Primary-level Party Organizations

Village-level Party organizations are the core of leading the masses out of poverty. A strong primary-level Party organization is indispensable for rural revitalization. In the past, the villagers minded their own business without caring about others. Most of the young and strong laborers left the village and chose to work in big cities, leaving the old, the disabled, women and children at home. Dawan Village deteriorated day by day.

大湾村（许昊 摄）
Dawan Village (Photo by Xu Hao)

　　事情的转机发生在 2015 年。这年 7 月，在金寨县中医院工作的余静主动请缨，到大湾村驻村扶贫，担任大湾村党支部第一书记、驻村扶贫工作队队长①。从驻村扶贫第一天开始，余书记就把帮助建强基层组织、协助抓好村"两委"②班子建设、打造"不走的工作队"作为最重要的一项工作。她认为，只有搞好基层党组织的建设，才能带领大湾村走向振兴。"农村富不富，关键看支部；支部强不强，关键靠头羊。"大湾村的"领头羊"可谓是"巾帼双英"，一位是余静，另一位则是党总支书记、村委会主任何家枝。曾经的何家枝，抱怨村干部工作难干，天天想着离开。但是余静找到她，请她担起"领头羊"的重任。现

────────────

　　① 驻村工作队是指由各级党委和政府选派到贫困村的第一书记和工作队，负责脱贫工作和乡村振兴工作。
　　② 村"两委"指的是村党支部委员会和村民委员会。

Everything has changed from 2015. In July, Yu Jing, who worked at the Jinzhai County Hospital of Traditional Chinese Medicine, took the initiative to volunteer to work in Dawan Village for poverty alleviation. She served as the first secretary of the Dawan Village Party branch and the leader of the village task force [1]. Since the first day of her arrival, Yu has regarded helping to build strong primary-level Party organizations, assisting in the construction of the village's "two committees" [2] team, and building a work team that takes root as the most important task. She believes that only by doing a good job in building primary-level Party organizations can Dawan be led to revitalization. "Whether the rural areas are prosperous or not depends on the Party branch; whether the branch is strong or not depends on the leader." The leaders of Dawan Village can be described as "double heroines". One is Yu Jing, and the other is He Jiazhi who is the secretary of the Party branch and head of the village committee. He Jiazhi once complained that the work of village cadres was difficult and thought about quitting. But Yu Jing had an in-depth communication with He Jiazhi and Yu asked He to work together to act as "bellwethers". Now in the eyes of the villagers, she is a "warmhearted sister" and "caring person". She treats the villagers as her own families. She is on call 24 hours a day, and always takes the people's affairs at heart. Yu Jing and He Jiazhi cooperated tacitly, and together they visited villagers' homes, talked about household affairs and policies, and got on well with villagers.

"I have never dreamed of it," Uncle Wang, a veteran Party member with 52 years of Party standing, said, "the friend circle of Party organization is getting bigger. In the past, the village Party branch held few activities. There were only a few meetings a year, and comrades in the branch did not even know each other." Primary-level Party organizations play a key role in ensuring the exercise of

---

① The village task force refers to the first secretaries and work teams selected by Party Committees to work in impoverished villages to be responsible for poverty alleviation and rural revitalization.

② "Two committees" refer to the village party branch and the village committee.

在的她是村民心中的"好大姐""贴心人",她把村民当自己的亲人,手机24小时开机,时刻把群众的事放在心上。余静与何家枝配合默契,共同去群众家走访,拉家常、讲政策,与群众打成一片。

余静(中)和群众在一起(陈力 摄)
Yu Jing (middle) and villagers (Photo by Chen Li)

"做梦都想不到。"有着52年党龄的老党员汪大爷感慨党组织的"朋友圈"越来越大。他说,过去这个村党的组织生活不多,"一年开不到几次会,甚至支部内个别同志彼此都不认识"。现在,村里的党支部是村里的坚强的战斗堡垒。即便是深夜,大湾村党总支微信群里也不缺操心的"夜猫子":"脱贫户的产业发展情况,是不是再摸底一次?"作为一名90后,村民周超曾在省会合肥从事互联网技术工作。何家枝数次登门将周超劝回。"我被她的执着和坚定感动了,回村扶贫是创业,也是我的价值。"周超说。2018年,周超高票当选村委会委员,并成为入党积极分子。多年来,大湾村党总支从能人大户、社会青年中培养入党

the Party's leadership. Even late at night, "night owls" in the WeChat group of the Dawan Village Party branch are still at work: "Should we check the career development of villagers out of poverty?" As a post-90s generation, villager Zhou Chao once worked in an internet company in Hefei City. He Jiazhi visited Zhou Chao several times to persuade him to return. "I was moved by her persistence and determination. For me, returning to help villagers is my career. It is worth it," said Zhou Chao. In 2018, Zhou Chao was elected as a member of the village committee with a high vote and became an applicant for Party membership. Over the years, the Dawan Village Party branch has developed many Party members from outstanding people and young people in the village. Currently, there are 113 Party members, and two thirds of the newly-developed Party members are under the age of 35. After the tenth election of the village's "two committees", Dawan Village has 6 village cadres with an average age of 43 years old. "Currently, everyone wants to fight for the future, is able to do things, and tries to be a pioneers," said the veteran Party member Wang. Nowadays, in meetings, everyone talks about new methods and new ideas of rural revitalization. Party members have a stronger awareness of taking the lead in development.

ii. Under the Party's Leadership, Agricultural Tourism Is Becoming More Popular

After exploration, the Dawan Village Party branch insisted the development idea of "growing tea on the mountain, welcoming guests at homestay and combining revolutionary scenic spots and green tea culture". A green leaf drives an industry and enriches villagers. Dawan Village is blessed with a moderate climate of distinct seasons, abundant rainfall, and it enjoys a long history of tea growing. It is a place of origin for the famous Chinese tea Lu'an Guapian. But in the past, the villagers produced common tea which could not form a brand and could not be sold at a high price. Now, with the help of the Party branch, Dawan Village has

积极分子，发展党员，如今党员 113 名，新发展的党员中有 2/3 的人年龄低于 35 周岁。在第十届村"两委"换届后，大湾村配齐村干部 6 人，平均年龄 43 岁。"现在大伙儿想干事、能干事、带头干。"老党员汪大爷感慨，如今村里开会，大家都七嘴八舌讨论乡村振兴的新方法、新思路，党员带头发展的意识也更强了。

（二）党旗下农旅"热起来"

经过探索，大湾村党总支明确了"山上种茶、家中迎客、红绿结合"的发展思路。一片绿色的叶子带动一个产业，富裕一方百姓。大湾村四季分明、雨水充沛，种茶历史悠久，是中国名茶"六安瓜片"的黄金产区。但过去村民自己生产的都是大路茶，形不成品牌，卖不上价钱。现在，在党总支帮助下，大湾村有了四家茶企。通过几年的建设，茶园面积也得到大幅扩展。大湾村现有

大湾村茶产业扶贫车间，村民正在炒茶（陈力 摄）
Villagers are roasting tea in a workshop (Photo by Chen Li)

built four tea companies. After years of development, the tea garden area has also greatly increased. Dawan Village now has more than 5,000 acres of tea gardens, including 2,000 acres of high-quality tea gardens. The average annual household income of villagers has increased by RMB 2,000. At the same time, the Dawan Village Party branch also makes full use of the advantages of tea production and tourism resources to vigorously develop rural tourism and leisure agriculture. The beautiful picture of "growing tea on the mountain and welcoming guests at homestay" has become a reality. Dawan Village has won the titles of China's Beautiful Leisure Village and Anhui's Most Beautiful Tea Village.

In July 2023, a group of international visitors from 10 countries including Australia, Italy, and the United States came to Dawan Village to participate in international youth exchange activities. "This is our first time here, and I am very amazed at how you have made full use of local natural resources to get rid of poverty and become rich." Nicholas from Bolivia felt excited. Wandering in front of the new houses in Dawan Village, these foreign friends learned that the per capita income of villagers has made a huge leap, achieving rural revitalization. In Dawan Village, international friends put on bamboo hats and carried small backpacks. Under the guidance of local villagers, they experienced the fun of tea picking and roasted the tea leaves picked by themselves at the Dawan Tea Factory. Seeing magical "oriental leaves" in the cup, Lorenzo from the Republic of San Marino said that it was very interesting to understand the process of picking and making tea. He did not expect that the lives of ordinary people could be greatly improved by tea. "I like it very much. The culture is very different from that of my hometown, and I have learned a lot. I like the people here very much and hope to have the opportunity to learn more about this place," said Philippe from Italy.

Dawan not only has green tea leaves, but also has a red revolutionary spirit. Under the leadership of the Dawan Village Party branch, the revolutionary tourism has also been flourishing. The Dawan Village Rural Folk Museum allows people to better understand the local farming culture and handicrafts. The Wang

茶园 5000 余亩，其中优质茶园 2000 亩，村民年户均增收 2000 元。同时，大湾村党支部还充分利用茶叶及旅游资源优势，大力发展乡村旅游及休闲农业。"山上种茶、家中迎客"的美好画面已成为现实。大湾村先后获得"中国美丽休闲乡村"和"安徽最美茶村"的称号。

2023 年 7 月，一群来自澳大利亚、意大利、美国等 10 个国家的国际友人来大湾村参加国际青少年互动交流活动。"这是我们第一次来这里，我非常惊叹于你们是如何充分利用当地自然资源实现脱贫致富的。"来自玻利维亚的尼古拉斯激动地说。漫步在大湾村一幢幢新居前，这些外国朋友了解到，该村村民人均收入有了极大的飞跃，实现了乡村振兴。山前屋后，国际友人们戴上了斗笠，挎上了小背篓，在当地村民的带领下，体验采茶乐趣，并将亲手摘下的茶叶在大湾茶厂里进行炒制。看着杯中一片片神奇的"东方树叶"，来自圣马力诺共和国的洛伦佐说，了解采茶制茶的过程十分有意思，没想到茶叶这样简单的植物可以极大改善普通百姓的生活。"我很喜欢这里，与我所在城市的文化有很大不同，我学到了很多。我很喜欢这里的人们，希望有机会能进一步了解这个地方。"来自意大利的菲利普说。

大湾不仅有绿色的茶叶，还有红色的革命精神。在大湾村党总支的带领下，大湾村的红旅之路也搞得精彩纷呈。大湾村乡村民俗博物馆让人们更好了解当地的农耕文化和手工艺术；六安六区十四乡苏维埃政府旧址——汪家旧屋则引领人们传承红色血脉和革命精神；红色书屋的建立让红色经典与红色书籍深入人心。大湾村以红色旅游带动乡村振兴，带动了沿线餐饮住宿等服务业的发展。红色旅游让更多村民吃上了"旅游饭"，也为村里经济插上了腾飞的翅膀。

中国共产党一经诞生，就把为中国人民谋幸福、为中华民族谋复兴确立为自己的初心使命。如今，大湾村党支部接过了前辈们的火炬，不忘初心，把带领村民谋幸福作为自己不变的使命。大湾巨变，离不开党组织的决策和引领。

family's old house, which was the former site of the Soviet government in Shisi Township, Sixth District, Lu'an, leads people to carry forward the revolutionary traditions and heritage. The establishment of the Red Bookstore has made red classics and red books deeply rooted in the hearts of the people. Dawan Village drives rural revitalization with revolutionary tourism, and the development of catering, accommodation and other service industries along the route. Red tourism has allowed more villagers to enjoy higher income and also helps the village's economy take off.

Since its founding in 1921, the Communist Party of China has always made seeking happiness for the Chinese people and rejuvenation for the Chinese nation its mission. Today, the Dawan Village Party branch has taken over the torch of its predecessors, stayed true to its cause, and led the villagers to seek happiness as its unchanging mission. The great changes in Dawan Village depend on the policy and guidance of the Party organization.

iii. Party Members Working Together to Help Revitalize

Yu Jing and He Jiazhi agree that if Dawan Village is to be revitalized, each Party member must give full play to his role. With their help, Dawan Village actively implements the "Four Helps Project", namely: production to help industrial development, employment to help migrant workers, regular contact to help solve problems in life, and encouragement to help improve villagers' state. All village Party members, volunteers, and able men take the initiative to contact the villagers to help, and the participation rate of rural Party members reached 100%.

Moving into a new home, villager Yang Xilun invited Party member Yu Shaoqi to visit. Yu Shaoqi was credited with transforming Yang Xilun from a man who was once regarded as a "slacker" into "Boss Yang" engaged in a number of industries. In the past, Yang Xilun worked in cities and his house was abandoned. Yu Jing took the initiative to coordinate with Yu Shaoqi, an experienced farmer

（三）党员齐心助振兴

余静和何家枝一致认为，大湾村要振兴就必须充分发挥每个党员的作用。在她们的带领下，大湾村积极实施"四联四帮工程"，即：生产联手帮扶产业发展、就业联动帮带劳力务工、经常联系帮解生活难题、思想联络帮提精神状态。全村党员、积极分子、能人大户等主动联系帮扶村民，农村党员参与率达100%。

搬入新居，村民杨习伦迫不及待地邀请党员俞绍奇上门做客。从曾经被看成"懒汉"到现在成为从事多个产业的"杨老板"，俞绍奇功不可没。以前的杨习伦在外地打工，老家房子也荒了。余静主动协调村里的能人大户俞绍奇指导杨习伦养殖土鸡。俞绍奇带动杨习伦赚得"第一桶金"。这慢慢激发起杨习伦自力更生的干劲。渐渐地，杨习伦俨然变了一个人，每天一大早就喂猪喂鸡，忙里忙外，家里还盖起了新房。在产业发展的一线、在帮扶农户的田间地头，村里党员都冲在最前面。"党员最热心。"杨习伦说。"党员们发挥了很大作用，大家都是铆足了劲，奔向富裕路。"余静说。

毫无疑问，如今这个美丽新农村已经成为乡村振兴图景中浓墨重彩的一笔。中国是农业大国，目前有4亿多农民，中国式现代化是全体人民共同富裕的现代化，"不能把农民甩在最后"。2016年，习近平总记在大湾村村民陈泽申家的小院里开了一场座谈会。"全面建成小康社会，一个不能少，特别是不能忘了老区。"习近平总书记的殷殷嘱托，温暖着大湾村干部群众的心田。乡村振兴风正劲，100年前的中国共产党在这片土地上点起了星星之火，100年后，大湾村不忘初心，坚定不移建强农村基层党组织，让党建成为引领乡村振兴的"强力引擎"。

in the village, to guide Yang Xilun in breeding local chickens. Yu Shaoqi drove Yang to earn his "first Pot of gold". This gradually inspired Yang's self-reliance. Yang changed. In every early morning he fed pigs and chickens and finally he built a new house. Village Party members are at the forefront to achieve the industrial and agricultural development. "Party members are all caring about us," said Yang Xilun. "Party members play an important role. We work together towards prosperity," said Yu Jing.

Today, there is no doubt that this beautiful new countryside has become an important part of the rural revitalization. China is a large agricultural country, with more than 400 million farmers. Chinese modernization is a modernization that brings prosperity to all people. Chinese modernization "cannot leave farmers behind". In 2016, President Xi Jinping held a symposium in the courtyard of Chen Zeshen's home in Dawan Village. "To build a moderately prosperous society in an all-round way, no one can be missing, especially people in old revolutionary areas." Xi Jinping's earnest instructions warmed the hearts of the cadres and masses of Dawan Village. Rural revitalization is booming. 100 years ago, the Communist Party of China lit a spark in this land. 100 years later, Dawan Village has not forgotten its original intention and firmly built and strengthened rural primary-level Party organizations, so that Party building can become a force for leading rural revitalization.

三、江淮汽车：党建领航企业提质增效

　　坚持党的领导、加强党的建设是国有企业的"根"和"魂"，是我国国有

江淮汽车技术中心〔李博 摄〕
JAC company (Photo by Li Bo)

III. JAC: Quality and Efficiency Improved under the Guidance of Party Building

Upholding the Party's leadership and strengthening Party building are the "root" and "soul" of state-owned enterprises, and are the glorious tradition and unique advantages of China's state-owned enterprises. JAC[①] continuously consolidates the primary-level Party organization building, actively promotes the in-depth integration of Party building and production, uses the "red torch" to unite the heart and soul, and comprehensively leads the enterprise on the path of high-quality development.

i. The Party Committee Holding the Right Direction

The Party organizations of state-owned enterprises must hold the right direction, manage the overall situation, and ensure implementation. As a large state-owned enterprise, the JAC Party Committee has a clear division of labor and a sound structure. The Party Committee secretary, deputy secretary and members are respectively responsible for various tasks of the Party Committee. JAC has

---

① JAC refers to Jianghuai Automobile. JAC is one of the important representatives of the Chinese automobile industry. It is a comprehensive automobile enterprise focusing on researching, manufacturing and sales of commercial vehicles and passenger cars.

企业的光荣传统和独特优势。JAC①不断夯实党的基层组织建设，积极推进党建与生产的深入融合，以"红色火炬"凝心聚魂，全面引领企业走上高质量发展之路。

（一）把方向的党委

国有企业党组织要做到把方向、管大局、保落实。作为一个大型国企，JAC党委组织分工明确，机构健全，党委书记、副书记和委员分别负责党委的各项工作。JAC设立了党务工作部门，负责全面推进党建工作。企业党委作为企业的核心领导机构，对企业的重大决策起着决定性作用。

打造轻卡智能制造基地（程兆 摄）

The smart manufacturing base (Photo by Cheng Zhao)

---

① JAC是江淮汽车的缩写。江淮汽车是中国汽车工业的重要代表之一，是一家以研发、制造、销售商用车和乘用车为主的综合性汽车企业。

established a Party affairs department responsible for comprehensively promoting Party building. As the core leadership organization of the enterprise, the Party Committee plays a decisive role in major decisions.

In the face of changes that are consequential to the world, to our times, and to history, under the leadership of the Party, JAC seeks greater development of the enterprise by opening-up. The JAC Kazakhstan project reveals the accelerated advancement of the Belt and Road Initiative. JAC has been actively exploring the Kazakhstan market since 2014. In 2019, the JAC Party Committee decided to jointly invest with CMC (a subsidiary of China General Technology Group) and officially became the controlling shareholder of Allur Group, which was the largest automobile company in Kazakhstan. JAC encountered great difficulties in selecting vehicle models to put on the market. The JAC Party branch in this project carried out detailed research, traveling to many cities in Kazakhstan and interviewing tens of thousands of local residents. They found that Kazakhstan had an arid climate and complex terrain, with deserts, grasslands, and mountains. Local residents are generally tall and they like to operate flexible and convenient cars and need to carry heavier loads. Therefore, the JAC Party Committee made the decision to choose a high-end light truck as the first product to put in the market. High-quality products have helped JAC gain a high reputation in the Kazakhstan market. In order to fully respond to the Belt and Road Initiative, in recent years, under the leadership of the Party Committee, JAC's exports have occupied nearly 100 countries' markets along the Belt and Road. It promotes not only the improvement of the technology and scale of the automobile manufacturing industry, but also the development of the economy of those countries.

In the work, the JAC Party Committee took the lead in solving the problem of disjunction between Party building and the actual development of the enterprise. The committee always regards the difficulties of reform and the development as the focus of Party building and insists "attaching equal importance to each". In accordance with the ideas "pursuing the grand course together, living in harmony

面对世界之变、时代之变、历史之变，本来正在形成的经济全球化的世界站在历史的十字路口上。在党的领导下，JAC 以更坚决的对外开放谋求企业的更大发展。JAC 哈萨克斯坦项目是加速中国"一带一路"倡议推进的缩影。JAC 自 2014 年起积极开拓哈萨克斯坦市场，2019 年，JAC 党委决定联合 CMC（中国通用技术集团控股子公司）共同出资，正式成为哈萨克斯坦第一大汽车企业 Allur 集团控股股东。在投放市场车型的选择问题上，JAC 遇到了很大的难题。驻地的 JAC 党支部展开了详细的调研，跑遍了哈萨克斯坦的大小城市，走访了上万名当地居民。他们发现哈萨克斯坦气候较干旱，地形复杂，有荒漠有草原有山地，当地居民身材普遍高大，居民喜欢操作灵活方便型汽车以及存在较大拉载货物的需求。所以在车型选择方面，JAC 党委拍板，首先选择了高端轻卡的产品组合投放市场。高质量的产品帮助 JAC 在哈萨克斯坦市场获得了良好的口碑。为充分响应国家"一带一路"倡议，近年来，在党委领导下，JAC 出口覆盖"一带一路"沿线国家近百个，不仅推动沿线汽车制造业工艺水平和规模的提升，还促进了沿线经济的发展。

在工作实践中，JAC 党委带头，解决了党建工作与企业实际发展"两张皮"的问题，始终把改革的难点、发展的重点作为党建工作的着力点，坚持"两手都要硬"。JAC 按习近平总书记指出的共行天下大道，和睦相处、合作共赢的思想，与世界各国的企业携手努力创造世界的美好未来。

（二）攻坚克难的党支部

近几年，我国打响了蓝天绿水保卫战，燃油车已经不能够满足当今市场的需要，也给环境带来了很大的压力。很多传统的汽车企业由于不能够及时转型，逐渐面临经营困境。JAC 党委领导果断决定转换赛道，响应政府号召和回应市场需求，转型投入新能源汽车生产。

and win-win cooperation" pointed out by President Xi Jinping, JAC works hand in hand with enterprises from all over the world to create a better future.

ii. Party Branches Overcoming Difficulties

In recent years, our country has launched a battle to protect blue sky and green water. Fuel vehicles can't meet the needs of today's market and have also put great pressure on the environment. Due to failure of transformation in time, many traditional automobile companies are facing business difficulties. The leaders of the JAC Party Committee are resolute to transform the production, respond to the government's call and needs of the market, and promote new energy vehicles.

After investigation, the JAC Party Committee decided to adhere to the idea of "Better Party building, better projects" and set up Party branch technical project teams for intelligent manufacturing, advanced energy conservation and others. The secretary of the Party branch played a vital role in ensuring the implementation of the projects on time.

In the first half of 2021, the pre-sale and launch promotion of JAC iC5 were put in the "Key Projects of the Party Organization". From three dimensions of personnel, vehicles and stores, a new sales mode with low investment, zero inventory, and fast turnover would be achieved. At the same time, brand influence and radiation would be expanded and new breakthroughs in marketing development would be achieved. The iC5 Party branch decided to take "improving project operating efficiency and management level" as the main test criterion for Party building work, and worked together on authorized dealer training, new media platform management system, etc. While focusing on creating value for customers, it achieved integrated development and promotion of both Party building and business. Facing with the task of building a stronger enterprise and improving the brand, JAC has shouldered the great responsibilities of advancing high-quality development. From the rapid development and launch of the WeChat App for

江淮汽车公司生产的纯电动"钇为 3"车型（方好 摄）
An electrical vehicle of JAC (Photo by Fang Hao)

　　JAC 党委经过调研后决定，坚持"围绕项目抓党建，抓好党建促项目"的思路，成立智能"智造"、先进节能等多个方向的党支部技术攻坚项目组，由党支部书记挂帅，保障项目按时落地。

　　2021 年上半年，JACiC5 的预售及上市推广被列入"党组织重点攻坚项目"，力争从人员、车辆、店面三维进行优化，实现低投入、零库存、快周转的新型销售模式，扩大品牌影响力和辐射力，实现营销发展新突破。iC5 党支部决定把提升项目经营效益和管理水平作为党建工作的主要检验标准，在授权经销商培训、新媒体平台经营体系等方面群策群力，在着力为客户创造价值的同时，也实现了党建工作与经营发展的双向渗透、同频共振。面对企业由大向强的新形势、品牌向上的新任务，JAC 扛起企业高质量发展的使命担当。从火速开发上线、与 iC5 预售同期发布的微信小程序预约试驾和在线订车，都能看到支部成

test drive appointment and online car booking for the iC5 pre-sale, Party branch members always take the lead and play an exemplary role.

iii. Party Members Taking the Lead

Faced with the uncertainty and fierce competition in the global automobile industry, how to gather talents? JAC's answer is to focus on Party building. It is the JAC Party members' original intention to make China a powerful automobile country. They make a determination to contribute to the development of China through industry and set an example for the high-quality development of JAC. With the pioneering and exemplary role of Party members, many JAC employees strive to become experts in their fields. Their talents are discovered and their work results are directly put to great use.

Engineer Wang Qing, a national model worker, is a veteran Party member of JAC. He came to JAC after graduating from college in 1994 and has been engaged in equipment maintenance ever since. In the past 29 years, he has worked hard as a technician, devoted himself to research, and strived to overcome problems. He is considered as a "miracle doctor" who uses high-precision equipment to repair the machines. How did Wang Qing develop his ability to locate and fix sophisticated equipment? He told us that the word "research" is the key. Once, a robot parameter didn't work and the error could not be found. Wang Qing debugged hundreds of parameters one by one, and finally found out the problem. In recent years, Wang Qing has also led other technical workers to carry out projects such as CNC lathe system transformation and hydraulic machine tool air cooling. "Party members must take the lead, and we must be a pioneer to overcome difficulties," he said, "At the same time, we have to keep in mind that teaching and training the next generation of technical talents for the country are of great importance." Wang Qing took the lead in establishing the Master Studio, which has trained more than a hundred highly skilled maintenance personnel and created an atmosphere of

员主动站位、发挥模范带头作用的身影。

（三）带头的党员

面对全球汽车行业发展前景的不确定性和竞争激烈性，如何凝聚人才核心力量？JAC 的答案是注重党建引领的作用。JAC 党员心怀汽车强国的初心、产业报国的决心，为实现 JAC 高质量发展树立了榜样。有了党员的先锋模范作用，很多 JAC 员工立足工作岗位，努力成为专家。JAC 涌现出了许多专家型人才，他们的工作成果派上了大用场。

全国劳动模范汪清工程师是 JAC 的一个老党员。他 1994 年大学毕业后来到 JAC，一直从事设备维修工作。从业 29 年来，他深耕一线技术岗位，沉下心搞钻研，铆足劲克难题，是大伙儿心中为高精尖设备把脉问诊的"神医"。汪清这一身高精尖设备诊断维修的本领是如何练成的呢？他告诉我们，"钻研"二字是关键。一次，一个机器人参数出现了差错，原因怎么都找不到，汪清在上百个参数中，一个一个动手调试，终于查出了原因。近年来，汪清还带领其他技术工人一起开展了数控车床系统改造、液压机床空气冷却等项目。"党员必须要起带头作用，攻坚克难我们要冲在第一线。"他说，"同时，我们也不能忘记'传帮带'，为国家培养下一代技术人才"。汪清带头成立技能大师工作室，培养了百余名维修高技能人才，在公司营造了爱专研、勤动手的学习氛围。

像汪清这样的先进党员在 JAC 不是个案，在这些党员的带头下，JAC 开展六西格玛人才、高技能人才、科技研发人才、质量专家等专项人才培养，为公司关键人才储备提供战略支撑。截至 2022 年底，公司共有技能大师工作室 37 个，技术首席专家工作室 8 个。"广大党员要推动发展中争做冲锋路标，带动整个团队不断进步。"江淮集团党委副书记王东生如是说。

百舸争流，奋楫争先。在江淮汽车发展的过程中，党的全面领导为企业发

dedicated research and hard work in the company.

Advanced Party members like Wang Qing are not an isolated case in JAC. Under the leadership of these Party members, JAC has carried out special training programs of Six Sigma talents, high-skilled talents, scientific and technological R&D talents, and quality experts to provide strategic support for the company's key talent reserves. As of the end of 2022, the company had a total of 37 master studios and 8 chief technical expert studios. "The majority of Party members must strive to be a model in promoting development, and drive the entire team to continuous progress," said Wang Dongsheng, deputy secretary of the Party Committee of JAC.

Thousands of sails compete, we should fight hard to be the first. In the development of JAC, the Party's overall leadership has pointed out the direction for the development of the enterprise. The cohesiveness and combat effectiveness of the Party organization provide inexhaustible "red power" for the prosperity of enterprises. By strengthening Party building, the vast number of cadres and employees have burst out with work passion and innovative spirit, which has promoted JAC to continuously improve economic and social benefits and achieve high-quality development. In the new era, JAC will strive to fulfill its glorious mission of rejuvenating the country through industry and serving the country through industry, and set a mode of high-quality development with the "JAC mode" of Party building.

Through in-depth analyses of the three cases of Party-building in Binhu Century Community, Dawan Village and JAC, we can see that they have distinctive characteristics. Binhu Century Community has always adhered to a people-centered philosophy. By strengthening the building of Party members, improving the organizational structure, and enriching activities, it has continuously improved community governance capabilities and service levels, and created a primary-level governance pattern of collaboration, participation, and shared benefits. Dawan

展指明了方向。党组织的凝聚力和战斗力为企业的繁荣提供了不竭的"红色动力"。通过加强党的建设，广大干部职工迸发出火热的工作热情和创新精神，推动了江淮汽车不断提高经济效益和社会效益，实现高质量发展。新时代，江淮汽车将奋力完成产业兴国、实业报国的光荣使命，以党建"江淮样板"树立高质量发展典范。

通过对滨湖世纪社区、大湾村和江淮汽车三个党建案例的深入分析，我们可以看到它们在不同地域和领域所取得的成功经验具有鲜明的特色。滨湖世纪社区始终坚持"以人民为中心"的发展思想，通过加强党员队伍建设、完善组织架构和丰富活动形式，不断提升社区治理能力和服务水平，打造共建共治共享的基层治理格局。金寨县大湾村注重发挥党员的先锋模范作用和基层民主建设，发展当地特色产业，实现了乡村振兴的目标。江淮汽车推动党建和生产经营活动有机融合，党建融入公司治理各环节，推动企业不断创新和发展。

合肥市滨湖世纪社区、金寨县大湾村和江淮汽车集团党建的成功实践为城市基层治理、乡村振兴和企业提质增效提供了宝贵的经验和启示。在新时代背景下，只有不断加强党的建设工作，发挥基层党组织的战斗堡垒作用和党员的先锋模范作用，才能真正书写好中国式现代化安徽故事的党建实践，为推进中国式现代化贡献安徽智慧。

Village in Jinzhai County pays attention to the pioneering and exemplary role of Party members and the construction of primary-level democracy, develops local specialty industries, and achieves the goal of rural revitalization. JAC promotes the integration of Party building and production and business activities, integrates Party building into all aspects of corporate governance, and promotes a continuous innovation and development of the enterprise.

The successful practices of Party building in Binhu Century Community in Hefei City, Dawan Village in Jinzhai County, and JAC have provided valuable experience and inspiration for urban primary-level governance, rural revitalization, and enterprise quality and efficiency improvement. In the new era, only by continuously strengthening Party building and ensuring the exercise of the Party's leadership by primary-level Party organizations and motivating Party members to become role models, can we truly write the glorious story of Chinese modernization in Anhui and contribute Anhui's wisdom to promoting Chinese modernization.

后 记

　　本书是中央党校（国家行政学院）中国式现代化研究中心和中央党校出版集团国家行政学院出版社策划出版的"中国式现代化的故事"丛书之一，是中共安徽省委党校（安徽行政学院）认真贯彻落实习近平总书记关于"讲好中国故事，传播好中国声音，展示真实、立体、全面的中国"等重要讲话指示精神，扎实开展对外交流工作的又一成果，校（院）创新工程专著出版项目为本书出版提供了资助。

　　中国式现代化的安徽生动实践中，方方面面的案例俯首可得、举不胜举，本书通过6个主题18个故事，以小切口、微视角展示江淮儿女谱写中国式现代化安徽篇章的奋斗和成就。故事虽小，也许不能完整、准确代表江淮儿女贯彻新发展理念、谱写中国式现代化安徽篇章的实践探索，但希望故事背后的逻辑和道理可以带给人们诸多启示；故事虽微，也许不能系统、全面反映中国式现代化建设的安徽成就，但希望大家能感受到安徽是创新创业的福地，是山水秀美的胜地，是内陆开放的高地。新时代的安徽正以徽风皖韵绽放时代芳华、以科技创新促进经济发展、以治理现代化建设"皖"美江淮。

　　本书由中共安徽省委党校（安徽行政学院）国际合作部的一批中青年教师编写，从策划、咨询、撰写，到付梓出版只有半年时间。这得益于这批中青年教师近年来参与涉外课程录制或者线上线下涉外交流合作项目等工作，有些故

Epilogue

This book is one of the series of books "The Story of Chinese Modernization" planned and published by the Chinese Modernization Research Center of Party School of Central Committee of C.P.C (National Academy of Governance) and the National Academy of Governance Press, Party School of Central Committee of C.P.C Press Group. Meanwhile, it is one of the new achievements of the Party School of Anhui Provincial Committee of C.P.C (Anhui Academy of Governance, hereinafter referred to as Anhui Party School) in undertaking foreign exchange and communication steadily by conscientiously implementing the important instructions of President Xi Jinping on "Telling the China's stories well, making the voice of China heard, and presenting a true, multi-dimensional, and panoramic view of China to the world". The Innovation Project on Monograph Publication of Anhui Party School provided funding for the book.

The vivid practices of Chinese modernization in Anhui are abundant in numerous cases on all fronts. Taking 6 themes and 18 stories as small angles of view, this book demonstrates the endeavour and accomplishment of Anhui in writing its own chapter on Chinese modernization. The stories are tiny and may not completely reflect the practical exploration of implementing new development philosophy and writing the Anhui chapter of Chinese modernization by the Anhui people. However, we hope that the logic and reasoning behind these stories bring the readers certain inspiration. The stories are micro and may not comprehensively

事由录制的课件或现场教学材料转化而来。本书由国际合作部主任方铭勇副教授编著，负责全书统稿，各章撰写分工如下：第一章由张铁松撰写、周俊翻译成英文，第二章由刘敏撰写并翻译成英文，第三章由邹永红撰写并翻译成英文，第四章由刘淑珍撰写并翻译成英文，第五章由叶红艳撰写并翻译成英文，第六章由方丽撰写第一二部分并翻译成英文、周俊撰写第三部分并翻译成英文，第七章由王悠然撰写并翻译成英文。感谢各位作者的倾力付出。

中共安徽省委党校（安徽行政学院）常务副校（院）长陈爱军自始至终关心、推动着本书的编写、出版；副校（院）长潘理权教授多次主持召开咨询会，确定了本书的主题内容、篇章结构、风格体例、写作要求；校（院）宣传部、科研处等部门承担了相关的组织协调工作。安徽日报、滨湖世纪社区等单位在资料提供上给予编写组全方位的支持。国家行政学院出版社做了细致的编辑工作。在此一并感谢！

编写供对外交流使用的双语读物，是中共安徽省委党校（安徽行政学院）的首次尝试与探索，由于时间较紧，资料受限、加之作者水平有限，缺点疏漏在所难免，敬请各位读者批评指正。

编者

2023 年 10 月

reveal Anhui's achievements in the construction of Chinese modernization. Nevertheless, we anticipate that the readers sense that Anhui is a promising place of innovation and entrepreneurship, a wonderful land enjoying the beautiful landscape, as well as a highland of inland opening-up. In the new era, the province is blossoming with the charm of Anhui style and rhyme, promoting economic development by sci-tech innovations, and building a magnificent Anhui by the modernization of governance.

This book was written by a group of young and middle-aged lecturers from the International Cooperation Department of Anhui Party School. It took them only half a year to plan, consult, write, and finally submit to publish. This was owing to the fact that this group of young and middle-aged lecturers had been involved in the recording of international communication courses and programs of foreign exchange and cooperation online and offline in recent years. Some of the stories were transformed from the recorded courseware or on-site teaching materials. This book is compiled by Associate Professor Fang Mingyong, the Director of the International Cooperation Department. The division for each chapter is as follows: the Chinese part of Chapter 1 was written by Zhang Tiesong and translated into English by Zhou Jun; the Chinese and English parts of Chapter 2 were written and translated by Liu Min; the Chinese and English parts of Chapter 3 were written and translated by Zou Yonghong; the Chinese and English parts of Chapter 4 were written and translated by Liu Shuzhen; the Chinese and English parts of Chapter 5 were written and translated by Ye Hongyan; the Chinese and English parts of the first and second sections of Chapter 6 were written and translated by Fang Li, and the Chinese and English parts of the third section were written and translated by Zhou Jun; and the Chinese and English parts of Chapter 7 were written and translated by Wang Youran. All of your dedication is deeply appreciated.

Executive Vice President Chen Aijun, from the Party School of Anhui Provincial Committee of C.P.C (Anhui Academy of Governance), has attached great importance to this book from first to last, promoting its compilation and

袁廉民 摄

Photo by Yuan Lianmin

publication. Professor Pan Liquan, Vice President of the Party School of Anhui Provincial Committee of C.P.C (Anhui Academy of Governance), has chaired a number of consultative meetings to define the book's theme, structure, and style, as well as writing requirements. The Publicity Department, Scientific Research Department, and other departments of Anhui Party School have undertaken the relevant work of organization and coordination. Anhui Daily, Binhu Century Community, and other institutions have offered the writing group a full range of support in the provision of information and materials. The National Academy of Governance Press has done meticulous editing work. Here, we would like to extend our sincere gratitude to you all!

It is the first attempt and exploration of the Anhui Party School to compile bilingual readings for foreign communication. Due to constraints in time and materials, and limited competence of the authors, drawbacks and omissions might be unavoidable. Cordially, we look forward to your criticism and correction.

Editorial Board
October 2023

图书在版编目（CIP）数据

皖美跨越：中国式现代化的安徽故事：汉英对照 /
方铭勇主编 . -- 北京：国家行政学院出版社，2023.12
（"中国式现代化的故事"丛书 / 张占斌主编）
ISBN 978-7-5150-2861-3

Ⅰ . ①皖… Ⅱ . ①方… Ⅲ . ①现代化建设—研究—安
徽—汉、英 Ⅳ . ①D675.4

中国国家版本馆 CIP 数据核字（2023）第 232045 号

书　　名	皖美跨越：中国式现代化的安徽故事	
	WANMEI KUAYUE : ZHONGGUOSHI XIANDAIHUA DE ANHUI GUSHI	
作　　者	方铭勇　主编	
统筹策划	胡　敏　刘韫劼　王　莹	
责任编辑	王　莹　孔令慧	
责任校对	许海利	
责任印制	吴　霞	
出版发行	国家行政学院出版社	
	（北京市海淀区长春桥路 6 号　100089）	
综 合 办	（010）68928887	
发 行 部	（010）68928866	
经　　销	新华书店	
印　　刷	北京新视觉印刷有限公司	
版　　次	2023 年 12 月北京第 1 版	
印　　次	2023 年 12 月北京第 1 次印刷	
开　　本	170 毫米 ×240 毫米　16 开	
印　　张	18.5	
字　　数	289 千字	
定　　价	79.00 元	

本书如有印装问题，可联系调换。联系电话：（010）68929022